Helen

The Duplicitous Bohemian

Susie Green

For K,F and N who have enriched my life beyond anything I deserve.

Contents

Facing reality - 1982

Standing back - Early 1983

Limbo - February 1983

Beyond belief - Late March 1983

Future becoming present

Consequences

Acknowledgements

Writing a book is by definition a solitary undertaking and a self-published book excludes the usual appreciative litany addressed to editors, editorial assistants, designers etc. who contribute to commercial publication. So, acknowledgements are few but no less sincere because the people I am grateful to are precious family and friends with whom I have shared my aspirations. They have been like the buffers on a pinball machine, enabling me to bounce my ideas along to this culminating point.

For example, there's my lifetime's friend, Hilary who triggered the whole process and was stalwart in her comments and suggestions. Earlier versions of the book were epic in their proportions (over 300,000 words), but she unflinchingly read and critiqued the lot and helped me to reduce it to a manageable length. Most importantly, she believed I had a story to tell.

Conversations with literary friends Jane, Jane and Camilla were always stimulating, not necessarily concerning the book's content, but in shaping the thinking behind it. And Robin Drury's design skills influenced the final version of the cover. Thank goodness too, for my darling daughter Fanny's word processing and editorial skills, but much more than that, her joyous enthusiasm for the whole enterprise. "Go for it Mum, it's brilliant !" was her comment after a preliminary read through. Finally, I feel duty bound to mention the main protagonist, the Duplicitous Bohemian, without whom there would have been no story.

Correspondence - 1966 - 1982

1. Day Hospital and the 'huh' of hindsight

Lorna was in her usual position, hunched over the antiquated switchboard in the reception area of the Day Hospital, deeply engrossed in conversation. The hospital had been the home of the celebrated Huxley family decades ago, but had somehow been purchased by the NHS and converted into a psychiatric day centre. It was a generously proportioned Victorian house and garden, with a solitary Catalpa tree standing in the middle of what was once a lawn. At the back the servants' quarters housed a nursing unit, where they did ECT and dished out Lysergic Acid in the hope that it would encourage patients to yield up their innermost secrets. The director of the hospital, like most of the staff, was Jewish, an archetypal Viennese psychiatrist of Freudian persuasion, complete with goatee beard and thick bottle-top spectacles.

In her mid-fifties, Lorna was elegantly glamorous enough for most men who set foot inside the door to feel compelled to flirt with her, which she loved. She created an atmosphere of intimacy, she and her switchboard so when she wasn't dealing with incoming traffic, she was purring into the mouthpiece with purposeful intensity. The switchboard was one of those old-fashioned wooden boxes with umpteen little compartments, each containing an eyelid flap which had to be flipped up after it had flopped down to announce an incoming call. Lorna would whisper intimately into her mouthpiece, meanwhile expertly detaching then re-

3

inserting an apparent viper's nest of leads which connected one eyelid to another.

"Who's the new Adonis ?" I had mouthed as I hurried across the hallway and past her desk. I'd just spotted a stranger going up the stairs beyond the reception area and knowing we were expecting a new psychiatrist to join the staff, wanted to get the low-down on him in advance of my colleagues. He certainly didn't have the anxious intensity of someone seeking therapy. Lorna, being the queen of the hospital grapevine was the best person to ask. She knew everything that went on in the Day Hospital which was a hotbed of intrigue and affairs. Young single staff were always on the prowl, including me. Older ones, whether they were married or not, were equally curious although they were perhaps more covert in their approaches or simply more experienced.

"Oh him ?" she nodded in the direction of the stairs. "Name's Dr. Urbanczyk but everyone calls him Zarek because they can't pronounce his first name. He's Polish and so far doesn't speak a word of English except for 'the English women, they are so beautiful'. Does all that hand kissing stuff too, so you'd better watch out."

"They have to try it on, don't they," she finished in weary exasperation as she turned her attention back to the switchboard and another call.

And I was soon to find out. Having recently detached myself from a singularly unlikely fiance' (architect, covert gay, died of AIDS years later), I was definitely prowling, and despite his inadequate English, Zarek and I were soon working

4

together. I'd been employed in the Day Hospital as an Occupational Therapist so while the psychiatrists did the fancy stuff with drugs and psychotherapy, I was attempting to help people lead so-called normal lives, shopping, cooking, keeping clean, looking after themselves, getting jobs, making friends and hopefully enjoying life a bit more. Amazingly Zarek embarked straight away on conducting psychotherapy groups and I was enlisted as a 'non-participating observer'. This meant sitting silently with pad and pen poised, attempting to capture verbatim, everything that participants said. For Zarek with little English, conducting the group wasn't as difficult as it might sound as reading people's non-verbal behaviour revealed as much as their spoken words. "Uh huh"………"mmm"…… "Mmmm ?"…… "and how did that make you feel ?" ………uh huh" was about as much English as he needed to know. His job seemed easy in comparison with my instructions to scribble everything down, reactionless, while group participants scrabbled over each other's pain and madness like hyenas at a carcass.

We spent a lot of time together, Zarek and I. There were two evening group psychotherapy sessions each week and they continued for months, several years even, just us and half a dozen patients. He taught me psychiatric theories and particularly about a largely forgotten American teacher, Sullivan, who sadly communicated in the class room, rather than writing about his ideas. These largely centred on the belief that we exist in relation to each other, that, as John Donne would have it, 'no man is an island.' Afterwards we would go through my notes and then, inevitably, go for a drink or a film and then after a while, of course, a fuck. Well.

For me it wasn't a fuck, it was love-making, the real thing. He was definitely 'foreign' - exotic, passionate, good looking too with prematurely grey/white hair, an en brosse haircut and oddly tailored suits in strangely patterned fabrics. I know this because after they had been hastily thrown aside and lay strewn on my bedroom floor, I noticed a variety of carefully positioned buttons, tabs and linings, underpinnings to show that the tailor had done his job properly. Not like the insides of other suits I'd seen. Me ? I was in love, but a lot needed to happen before we could establish any kind of life together. And I was naïve enough to think that falling in love enabled one to overcome apparently insurmountable obstacles which would inevitably lead to living happily ever after. Certainly in my head I was committed to a future with him in spite of huge barriers to it ever happening; his awareness of these barriers may have made his own commitment to this future at best, wobbly.

Many years ago, my mother died as a result of having Alzheimer's disease. It has always saddened me that the memories of her that linger in my mind are of a poor dotty old woman, rather than the lovely feisty lady she once was. It's the same with a failed marriage which is what this book is about. My prevailing memories are of its deterioration whereas we were once joyously happy together. We fought, yes of course we did, but only with the knowledge that our emotional investment was for life and therefore apparently indestructible. And the good times, especially in those early days, were very good. I suspect that I was as much seduced by the introduction to Zarek's rich and magical cultural world as I was by the man himself. I can remember mushrooming in Epping Forest, usually early on a Sunday morning, when we would meet other Eastern European nationals, each with their eyes cast to the ground, silently searching for boletus mushrooms, with great concentration. Then, if we had been lucky, returning to my bed-sit with the mucky and probably maggoty products of our search (some had suspicious looking teethmarks in them too), which, with the help of a few bits of bacon and some sour cream, Zarek converted into a truly delicious lunch. I was wary at first, imagining that with every mouthful I would be poisoned. But it never happened and I grew to trust Zarek's knowledge and confidence.

Food seems to have been a preoccupation, possibly due to the deprivation he had experienced as a child during the second world war. For example, we camped once in Southern Ireland by a lake where he caught eels and delighted in degloving them by hooking them up through their chins and then pulling downwards on their skin. After that the chopped up pieces were fried in butter. Once more I was wary, but this time it was because they writhed as they lost their skins, and in the pan as they were cooked, which had me squirming too. Then in Dublin we had bed and breakfast with Mrs. Ball of Ballsbridge in her basement kitchen with its huge condiment-laden Victorian dining table.

Daquise, a restaurant outside South Kensington tube station, served authentic food to an appreciative Polish clientele, including wonderful cakes and pastries. I'd only ever seen poppy seeds sparsely scattered on loaves of bread but here they were the main filling ingredient for the best pastry of all. Another favourite for me was 'chlodnik' a cold version of barszcz (beetroot soup) with dill, chives, prawns, beans and sour cream all stirred in; a delightfully refreshing antidote to a dusty, hot summer's day in London. Oh dear, to this day I can still get carried away by the delights of Polish cuisine but the wonderful Jewish wedding we went to at the Savoy stays in my memory because of the simultaneous appearance of waiters at the four corners of the room bearing aloft...... souffles ! Actually that event is also remembered with embarrassment as Zarek , having donned the white paper Kippah (small cap worn by Jewish men) for the prolonged Yiddish grace that preceded the start of the meal, chattered and joked audibly and disrespectfully throughout as if to demonstrate that he wasn't one of them, not a Jew.

We took advantage of all that London had to offer - theatre with the Mazowsze, a wonderful state troupe of dancers, cinema where we once met an old school friend of Zarek's, the actor Vladek Sheybal at a showing of Wajda's film, the Wedding; concerts which inevitably tended to focus on Polish composers, Chopin of course but also others, less known in this country, Lutoslawki, Penderezski, Szymanowski. At Christmas time we went to Westminster Cathedral for a special service of carols for the Polish community. I am glad that I have kept an ancient vinyl record (and the means to play it) of these lovely carols as they have remained an essential part of my seasonal traditions.

Friends ? Well, Zarek had many anxieties. He had left a wife and child in Poland so there was his association with me and the possibility of divorce, not to mention the ambiguity of his status in England. This meant that contact with work friends was non-existent but he had a relative by marriage, a tiny bird-like widow, who immediately after the war had managed to settle in north London. Ciocia Marysia was an expert seamstress who made exquisite gowns for Princess Diana among others. Anything that she did, whether it was sewing, baking, cooking, gardening, was immaculate, as though it had not been touched by human hand. I came to love her dearly and was heartbroken when she died. In later years, after being banished from the family home, I saw little of her but knew, because she always asked the children about me, that she had not been taken in by the bad press about me that Zarek had circulated.

Our closest friends in those early days were James and Janet. She was a psychologist and he an Australian psychiatrist who had come to England in search of a Cambridge degree in musicology, funded through his clinical practice. He saw himself as a gourmet with an appreciation of fine wines, notwithstanding also a weakness for chocolate and ice cream. His main passion however, was for music, especially of the seventeenth and eighteenth centuries and J. S. Bach in particular. It was obsessive. He currently is the proud possessor of over thirty keyboard instruments of that period, all expertly restored and used for an annual series of subscription concerts and broadcasts, in Sydney, Australia. Together we spent endless evenings comparing and contrasting different performances on his super-duper sound system, installed in the rather shabby flat that he and Janet shared off the Finchley Road. They were culturally, incredibly rich and stimulating times.

I owe to Zarek, my appreciation of all things European and although Lorna's cynicism about the hand-kissing stuff was probably justifiable, I was half her age, naïve and totally seduced by the gallantry and cultural breadth which accompanied it. This handsome, swashbuckling foreigner had completely swept me off my feet.

But what of the barriers ? There was the wife of course, and their young daughter, left behind at the mercy of his fierce mother-in-law in Warsaw. More complicated was his own status both in Warsaw and this country. His original plan, so he said, was to return to his consultant post in Warsaw with new ideas but in fact he never went back. The reason for this was that his approach to psychiatry in Poland had been seen as radical and politically challenging. Had he wanted to progress further up the career ladder, it would have been necessary for him to embrace with rather more enthusiasm than he could muster, the Communist ideology that was endemic in Poland at that time. Having arrived in London, ostensibly to study the Day Hospital movement in this country, he'd outstayed his travel arrangements and had become stateless. The Day Hospital soon found him a temporary job but registration with the General Medical Council, which authorised foreign doctors to practise here permanently was another matter. It was 1966 and reciprocity between EU countries enabling recognition of qualifications and opportunity to work in participating countries simply did not exist. So, in order to remain and get a job, he would have to start again and become a first year medical student, with all the qualifying exams ahead of him in a language and an examining system that were both unfamiliar. Telling English women they were beautiful wasn't going to get him very far in this endeavour.

I might have thought twice if I'd realised what I was letting myself in for but I was in lurve and thought that this would conquer all. My Mum and Dad were less sure but having tried always to show trust, patience and tolerance, they sat and waited anxiously during the five years that it took him to achieve his British qualification and citizenship and his divorce. Only then were we able to marry and get on with living 'happily ever after'.

Huh.

.......that's the 'huh' of hindsight; the huh that offers a portent of things to come, that the ever after might not be quite so happy after all. How do I know this ? Well, this is a true story; a memoir of a series of events in my life that happened many years ago. So Lorna and her switchboard, the Day Hospital with its Catalpa tree and swirling history of excitement, discovery, pain, sadness and joy, all existed. They were real and could tell many stories of their own. But this one is mine. It is of course, only true as I experienced it. Each of the other protagonists will have their own truth, their own experience of what happened, their own story to tell. This makes me wonder if there is any such thing as a "true" story, one that can be recognised by all its participants. In general, yes, but in detail, feeling and how it is presented to others, I'm not so sure. Although we inhabit a shared world, it is a different and unique place for each of us, so I am the only one who can tell this particular story.

11

Why do it ? Well, as any climber will tell you when asked why they risk life and limb to scale yet another apparently unconquerable mountain, it's because it's there. It all happened. I'm certainly no celebrity, nor have I distinguished myself in any particular career or field, created a work of art, or done much to enrich people's lives, all of which are more usual triggers for a memoir. I'm simply Mrs. Ordinary of Shropshire, with three children and umpteen grandchildren, with a compulsion to write. But this story, by its very existence on paper, demonstrates that even when the most utterly devastating things happen to us, we have the capacity to survive and work our way back into a meaningful life. I often wonder, as I walk the streets of the pretty little town where I live, greeting both friends and strangers, how many of them carry with them their own invisible heartbreaks and tragedies, complications of both body and soul. None of us is immune. We smile, we greet each other and respond when asked how we are, with "Fine, thank you", knowing deep down, the challenges we have had to face and how tough life can be. But at least we have it. And surviving these tough experiences can make us strong.

My own story raises many tough issues. Relationships between men and women for a start, and toughest of all, marriage. It's also about women's role in society, attitudes to how we bring up our children, how our expectations are shaped. It's about guilt, divorce and the painfully unsubtle way the courts deal with it but also the impossibility of making a 'right' decision. Think of the judgement of Solomon where two women both claimed ownership of a child. He pronounced that the child should be cut in half so that they could have an equal share but the true mother immediately offered to relinquish her half so that the child could live. That's the sort of thing courts are faced with and to my mind, in present day circumstances, they are sometimes having to make impossible choices. These days the needs of the children are rightly paramount so it can be one or other of the poor disputing parents who can be left feeling that they have been emotionally flayed.

Admittedly what I am describing happened forty years ago and although there have been huge technological advances and attitudinal changes, the fact that one of my daughters has recently undergone a similarly heartbreaking conclusion to her divorce, suggests to me that things haven't moved on as much as we think. My story is set in a time when there was no internet, no mobile phones, no You-tube, Facebook, tweeting or blogging and before reality TV shows. In the NHS it was considered unprofessional to use anything less formal than one's surname so to the patients with whom I had daily contact, I was always Miss Mayhew, never Lizzie. For us, the telephone was firmly fixed to the wall and the arrival of the postman twice a day, was the only other means of remote contact.

Significantly, attitudes and expectations, particularly in relation to sexual behaviour have changed dramatically during that period. At that time, unmarried mothers weren't necessarily condemned but they were certainly noticed and probably pitied. The contraceptive pill had only just gone into circulation and was rather less available to single women like me who were desperate to dispense with their virginity, than to those who were safely married. 'Living together' was more the exception than the norm but sexual intercourse, sleeping together, has obviously never gone out of fashion. It was just that people kept it to themselves and they may have been less comfortable doing it, canoodling in cars and elsewhere, furtively for fear of discovery. Then, the litigious society was in its infancy and most of us had yet to be challenged by the Big Brotherliness of the electronic world which can photograph us, DNA sample us, list us, register us, pursue us in any number of ways we could barely have guessed at in the 1970s and 80s. Nevertheless, issues remain which you, as reader, may well identify with through your own experience or that of people known to you.

I had thought that identities should be concealed, sensitivities protected but with the distancing of time, I now see no reason although I still feel ambivalent about it. The sensitivities are buried under the passing years and some of the people I have written about are long dead. Others I have lost contact with and therefore cannot know how they might view this exposure of the part they played in my story. For their sakes I have used different names but my personal feeling is that we move on and are gone too soon for it to really matter. Protecting people's identities by giving them different names is hard. One's name is part of who one is, both for oneself and for others. But, as I have lost contact with many of the people who were a part of my story at this time, and I cannot know who might pick up this book, and the feelings it might arouse, it has to be done.

There's another reason why I am telling this story. I'm tidying up. During the adult part of my lifetime, I have moved house eight times. Although my possessions have waxed and waned over the years, every move has been accompanied by two bulging and very precious plastic bags, full to bursting with letters. Until now, they have been shoved to the back of a cupboard or the bottom of a drawer, waiting for the time when I could decide what to do with them. Throw them away and move on ? Good God no. They were a part of me.

You will find out more about these letters and read many of them later on. Suffice it to say that they were mainly between me and a man who subsequently became my lover and a key player in this story, both of us compulsive scribblers. These letters largely determined the course of events and played a hugely important role in this story. This is why I kept them. I have always known when the time was right that they would demand to be exhumed and brought to life. That is now, so please, read on......

2. Letters to Hilda

I've already described myself as a compulsive scribbler, a compulsive correspondent. My best friends, whether leftovers from schooldays, college or any time thereafter, were all people who shared this passion for writing. That's how we'd stayed in touch over the years. Hilda was one of them, in fact she'd made it her career. We were at college together but she soon gave up her not-very-successful attempts to be an Occupational Therapist and embarked on an exciting life of travel. Coupled with writing, this had given her lots of adventures and no little success. Although we shared interests in books, theatre, cinema, the arts generally, our lives had gone in very different directions but our early shared experience cemented what has been the friendship of a lifetime.

Christmas 1972 Surrey.

My dear Hilda - what a shame that you couldn't have been with us to celebrate our November marriage, at long last. It feels like half a lifetime rather than five years, since I was writing ecstatic letters while you were in America, having detached myself from Jim and then becoming involved with Zarek. We thought we were being discreet but the attraction between us must have been obvious. In the middle of a community meeting in the hospital with all the patients looking on, one of them once asked "why does Dr. Urbanczyk keep looking at Miss Mayhew ?" A perceptive question but I guess we weren't about to own up that it was because we were both thinking about what we had been doing the night before ! I must confess though, that it really surprised me prior to our wedding and before his citizenship was confirmed, when I received a visit from two gentlemen in trench coats from the Home Office, wanting to know if I knew he had been married in Poland. It made Zarek's caution more understandable - fearing always that somehow his intention to establish a new life in England might be communicated to authorities in Poland who would then magically drag him back behind the iron curtain for retributive punishment. We've joked about how hard he finds it to believe _anything_ he reads, even a recipe in a cookery book, such was the paranoia generated within the communist regime.

Anyway, after obtaining two divorces, one British, one Polish just to be on the safe side, British citizenship and full medical registration with the General Medical Council, we are now man and wife, residing in what is known as a leafy suburb, in Epsom. For me this means getting used to being called Mrs. 'Urb...........um' since anyone who attempts his Polish name always stops short when they realise they don't know what to do with the final 'czyk' bit !

We had such a lovely wedding. Those who knew what had been required of both of us, Zarek to obtain legitimacy in this country, and me, to wait patiently and loyally while he achieved it, were as jubilant as us - it was a very fine celebration. The dress ? Well, at 29, I didn't consider virginal white to be quite my style so opted for a lovely oyster silk Edwardian style top joined to a long skirt made of oyster coloured furnishing fabric, which worked brilliantly except *for one thing. The huge leg 'o' mutton sleeves started at the waist and as soon as the first tear rolled, I had quite a problem retrieving my Grandma's lace edged handkerchief which I knew I would need and had tucked up my sleeve for safe keeping, which had disappeared somewhere round my middle ! In the end the Registrar passed me a tissue. And then several more as I wept the whole way through. We held the wedding reception in a place in South Kensington which is aptly called the Polish Hearth. It's a club for Polish emigres, peopled with elderly gentlemen playing chess or reading Polish newspapers and pretty, older ladies often with bleached yellow hair, lots of makeup and an over-arching confidence in their femininity. There's the quiet shushy, szuszy buzz of the Polish language and huge murals of whirling dancers in brilliantly coloured folk costumes, with ribbons and pigtails flying. There are also lovely papercut pictures of the greatest intricacy which are supposedly made by country farmers using the same shears that they use on their sheep ! Of course in the restaurant they only serve Polish food - buckwheat (kasza – I'm showing off here !), beef olives (zrazy), stuffed cabbage leaves (golabki), tripe (flaki) and wonderful cakes. My favourite has a filling made with poppy seeds which seems a pretty insubstantial ingredient ! You can buy Polish books there too but they look universally uninteresting as they are all bound in the same dull cloth - a consequence, so Zarek says of Communist frugality.*

Anyway, our wedding reception was lovely, all a bit impromptu because of this 'foreign' environment but we did the usual things - cutting the cake, toasts and speeches for which my father had taken the trouble to learn some Polish !

Our honeymoon was in Tenerife - the only place Zarek could find with plenty of sunshine in the middle of November. After a relationship which had taken root five years earlier, we were hardly in the first throes of passion but suffice it to say that our lovemaking was everything that I could have wished for my honeymoon - and some ! Zarek is a superb lover.

And I really do love this man in a way I haven't before experienced. How do I know? Well I've never before wanted anyone else's children as much as I'd like him to be the father of mine. It's that simple. It could be just a case of broodiness, particularly in view of my age but it doesn't feel like that. I'm assuming that our children would be like Zarek, intelligent, cultured, interesting, handsome etc. - definitely good enough, so I hope we don't have to wait too long. Of course we have arguments, all couples do, but marriage enables you to weather the storms with so much more confidence. And this one has made a whole new cultural world available to me which I delight in.

The house we have bought in Epsom required complete renovation but with the help of one of Zarek's patients, a young lad who was ready to start work but couldn't find any, we've been stripping off wallpaper, sanding, painting, paperhanging and waiting for the various purveyors of carpets and furniture to deliver their goods. So now we have a home ! An early purchase was a piano, so that I could accompany Zarek on his violin with passionate renderings by conspicuously musical Poles - Chopin, Wieniawski, Paderewski, or as a musical friend of ours refers to him "that famous Irish politician, Paddy Rooskey !" I love the elegant

19

and stately Polonaises which Zarek plays with authentic gravitas but his interpretations of English music are questionable, in fact he drives me barmy with the triplets he insists are appropriate for Greensleeves instead of playing a dotted quaver, semiquaver and quaver. Grrrrr ! I have also acquired a taste for very cold Polish bison vodka and have learnt to appreciate that a few old cabbage leaves, some wrinkly bacon, a sausage past its sell-by date and some of last week's stew are the perfect ingredients for Bigos - a sort of Polish cabbage stew that has everything stirred into it. I'm really enjoying learning about the culinary culture of another country although I wish Zarek was a little more tolerant of ours - "Roast beef and Yorkshire pudding ?" "No, it does not go," he says.

I can't imagine what it must have been like, leaving his Polish life behind, not to mention his eight year old daughter whom he adored. I've been making her clothes and with every parcel that gets sent to Warsaw, photographs are returned showing her wearing whatever I have made, including her first communion dress. Not of course that Zarek is religious. In Poland, Catholicism is as much a political statement as a religious one.

So yes, although I haven't relinquished my Englishness, I've certainly embraced his Polish culture with genuine enthusiasm and excitement. Such is the political climate at the moment, he doesn't dare go back but maybe one day it will change and enable us both to visit his country and his family. I can't wait ! Lots of love Hilda, Lizziex

Summer 1973 Hampshire.

Hilda - I'm so excited ! Zarek has finally got back to where he was before leaving Poland. He's got a Consultant post in Portsmouth and we've bought a house in a village a few miles away, which feels like a palace ! We see it as our long-term future home - a place for bringing up children and becoming part of the local scene. I can't wait for you to see it - detached with four bedrooms, a study, large living room, kitchen and sitting room and on a corner plot so there's quite a lot of garden on two sides and then a sizeable piece at the back with fruit trees, a shed and well planned and planted herbaceous border down one side. The people who were selling it have moved into an even bigger house in the same village so have passed on local knowledge, such as when the travelling butcher and bin men call, and social contacts too. It feels as though they want us to enjoy all the village amenities as much as they do themselves. A good start.

Moving here has meant for me, abandoning any professional aspirations. As a consultant, Zarek's income is more than adequate for us both and all that we want to do in the house. So yet again, we're painting and papering like mad although this time it's easier because the house is in much better condition than the Epsom one. It has been well maintained, it's just that we don't share the same taste as the previous owners. And it's big so we need more furniture. We veer between antique - a lovely Victorian sofa, beautiful if slightly threadbare Afghan carpet, Edwardian mahogany corner cabinet and a Georgian bookcase/writing desk which has yielded a secret compartment, and the practicality of Habitat, anticipating the future needs and demands of an increasing family.

There is nevertheless, the small matter of achieving pregnancy and we have resorted to regular sex 'sessions' preceded by an appointment with a thermometer to see if the temperature indicates fertility and the right time of the month. Neither love nor lust really come into it - we're having sex and just want to make a baby. Having started to look hungrily at other women's babies in the supermarket, I can fully understand the obsessive desperation that overcomes some women when they fail to conceive - I'd stop short at baby-snatching, but I can identify with the feeling. Anyway, there's plenty to do to create another home so no real urgency, except in my head.

The village itself is small, only about 2,500 people most of whom are either associated with the navy or IBM in Portsmouth. It sports golf and tennis clubs and several roads of large houses set in their own grounds so you can imagine the sort of place it is. I think you should come and see for yourself, don't you ?! Lots of love, Lizziex.

July 1974 Hampshire.

Dear Hilda

This letter has been incubating at the back of my mind for ages and was all ready to hatch out when I suddenly realised that, horrors, I had no paper ! A quick rifle through Zarek's imposing desk produced the necessary, so here we are, raring to go.

Well now. The solitude of domesticity ? Yes, but there's so much else going on in our lives - books, culture – such a rich diet ! I finished Balthazar B. and am grateful to you for helping me to overcome my intense dislike of Donleavy, based on a single reading of the Ginger Man. I hated it so much that I couldn't bear to finish it and as you know, I am normally much too mean, having purchased a book (theatre/cinema ticket) not to sit it out, at least to see if it can produce any redeeming features. But for you, I would have turned my back on Donleavy FOR EVER !

Culture ? Well, apart from Chichester Theatre, the high spot has been Glyndebourne which I was taken to by discerning friend Jonathan, who has been many times before so knows the form – where to deposit one's picnic hamper, what to drink and when ie iced coffee and chocolate cake on arrival and Pimms no. 1 on departure. We saw/heard The Marriage of Figaro – an exquisite experience for all the senses – supremely sophisticated and all in this uniquely English, slightly decadent picnic hamper setting with the sheep bleating among the thistles, beyond the ha-ha and bats zooming in and out of the auditorium as the light faded.

Don't be surprised that I should only mention the word 'pregnancy' at this stage in my letter - we have to get our priorities right ! All goes well and the little infant bobs around in my abdomen which proceeds to grow at the approved rate. Pregnancy is so much an attitude of mind (no it's not, it's the fertilisation of an egg by a sperm which then grows to maturity, and is expelled from the mother's body via strong muscular contractions) and with so many other things to absorb my interest, I barely notice the swelling of breast and belly. Initially I devoured information voraciously. I was excited when it first moved, excited going to the hospital to be prodded, excited when I felt securely enough pregnant to go and buy baby things. But now I've got used to the idea and when I don't feel tired and fat, I wonder if I'm pregnant at all. However, I AM worried about it getting out and also whether I shall feel I have lost my freedom.......

Zarek is such a controlling person that sometimes, tucked away in this little village and being so dependent on him for the sort of life we lead and the people we meet, I feel as though we're living his life and not mine at all and I'm wondering if I've relinquished more of my freedom than I realised. Maybe this is all part of the necessary process of adjustment, and motherhood will bloom and flourish in January to give meaning to it all. In any case, when you have got what you want, it's silly to start wondering if you ever really wanted it after all!

Zarek's latest acquisition hasn't helped. It's a 24 ft. cruising BOAT. Having been talked into it by friends and then doing a beginners' one week sailing course in Fowey (very scarey), he reckons that the sea is in his blood but mine has turned to watery shit at the various experiences we have had so far.

Consider this. Our first solo expedition ended on a mudflat where we were stranded for 24 hours having run ourselves very much aground - no food, no sleeping bags, not even a comb – and an abortive attempt at 4.00 a.m to pull the boat off when the tide rose. We failed, so she had to remain there for ten days until the next Spring tide and by that time Zarek and a friend, a Real Friend since no other would have done it, had to dig her out. The engine broke down too so that our poor little 'Seagull' finally arrived back in the yacht basin, lashed to the side of a rescue launch with Zarek and Real

Friend trouserless, and caked to their underpants in mud. Janet (R.F's girlfriend) and I had gone to meet them at the yacht basin and we both had to turn away when we saw them, we couldn't stop laughing !

Our second voyage was no less hazardous. Having miscalculated the time it would take us to return to our moorings, we found ourselves travelling in the dark along an unfamiliar channel littered with boats, buoys and other watery 'furniture' – my night vision is AWFUL at the best of times, which this wasn't. Zarek was over-confident which made me fractious and naggy which made him irritable so life aboard was…. bloody. Pregnancy adds to my feelings of vulnerability and I feel as though I'm being pushed beyond limits I haven't yet had the opportunity to consolidate. OK so we've found out how not to go aground and how to sail in the dark but I'd rather not find out the hard way. Supposing one of us goes overboard ? Ugh. For me, baby comes a long way before boat and I wish he'd bought a second car instead.

Aha. I hear the sounds of the Master arriving. Away, away, exeunts off. Lots of love, Lizzie.

December 1974 Hampshire.

My Dear Sniffy Friend

I'm sorry you are so miserable at being marooned in Capetown for Christmas while your dear bloke Hugh is in Brazil and your family are having their usual traditional Christmas in Chandler's Ford. I guess it's a time which can exaggerate one's sense of loneliness, especially as you have always had lovely family Christmases at home in England but as you seem intent on becoming a professional traveller, it may be something you will have to get used to.

This is just a quickie to wish you seasonal joy and to say that on New Year's Eve (as you may not receive this until then), we shall drink a toast to absent friends and think of you, probably sunning yourself on some balmy beach, surrounded by hunky life-savers to keep the sharks at bay.

Hopefully also, most of the aftertaste of your separation will have faded and you will be anticipating Hugh's delayed arrival with excitement rather than mourning his absence. It interests me greatly how one is brainwashed into believing the 'two bodies, one mind' aspects of marriage. Both you and I would be the first people to value our spiritual independence which I'm sure our respective husbands would stoutly confirm and say that they shared this value but when it comes to doing it/living it - ouch, it can feel like a tight shoe !

Here's an example. Zarek came home with two paintings he'd bought at the village Christmas Fair. There had been an exhibition by local artists and he'd chosen not just one horrible bit of kitsch but two by the same artist. I can see no merit in either of them and it grieves me that other people will see them on the walls of our home and will think they reflect my taste as much as they do his. I'm saddened because we have some really fine pictures and it corrupts their value - not even loving him can make me accept them - they are AWFUL ! Two bodies with but one soul ? Not a bit of it. I had thought I understood his foreign-ness, the fact

26

that he'd been brought up with different cultural traditions, different tastes but it was quite an eye-opener to see this blatant example of how very different they are !

Other things are better. Having survived the early horrors of boat ownership and our disastrous experiences, and thank God we managed to stop short of ramming anything or actual capsize, I think we were both relieved when the sailing season ended in October. Zarek's relief at no longer having to pit himself against the elements (generally a losing battle) was considerable although sociologists maintain that a certain amount of stress and anxiety in life can be healthy and productive.

However, no longer having boat worries on our minds, we're both looking forward to the arrival of our baby with undivided pleasure and it touches me to the core to see the fond smile of potential paternity and a special gleam in the eye (different from his other repertoire of gleams !) appear when he regards my ever-increasing girth. Occasionally I get caught out by all this cow-like contentment and the permanence of our life here, mapped out for years ahead. What happened to that spiritual independence I was talking about earlier ? D'you know, I can't be bothered to think about it ! Happy Christmas Hilda, happy new year, love Lizzie.

3. First baby

I'd gone into the village shop when Lucy, who was working at the till said "Oh, you're expecting. When's your baby due ?" and when I said "In three days' time," there were gasps of astonishment all round because nobody had noticed, nobody knew. In a way it's not surprising. I wasn't hugely big. It was January and winter clothing can conceal a multitude of ….. sins. The pregnancy had been uneventful, much to the disappointment of the obstetrician that I saw regularly. Doctors looking after doctors' families, love there to be complications so that they can show off their expertise to their colleagues. It's definitely a two tier system. None of that queuing in public corridors with a dozen other prospective mothers, wearing flimsy hospital gowns and seated on clammy plastic chairs. No, I went to the Consultant's comfortable private suite at his house in the village where we both lived. Our baby seemed reluctant to detach himself from my cosy womb so in the end, the only additional intervention, two weeks after the due date had passed was an induced labour. With hindsight, I can say that Greg, my first child, has always needed rather a lot of encouragement to get on with things, even being born.

Not too much fun, giving birth. Nobody tells you about the excruciating pain or if they do, it's impossible to understand until you have experienced it. It's like nobody telling you about the relentlessness of actually looking after the babies once they have arrived. Perhaps it's our hormones that deceive us into thinking that children are what we most want but by the time we have struggled to look after them, even for five years, let alone the ten, fifteen, twenty that follow, we are longing for privacy, independence and a bit of freedom all of which are relinquished in the interests of bringing children into the world.

Anyway, I went through the birthing process uneventfully even though with hindsight, I can hardly believe that my mind was present at such a fundamentally physical performance of my body. Leaving the hospital was pretty fraught with Zarek cool and aloof, staring into the middle distance as though it was nothing to do with him. He then decided to call at the fishmongers to purchase a dozen fresh herrings for me to pickle, Polish style - not exactly my top priority on arriving home with my firstborn.

April 1975 Hampshire.

Dear Hilda,

Forgive me if this letter becomes progressively more incoherent. Zarek is at some home-made wine tasting 'do' down in Portsmouth and Greg was supposed to be parked with friends so that I could go too but at the last minute his feeding routine fell apart so I had to stay behind and he's been awake until ten minutes ago.

Babies are death to one's social life. I'm here consoling myself with whisky and the pen – if Greg's behaviour persists, I'm in danger of becoming alcoholic. I don't actually mind at all because he's such a loveable little baby. Also, I'm becoming aware of an interesting phenomenon that I only noticed when an academic friend of Zarek's came to stay with us. We'd had an evening of fascinating 'clever' conversation, good food, drink flowing etc. with lots of obscure ideas being tossed around much too quickly for me to keep up. I had to go upstairs and feed Greg and I had this strange feeling that there with my baby at my breast was a much more real world than the one of concepts and abstractions downstairs.

Zarek is much better and much worse than I'd anticipated. He's better in that his love for Greg is both profound and spontaneously expressed. He constantly remarks with real joy on what a lovely little son I have given him. It's a great pleasure to live with this enjoyment, an added bounty. On the other hand, and I'd sort of anticipated this, there's nothing he doesn't know or have an opinion on, in relation to baby care. I sometimes feel as though I'm barely being allowed to mother my own child. Breast feeding is the only thing that Zarek can't do and I really reached explosion point one day when he started to criticise how I was doing that ! He's so very controlling, I sometimes feel really frightened, especially when I remember how much I enjoyed my independence. Now there's nothing I can do without his permission and he's always hovering at my elbow to 'advise'.

We've now purchased a second car and although it's a performance getting baby, pram and baggage aboard a VW Beetle, for the first time in our married life, I'm actually doing the weekly shop. Working close to a supermarket had made it more convenient for Zarek to do but it effectively insulated me from the outside world. OK domestic shopping is a frightful bore but it was another aspect of the control that Zarek maintained over our lives which I resented. He's still inclined to demand and question where I'm going and why and we probably argue over the route and where I shall park but once I'm in the car, who cares !

As you may have gathered, one devastating aspect of having a child is the effect it has on one's relationship. Zarek was fantastic when Greg first came home, but having had a child by his previous marriage, and one who is likely to bear emotional scars from that unsuccessful liaison, he's determined that we should be 'perfect' parents. This has caused him to fuss quite dreadfully and at times I've wondered if it was really worth it. Then I look at Greg and see Zarek looking at Greg and it dispels all doubt.

In addition, he's had an enormous amount of stress at work recently, he's been trying to get that damned boat ready to go back into the water for sailing and we also started to paint the kitchen, all without realising how much of my day was taken up looking after Greg. Zarek seems to live in a fantasy world - a big house, a permanently sunny garden, a happy, compliant wife emerging from a kitchen smelling of good Polish food, lots of little children gambolling around, a boat moored snugly in the harbour ready to carry him round the world should he wish to go, good friends, music, cultured evenings etc. etc. What he forgets is a) it all costs money, which has to be worked for and b) turning the fantasies into reality is really hard work, both practically and interpersonally. In consequence Zarek slaves desperately to earn the money and I slave, equally desperately to keep the practical side of things going and if anything suffers, it's the interpersonal bit. Our salvation comes with the knowledge *that without each other, there is nothing else and we both feel this very deeply so we <u>have</u> to make it all work, financially, practically and interpersonally. One thing we are agreed upon is that Greg shouldn't be the only focus for all our neurotic expectations so we hope for more children before too long - completing the fantasy again of course !*

I'm embarking on a bit of independent action with the resumption of my music lessons. I might even eventually get a teaching diploma, which will make me an expert in one particular thing rather than a jack of all trades which is how people tend to see occupational therapists .

Enclosed are some photos of Greg – the most beautiful, intelligent and well-developed baby ever – don't take any notice of his haggard looking Mum ! He's becoming delightfully responsive and laughs and wriggles happily when tickled. We have funny growling conversations which make me feel like a lioness with her cub. Why is it that our family photos always seem to include the dustbins, the coal bunker or the washing machine ? Hope you are well and happy and that Hugh has arrived safely, lots of love, Lizzie.

August 1975 Hampshire.

Dear Hilda,

Don't be insulted when I say that you are my holiday task for today ! You see it has become a positive luxury to write conversational letters. Recently my correspondence has been limited to sending off cheques to pay tax bills or phoning the tax man to persuade him that we aren't really trying to defraud him and if we have done so, it's because I am dim and Zarek uninterested ! Which makes this particular missive a sheer indulgence.

I must confess that I'm beginning to notice in myself a worrying hesitancy, diffidence, inarticulateness in conversation that I have noticed in other mums, wives of professional men who spend their time at home looking after families and making things comfortable and secure for their industrious husbands. The symptoms are lack of conversation about anything other than domestic issues, anxious glances at their husbands when they dare to voice any sort of opinion, no matter how conventional and a tendency to offer their sentences to other people to finish as though they weren't convinced that what they had started had any validity. I notice I'm doing this and wonder if one eventually reaches a terminal stage of mutism !

However, as they say, "mustn't grumble !" Having another car has transformed my life. Greg and I now go to regular swimming sessions with much wriggle and splash – he loves it. And at this moment we are at the seaside in Essex, visiting my parents who are of course, overjoyed to show their first grandchild off to their local friends. The wheels have given us all greater freedom as Zarek now takes himself to the yacht basin where he has friends who are prepared to crew for him and do blokey sorts of exploration of the Solent. The summer has been fantastic – days and days of sunshine and balmy weather, ideal for inexperienced sailors ! Greg and I have been sailing once or twice and actually got to the Isle of Wight, while Zarek has been out on the boat nearly every weekend. My anticipation of a *summer of endless conflict and anxiety about boating activities has been very happily frustrated.*

Also, now that Greg has established a sleeping routine, it means we are able to enjoy entertaining without fear of interruption. Last week I actually achieved a successful baked Alaska with a pineapple in the middle, or rather sitting on a sponge cake base, surrounded by ice cream and then insulated all over with meringue. Could hardly believe it when I cut into it and the ice cream was still firm after a quick blast in the oven ! What's more, I've even managed strudel pastry - much stretching and pulling required, also a bit of confidence but definitely worth the effort as it tastes so much better than anything you can buy.

So, it's been glorious – lots of guests coming for brief visits with a bit of recovery time in between. Having a new baby is a bit like moving house – everybody wants to come and see you and check it/him out ! We are so lucky with Greg – equable temperament, enormous and easily satisfied appetite, good health and an ability to fall asleep and stay that way whenever he is supposed to. Long may it continue. I guess we are now reaping the benefit of this fundamental change in our lives.

I've just re-read your last letter and the bit about you and Hugh avoiding conflict at all costs and him ventilating his difficulties in the relationship, to his mother rather than you. I hope this is an anxiety long forgotten but I think you really ought to discuss things that bug you rather than sweeping them under the carpet. Sooner or later there's going to be a mighty big heap of dust and one of you is going to trip over the bump that it makes. I really shouldn't interfere, especially as I'm unsure whether our method, which is to periodically yell at each other and get it out of our systems, is any better. That hurts quite a bit too. Loads of love Hilda, from Lizxx

Sad to say, sweeping it under the carpet definitely didn't work for those two. Although what Hugh did, which was to put a letter in Hilda's suitcase, on one of her periodic visits from America, saying their marriage was over, struck me as cowardly in the extreme.

4. Duplicitous Bohemian

He wasn't really my type but in any case, one of the first things I noticed about Chris, as you do at the age of nineteen, was his wedding ring. A married man so off-limits. Even so, he was good-looking, clean-shaven, lots of curly hair and with evenly chiselled features and odd socks. Always odd socks in bright colours. He was employed as an itinerant pottery instructor in the Art Room of a south London mental hospital where I was doing a student placement as part of my Occupational Therapy training. His small neat stature belied the size of his personality and his talents included not only pottery but drawing, painting, poetry writing and folk-singing, all of which he used to much more than therapeutic effect with the patients. Art was definitely on the therapy list so they were encouraged to spend time in this large semi-basement room. Although a bit gloomy, they liked going there. It was a good bolt-hole, more relaxed than the starchy ward environment, a place to sit and smoke and chat and maybe draw or paint if you felt the urge. This was a long time before Zarek of course, but Chris and I became friends and he soon introduced me to his wife Annie and gang of creative mates he'd been at college with. They seemed to have a lot of fun.

 For many, he brought rainbows of colour and laughter into their dreary worlds, as he did mine. He was friendly and entertaining and I soon met Annie and the rest of their crowd, all of whom had come from the creative, free-spirited art school world that I had so nearly embraced myself before starting my training. I could never have imagined at that time, the danger that he would subsequently represent for me. Chris had one other significant attribute - he was a compulsive letter-writer.

By the time Greg was born in 1975, Chris was already divorced from calm and dreamy Annie who had seemed like the ideal foil for his ebullience, an event which had startled and saddened me. His mother had been widowed when he was a baby and he'd been brought up lovingly but firmly within the Plymouth Brethren church in a family of women, his mother, his aunt and his older sister. Christian fellowship had been the backbone of their existence. As a child he had been compelled to attend church three times every Sunday and as a teenager, he'd run church youth groups and preached the gospel in the streets around his home. His knowledge of Scripture was encyclopaedic and his ability to parry quote for biblical quote, confident and unswerving. He happily took on missionaries of any denomination who happened to call at the door seeking converts. Against this background of committed Christianity and certitude, the failure of his marriage must have distressed his mother and I doubt if he ever dared to hint at the morass of sexual shenanigans that undermined it, it would have hurt her too much.

As a fellow scribbler, Chris and I were tied by an inky thread, sharing that which was intimate and painful as well as positive joys and successes. For example, we both acknowledged how in the early excitement of a new relationship, we looked for, found and celebrated all the similarities between ourselves and our beloved. Learning to live with the other person introduced us to the differences between us and that could turn the whole situation on its head. This was definitely a struggle for me and Zarek, but I'd decided that one had to accept, trust and respect the differences, rather than seeing them as rocks on which the ship could founder ……. life was never meant to be a bit of cream cake. It's a rich and sumptuous meal full of variety and surprise, with occasionally a touch of indigestion too. Undeterred, Chris had found a new partner, Vanessa who he married in the summer of 1976.

This was the year that Daisy was born, seventeen months after Greg. We'd anticipated a narrow gap between the birth of first child and second. With me at 32 and Zarek thirteen years older, there was no reason to delay but we were quite unprepared for the immediacy of this second pregnancy. It was summertime with the most intense heat the century had known and our home, with two thirsty willow trees in the front garden, started to subside. This caused a whole string of problems and continued contact with structural engineers, surveyors, insurance agents and builders. The combination of heat and advancing pregnancy made me lethargic and relations between me and Zarek withered, not helped by Greg's sleepless nights. We were both frequently tired and over-sensitive. At that time Greg was walking, exploring his new world with all that curiosity and adventurousness of infants who know no fear, but I began to wonder how I could ever cope.

One boiling hot day after I had finished cutting the grass, I went into the larder to be greeted by Greg's contribution to lunch - a mess of broken eggs and cream on the floor in front of the open fridge door. Domestic chores, busy toddler, new baby ? My feelings of excited anticipation which had heralded the start of the pregnancy began to turn to anxiety and then fear. Zarek at this time was distinctly unsympathetic, offering help with neither household chores, nor small child. I'd find myself ironing his shirts at midnight or waiting on him with his meals. This time I went into labour spontaneously and was anxious to get to the hospital to get on with the job. Zarek's reaction was not wonderfully helpful. "Oh but you can't go yet because someone has to look after Greg while I do my violin practice."

 I once had a cleaning lady who said her daughter looked like a bundle of sausages when she was born and although seeing the thick cord and skinny little arms and legs of my daughter, I could see exactly what she meant, for me Daisy was the most beautiful little baby ever. Greg thought so too. He was immediately curious about his new sister, peering into her cot with his face wreathed in smiles and saying "baby, baby" with great excitement.

Having swiftly accomplished the birth, yet again Zarek arrived looking tense and out of key with the situation so our departure from the hospital was once more both abrupt and surly.

5. Family tensions

From the end of 1976 and for the next two years, the demands of two very young children and an idiosyncratic husband meant a relentless round of attempts to meet all their needs and keep them happy. Baked Alaskas and strudel pastry became a thing of the past and Christmas 1976 simply didn't exist because both children were ill and needed cuddles and care. Time passed, punctuated by an increasing litany of complaints and criticisms from Zarek, which I wrote down, they seemed so bizarre.

"You're breast-feeding that child wrongly, her head should be at this angle in relation to your nipple, not that otherwise she can't breathe." Daisy had already proved herself well able to breathe and suck simultaneously and was a perfectly well-nourished infant.

"Why do you buy that expensive stuff (Napisan which everyone was using at the time) *to soak the nappies in. My mother used a mixture of this, that and the other and so should you."* If he was a baby in nappies, how on earth could he have known what his mother used ?

"You have put the wrong clothes on Greg. They are insufficient/too heavy. They must be changed."

"Greg does not appear to be settling," (tired, sleepy whimperings coming from his cot), *"he is not tired, you must get him up immediately."*

"If Greg does not want his cereal for breakfast, then you must give him something else. I will prepare some noodles, the same as my mother used to make me." Greg doesn't want the noodles either, or the scrambled egg, or the apple grated in yoghurt with which Zarek attempts to entice him. Could it be that Greg isn't hungry, or maybe is enjoying the game ? And again, which of us remembers what we were fed in our infancy or how it was prepared ? The only things that I know for certain that I ate as a baby (because it became part of family folk lore) was the cat's dinner from a dish on the floor where I was crawling and sand from the beach during a seaside holiday which gave me worms. Oh, and a drawing pin.

"That drug which you have obtained from the doctor for Greg's cough is not right. You must go back and ask for something different."

"Why have you put so much food on my plate ? I cannot eat any of it."

And he moved out of our bedroom for a month.

I had hoped that the difficulties I had experienced in coping with Zarek's excessive need to exert control over his family after Greg's birth and which I had tried so hard to rationalise to myself and my friends, would diminish as he became more aware that I could cope and was able to be an adequate mother. Another child, I had thought, would spread the focus of his attention so that he could surely see how much I enjoyed being a mother and was perfectly competent.

At that time, I never imagined that I wasn't, but now I find myself wondering. My role model was of course my own mother and my personal experience of being mothered. I remember little detail of my own early childhood but my sister and I were definitely loved, we were well provided for and our home was clean, tidy and welcoming. Is that not enough ? I had also spent some months before becoming a student, as an au pair, to friends with four small children under the age of five. Rachel their mother, was a doctor. She was witty, challenging, highly intelligent and a good cook and although that household was good-naturedly chaotic, I loved and respected the family and learnt much from them all including the children. They were a delight.

"Why have you washed my woollen scarf in the washing machine ? I told you not to – it is completely matted and now you have made a hole in it." Did I ? In my opinion the scarf was beyond redemption anyway and I deliberately put it in the machine on a woollen wash setting thinking that if it survived, well and good, if it didn't, it was no great loss.

"As you use the water pipes in the utility room most for the washing machine, it is you who should lag them." I'd already done most of it anyway.

"I earn the money, so I make the rules."

"Have you salted the potatoes ?" "Have you salted the potatoes ?" Every bloody time, *"Have you salted the potatoes ?"*

"In my home, potatoes will always be peeled before they are cooked."

"In my home, the frying pan will always be washed every time it is used."

Maybe he was right; maybe I wasn't very good at it or thought I was better than I actually was. Certainly I felt perfectly able to cope with the children, but perhaps my ability to cope with him was the problem ? He could reduce me/arouse me to incandescent rages when I lost the ability to articulate my anger and simply lashed out. It didn't happen often because he would hit me back, a man's hit, a hit that was intended to hurt and beat me down, a frightening hit.

Before I go on, I am struck by this litany of negativity and the possibility that by only listing nastiness, I am ignoring sunnier aspects of our relationship. Had they ceased to exist ? And what had *I* contributed to this huge hostility that I seemed to stimulate in a husband who at one time seemed to have loved me ? By January 1978, I was writing this in the notebook I had started to keep because I had no other outlet for my frustrations.

I can no longer cope with the choked feeling I get wondering when he comes home whether it will be 'alright to ask him now?' Waiting for the grumbles and constant criticism, the suggestions which are orders, the continual denigration of my efforts and the stifling of initiative and responsibility for the management of our home and family. Zarek treats me like a half-wit, incapable of original thought. His word is law, mine unworthy of any consideration. We don't go out together now because any decision making processes have become too painful. We add nothing to our home, we simply survive. We no longer entertain because the tensions are intolerable and it is easier to muddle on involved with nothing but the basic care for our two little children.

"Why are you only putting cream into that sponge cake for the children's tea. It should be cut into four layers and soaked in rum." Sounds good, but, children's tea ?

During the course of conversation at a formal dinner party given by a doctor from the hospital where Zarek worked *"Don't listen to her* (me) *- she is stupid."*

"You can have a new kitchen when you are a better cook."

"You are a careless mother and have purposely inflicted a whiplash on Daisy. You are neglectful, incompetent and violent." This was after an evening when I was so tired I just wanted to drop. Daisy had been fretful with a cold and hadn't settled to sleep so I had sat cradling her in the big armchair in our bedroom, hoping that she would drop off. She was very sleepy by then but Zarek came in, just as I was standing up to put her back in her cot. In doing this I had slightly over- balanced and yes, her head had fallen back more sharply than I expected. But whiplash ? To my precious little baby ? No way.

Another notebook entry, May 1978

Suddenly, I see the problem.

"I don't want to have anything to do with the Ashtons" he says. *"He is boring and thick, and she is a gossip."* And as clearly as the sun is shining outside, I realise that I am

having to live with two differing realities, mine and my husband's.

Over the preceding year, Zarek had successfully managed to insult to their faces or denigrate to me, all the people invited into our home whom I considered to be old friends. He reduced Tess who I'd known since I was four, to tears on her first evening with us by saying that her father was a senile geriatric who with his bad heart wouldn't last much longer. And this about a charming, intelligent man, a company secretary and truly a gentleman.

He called Chris who visited us after his brief marriage to Vanessa and one or two casual relationships, a male prostitute.

To Jeanie and Charles, dear and much loved friends who so generously shared their happiness during that long waiting period before Zarek and I could wed, he demonstrated a splendid indifference but privately made snide remarks. And the same with my family. He taunted and goaded my zealously religious sister and intimidated the others with his overweening confidence.

What was extraordinary was that this man was a psychiatrist who supposedly understood the human condition, mental health and therefore mental sickness, enabling him to diagnose and heal people whose problems were serious enough to make them seek help. He could deprive people of their liberty by committing them to institutions, advise the courts and the Home Office, and administer or prescribe alarmingly brutal treatments like Electro-Convulsant Therapy and powerful drugs. What's more he was doing Marriage Guidance Counselling - physician heal thyself for goodness sake. Maybe I was insufficiently sensitive to the demands made of him, doing this hugely responsible job but he rarely if ever, talked about his work or shared his anxieties. And maybe his daily encounters with his patients' imperfect worlds, made him determined that his own should be a model of excellence. In this, by his account I clearly failed him miserably.

Although I could not get feedback because people respected loyalty between husband and wife, I saw the looks on their faces. And they knew that I knew.

Gradually, my awareness of the discrepancy between our two worlds increased and could only be reconciled by us seeing no-one and living an existence divorced from the outside world. And yet I could not discard so many dear and loving friends whose world was so much more real than the one I was obliged to inhabit. If Zarek's interpersonal perceptions were so distorted, or at least, so unlike mine, should I remove myself and the children straight away or should I somehow struggle on, trying to help them find a sort of continuity and sanity in their lives ? Could I go on straddling these two worlds ? I could not decide.

Well, my indecision and our isolation must have continued throughout the following year as there are no letters to reference nor any notebook entries until this in November 1979:

A choice of worlds.

There have been false alarms in the past, agonising days of worrying, wondering, hoping - a delayed period, a bit of sickness, big tits – and then suddenly hopes dashed by the appearance of a period. Back to despair and desperation that one has to keep on trying. (And that's a telling phrase isn't it, having to keep on trying as though we might not want to do it at all, if we, or rather I, hadn't wanted another child.) *But this time, I thought it was for real. Since having my coil removed in February, we had passed through many stages of loving and hating and being indifferent. This was underpinned by certainty that I wanted a third child but Zarek's ambivalence had made it difficult to follow through since parenthood by definition requires obvious co-operation between prospective father and mother. Interestingly enough, both Greg and little Daisy seemed to accept the inevitability of our having a baby in the family. They were simply waiting for Mummy to get a big tummy, that was the sign.*

This particular meeting of sperm and ovum must have taken place to the strains of Leonora and Florestan since we attended a performance of Fidelio that critical weekend. The very next day I felt hugely nauseated so that I could hardly eat and this continued on and off for weeks. The day my period should have started came, and went. And the next. Then several more. By the 25th day after conception the books say a little heart will start to beat. That day was our eighth wedding anniversary.

6. Third time lucky

Dear Chris,

Thank you for the delightful pooping plane you sent the children for Christmas - it has been seized upon by one and all with great delight and has withstood considerable over-enthusiasm from the little ones – not one of those toys that collapse in a heap of bent springs and broken plastic the minute it is unwrapped.

This Christmas with the children has been lovely. Greg at nearly five, knows we bought him some toys but he still believes Father Christmas was responsible for the whole show and swallowed my excuse that there wouldn't be any Space Lego this year because Father Christmas hadn't organised the factory too well – actually pretty near the truth since according to the shops I tried, Space Lego has been in short supply since LAST January. Greg woke at 3.30 on Christmas morning, full of indignation that his empty stocking had been moved from the chair by his bed. I was able to steer him into our bed and back to sleep without him realising that his stocking was already bulging enticingly at the <u>end</u> of his bed. I'll bet that doesn't happen again !

Although Christmas was lovely, it was over too quickly and was insufficiently relaxed to be truly enjoyable, but maybe that is in the nature of our family Christmases. The children were fine, it was the adults who were the problem, me included. My parents anxieties were that they were imposing on us and upsetting Zarek, his that he would be put upon by them, my sister's that he would challenge her religious beliefs, and mine that with such an explosive mixture, it would be impossible to keep the peace.

We always start with a traditional Polish Christmas Eve supper which is the meal I usually enjoy most since one hasn't got bogged down (ha ha) by that familiar feeling of starting yet another feed while the memory of the preceding one is still too recent. The Polish meal is meatless, starting with wild mushroom soup then little hand-made ravioli things called pierogi filled with chopped mushrooms and cabbage, different sorts of fish (that should include some fresh carp, not often possible in this country) accompanied by a variety of sauces and apple strudel or something similar with fruit and nuts to follow. The meal is supposed to be served as the first star appears in the sky (ours is never ready in time !) and before we start, we pass round a piece of Christmas bread (like a communion wafer) and exchange tiny pieces with each person at the table, wishing them something special, personal and valuable for the coming year.

My special, personal and valuable thing for the coming year is easy – we are expecting our third child in June ! That's if it survives the test I'm due to have in a couple of weeks time – being what they call 'elderly' in the obstetric clinic. We're delighted, if a little apprehensive about the chaos in triplicate - duplicate is bad enough !

I'm very sad that you are finding your relationship with Jodi so worrying — it ought to be a joy but it's entirely understandable. Vanessa's abrupt departure, after you had already been married once, must have caused you such pain, it would be foolish and irresponsible not to be cautious about embarking on another relationship, especially with someone so much younger and less experienced than yourself. It sounds as though Jodi loves you very much and is experiencing that omnipotence which makes one feel that love will conquer all, that it would make another marriage work, despite your reservations. I can certainly identify with that.

The hardest thing to get one's head round when one feels like this is that marriage and permanency won't change anything, it will just seal for a lifetime the imbalance in your feelings for each other. It's a sort of delusion that one can somehow envelop the partner in love and that their feelings hardly matter as long as one is allowed the satisfaction of giving that love to them.

I know this doesn't work, and sadly and cynically, my experience tells me that "being in love" is a bit of a con, which can lead you very much up the garden path.

Not that I'd have missed it for the world, but it definitely distorts one's judgement. Having said that, I find I miss the excitement which an intense and passionate relationship brings into life. OK so I've got lovely children (and for me, childbirth leaves being in love standing as far as meaningful experiences are concerned), we're secure and well provided for but in a way, I feel as though I've almost ceased to exist as an individual . Guess it's simply not possible to have one's cake and eat it ?

So, enjoy the rest of the year's bread and butter, and thank you again, much love from us all, Lizzie.

April 1980 Hampshire

Dear Hilda,

I'm not sure I'm feeling sufficiently morose to write to you now since you always say I write my best letters when I'm low, but I'll try ! Zarek has made his contribution by refusing to take the children off my hands this afternoon when I'd dearly have liked a rest after being out with them all morning. Because of the rain, I couldn't turn them loose in the garden so we went on a long and arduous shopping expedition which left me thoroughly exhausted and bad-tempered.

I suppose the reason I'm not feeling morose, just a bit crotchety, is that I've largely detached myself from the relationship so that when he's being bossy, or mean, or hurtful, I just switch off. The trouble is that poor little Greg often bears the brunt of my irritation even when he doesn't deserve it – and quite a lot of the time he does ! He's a mischievous handful, there's no doubt, but he's also open and affectionate. How I wish Zarek and I could care for each other in the way that we do for our children. They are very excited about the baby and I am too. It's perfectly true, it is me that wanted it and I still do, very much. Despite our differences, Zarek and I have an overwhelming mutual interest in our children and even while there are only two, any sort of dissociation is out of the question so we might just as well indulge ourselves with a third. Which the amniocentesis revealed is to be.......a GIRL !

I'm almost ashamed to admit that I have a very primitive feeling that boys are sort of .... more important. But apart from that and in all other respects, girls are so much easier/nicer to cope with. And this seems to be general experience, as well as mine with Greg and Daisy. Until one experiences parenthood, one has this odd idea, perpetuated by parents because it's too difficult to explain, that all children in a family are loved equally. Well perhaps they are, but they are certainly loved differently and one cannot balance it out or say whether it is more or less. I feel pride in Greg's vigour and masculinity and he's a very loving little boy when the mood takes him. Daisy arouses much softer, gentler feelings in me - totally different. I wonder what the next little cherub will be like ?

This is only a snippet of a letter - perhaps I'll do better when I'm more miserable ! Lots of love, Lizzie.

Unlike my two previous pregnancies, the initial weeks of this one were distinctly unpleasant with lots of nausea and tiredness. One Friday evening when I collapsed in front of the television, having done a round of cleaning after getting the children to bed, and was totally incapable of any more energetic form of activity, Zarek had asked me what was the matter. Sensing a trap (it was), I said nothing. He persisted and when in final desperation I said "Look, I'm ten weeks pregnant and I feel lousy," his reply was "well, what did you expect, it was what you wanted." Sod him.

What's more, a couple of months later, I went down with pneumonia. Apart from taking me to the hospital for a chest X-ray where I was enveloped in a bulky lead 'apron' to protect the baby, Zarek did nothing, absolutely nothing to help, so I had to stagger around, feeling terrible, exhausted and with an aching chest, to keep things going for the little ones. Anyone who has had pneumonia will also know that it takes weeks to feel anything like normal again. Ugh.

The next thing was his sudden anxiety that because of my age, the baby might not be normal so I reluctantly attended the hospital for amniocentesis. The result seemed to take an age although it was actually only three weeks and when I telephoned to see if the test results were alright, I resisted the temptation at that point in time, to discover the sex of the child. This made Zarek furious, I'd guess because I was controlling the situation, although he could easily have telephoned himself to find out.

I hadn't wanted to tell anyone about my 'blessed state' until I was sure everything was OK. This reticence became a habit and with the concealment afforded by bulky winter clothes, my pregnancy remained virtually unknown until the last few weeks. Shortly after receiving the result (no Downs Syndrome, no Spina Bifida thank goodness), I paid a routine visit to the hospital and, reading the inverted result on the doctor's desk, discovered it was to be another daughter. My initial guts reaction was faint disappointment. Yes, I'd hoped for another little boy but at least my baby was healthy and in any case, Daisy had been a much easier child than Greg, partly because Zarek had interfered so much less in her upbringing. So, mixed feelings but primarily one of relief that there was no need to even consider the possibility of a late abortion.

Zarek and I had recently had many arguments and my feelings of isolation were heightened when I glanced at the first few chapters of the Lamaze Easy Childbirth book which stressed the co-operation and involvement of the husband. Even if we were on reasonable terms and I'd shown it to him, Zarek would have been totally dismissive. I felt no doubts about having this baby, just grateful that we had managed it in time as there wouldn't be another pregnancy either by Zarek or anyone else. And I felt desperate about our inability to see anything in the same way. We avoided any sort of discussion or decision-making process because it inevitably led to conflict.

This baby could be seen by some as a naïve attempt to consolidate a relationship which was already beyond hope or help. How I longed for the company of a man who would actually listen to what I was saying rather than twist my opinions into what suited him, some man who would ask about my choice of TV programmes rather than always watching his own, some man who wouldn't bully and dictate every little incident in our day to day existence, some man who wasn't so mean as to say that I didn't need a holiday because I was always on holiday, didn't 'deserve' a new kitchen because I wasn't a good enough cook, didn't need books to read. In short, some man who thought I was good enough as I was rather than forever trying to improve me in the way he thought was good rather than what I wanted for myself. I was an object of pity among those who knew us and could see how destructive he was. I was glad to have had his children but that was all. Was there a way out ? Did I want it ?

Dear Hilda,

Our baby has safely arrived ! And little Alice is of course, the most beautiful baby in the world, in fact I've come to the conclusion that all babies are born beautiful in their mother's eyes, even the very ugly ones !

First a surprising bit of emotional scene-setting. As I've already told you, Zarek had made absolutely no concessions to my pregnancy and we were on such bad terms most of the time that our communications were of the most perfunctory pass-the-salt variety - no chance to talk about names for the baby or if he wanted to be there when she was born - a sort of total detachment. An earlier planned trip to Belgium couldn't take place because our friends, who lived there and were both musicians, had concert commitments. They suggested an alternative date, four weeks before the baby was due and when Zarek said he might go on his own, I gave him every encouragement. I almost wished him never to return he was being so foul, not that the plane would drop into the sea, that would be too cruel, but simply that he would vanish out of my existence. Anyway, return he did, a changed man.

The old school friend he'd been staying with is the most charming, courteous, supportive gentleman you could wish to meet and Zarek had obviously noticed how he treated his wife and admitted that he wished he could emulate him. So, to my amazement I found myself with a charming, courteous, supportive gentleman of a husband who was actually treating me like a human being. Sadly it only lasted a month and he has now reverted to his usual beastly self but that month was fantastic and contributed to an all-time maternity high.

For various, to me quite unnecessary reasons, the obstetrician who was supervising my care decided that I should have labour induced a few days in advance of my due date. Having no choice, I presented myself at the hospital one evening with Daisy in tow, eager to know if they were "going to take the baby out now ?" as though it was the same as having a tooth out. I was duly 'processed' – the usual form filling, health checks and 'hot and high' enema. It seems that, as with Greg's birth, this is enough to set me off as Alice was born at 6.38 am next day, the 27th. June – perfectly mature and very lusty. She had kicked and heaved prodigiously throughout pregnancy and continued to do so during labour. This is a bit unusual as babies tend to go quiet just before they face that final journey out of the security of their mother's womb. It was the usual excruciating grunt, bellow and push performance - how these women give birth and serenely smile at the TV camera the minute the baby is out I really don't know, but somehow none of that matters – it is amazing and fantastic. Over the years of my childbearing experiences, processes have changed quite a lot and this time I was given my baby to suckle straight away whereas in the past, they have been taken away to be washed – a separation that feels very intense. I had quite forgotten the joy of having a new baby – it's wonderful.

The other two are coping well although Daisy is given to screaming demands for my attention and Greg is being a bit more mischievous than usual. The childbirth high lasted about a fortnight when I felt physically and emotionally magnificent. Since then, we've had one vile row in which we came to blows so communications are again minimal and the slight but inevitable decline in my physical well-being has set in. For me, it tends to hit an all-time low about four months after delivery when I look really haggish but then recover a bit. However, my gut feeling is of profound happiness and oddly enough, a sort of independence at having achieved this third child. I feel satisfied and complete which I didn't after having Daisy. It's definitely the baby that makes the whole pregnancy business worthwhile - if you don't want that precious child, then it really must be awful.

A few days after we came home from hospital, a friend said to Daisy, "I hear you've got something new that I haven't seen yet," to which she replied "Yes, we've got a bunny hutch but it hasn't got any bunnies in it until next week "!

On which cheery note, I'll sign off – hope you are well and happy, see you in the autumn, love Lizzie.

August 1980 Suffolk.

Dear Lizzie,

The first thing I do in the morning - well, that is, after stumbling over the cats waiting outside the bedroom door for their breakfast, and having a pee (me, not cats) is to see what the postman has brought. Two nasty brown enveloped bills but, sandwiched between them like choicest ham in the most tasteless bread, was your letter - quite unexpected and all the nicer a surprise.

WELCOME to the world little Alice, and congratulations to you and Zarek. I'm so glad for you all - three women in the family to keep Zarek and Greg in place is just right. Do hope mother and baby are doing well.

Lizzie you really are a dear person. I feel like rushing down to Hampshire to give you a big hug ! I've always been strongly attracted to you physically, but particularly the you that is inside and can be so understanding and sympathetic and tolerant and thoughtful. And you only seem to become more so as I see you at intervals and the years drift by. It saddens me to see your growing disillusionment, admittedly without bitterness and resentment and as you say, the children have come along and compensated in a way. But there have been many times when I've envied Zarek, feeling very much a kindred spirit in you, and letting my mind wander off into gentle fantasies of what life with you might be like.

What is the key I wonder ? Obviously companionship before sex, but perhaps even before companionship, what it depends on most is compatible attitudes and values. And it's your attitudes which time and again touch mine so directly and immediately. So I treasure secret thoughts about you, reinforced as they are on the occasions when we meet and by the superb letters you write, knowing that they can never be spoilt or taken away, or - and I don't mean this cynically, that there's the remotest likelihood of them ever having to be proved.

Jodi, my American girlfriend and I have been seeing a lot of each other – she's been studying pottery and I've helped her to set up on her own near Cambridge where she is living. She's sweet, very pretty with long dark hair and …. I'd guess you'd describe her as well rounded but I'd say cuddly! It doesn't seem like three years since we first met - that was when Vanessa was still deciding whether she was going to walk out of our marriage. This last year, Jodi and I have been battling with the Home Office to try and extend her stay in this country. We have great fun together and I'd miss her a lot, so if the worst comes to the worst, the last resort would be marriage number 3. That must sound horribly pragmatic but it's the way I see marriage now. So does Jodi fortunately. She's a very down-to-earth bird whom you'll have to meet. She works really hard at her pottery and is selling well - we've grown very much together during the past year with all the other 'emotional pressures' off and we have lots of laughs. We also have had amazing rows, quite violent sometimes, but thank God, she's no 'brooder' - a very open person and very positive. There are slight communication problems due to age (18 years difference) and being American, but I've great hopes even though I feel deadly cautious about getting married again. I just long for a quiet life now with no more hassles – reasonable at 45 !

But I mustn't be self-indulgent. I'm very touched by your concern for my 'situation' but feel a little guilty too as I frankly feel happier and more settled than I've done for years. It's tough on Jodi after all my emotionally painful messy comings and goings that I'm so pragmatic about relationships. I've poured 'romance' and poems and perfumes and candlelight and pretty knickers over half a dozen lovely women over the last fifteen years and it's all ended up back at square one even though it was beautiful and marvellous when it was happening - and I molly-coddled Vanessa almost out of existence. The facts for Jodi are different. There are so many reasons for her to stay in this country, she is such a worthwhile person, makes such a valuable contribution, is so appreciative and so willing to absorb our culture and blend it with her own that I feel compelled to marry her. If I didn't and she had to go back to the States, I'd miss her very much indeed. Hate to think of being alone yet again - I'm absolutely hopeless on my own.

Our first Christmas dinner together was a hoot ! Preparations went on and on and on - I think she wanted to impress me. We'd aimed at eating at six-ish, but finally sat down at 9.30 having started cooking at 3.00. By eight o'clock I was quite groggy with washing up for hours and at that moment, the candle on the pud set light to the holly in a great spluttery bonfire. We'd been nowhere near starting the meal but I'd lit the candle as a reminder to my begging stomach that sustenance was somewhere in the offing. Within an instant a pan of fat caught light. I saw it and shrieked, Jodi saw the pudding and shrieked - the shock after five hours of intensive washing-up on my concave simpering stomach was shattering. We ground to a halt, surrounded by a great mountain of superbly prepared fowl and vegs. and sauces and God knows what, things I'd never have thought of doing to the most humble ingredients, about midnight. Then to my dismay, I was too utterly exhausted and bloated to enjoy the delights of Jodi's body, wrapped deliciously in her new Christmas nightie !

The sad and strange thing is that I can't bring myself to use the word 'love'. Jodi longs for me to whisper it to her, but I just can't and don't think I could say it to anyone again. It's the D. H. Lawrence thing "I'm tired of the effort of loving" - I think that's what he said. But she's so endearing - a real old softie and her tears come easily. She loves kids and beasties but can be amazingly dismissive about people sometimes. So I'm frequently coming to her rescue and wiping tears away and I have to admit there have been times when I've looked down on the top of a dark head on my shoulder, gently sobbing and it's taken me a moment to recall if it's Jodi or Vanessa, whose ghost is still with me.

Don't be sad for me though, Lizzie. The ending with Vanessa and the various ons and offs with her strung me out to the limit and I'll never know how I didn't snap. Jodi has stood by, kindly and patiently for the last three years and I'm lucky to have her and be loved yet again. I would be a fool to turn her away. Anyway, I've always delighted in life and see the downs as equally relevant and acceptable as the ups which are therefore even more of a delight.

And with friends like you, who gives a damn about the downs ?!

My love to you, and thanks, Chris.

From my notebook November 1980:

"Greg, if you put the towel in the bath, I shall smack you."

"Greg, I've warned you. You know what will happen."

Greg puts the towel in the bath and so I smack him. (This was in the days when one could beat one's children black and blue providing it was administered as a justifiable rebuke rather than an expression of uncontrolled anger. I didn't.)

I get slapped by Zarek, witnessed by Greg. Zarek says I have smacked Greg enough that day. Once was it, or twice ?

"Don't blow Greg's nose on the towel we use for drying our hands" I say, and I am laughed at.

And a few days later, the most awful altercation, which was witnessed by friends who had come to supper. Daisy, who was three at the time and normally settled very easily at night, had decided she wanted to play hostess too, so she was allowed to stay up. In spite of my mounting irritation, because I knew she would soon fall asleep once put to bed, Zarek insisted that she should remain with the adults even though I felt he was encouraging her wakefulness and wanting to demonstrate what an indulgent parent he was, as opposed to nasty old me. At 10.15 after she had spent the whole meal with us, effectively destroying any relaxed atmosphere I might have hoped to achieve, my patience finally gave out. I went to take her from Zarek who had been making what seemed to me, an undue fuss of her and was hit by him with all his strength and told to mind my own business. This was irrespective of my feelings or those of our guests, or the effect on Daisy, caught in the crossfire. At which point, friend Laura left the table in tears.

Then, a bit later on I was hit again and menaced for insisting that Greg didn't go to school because it was his second spotty day with chicken pox. Our paediatric book stated that the most infectious period was 24 hours before spots until six days afterwards. Despite this, Zarek maintained that the infectious period would have been two weeks previously. Whether he was right or not, even the children cowered in fear at the vehemence with which he felt obliged to make his point.

December 1980 Suffolk

Dear Lizzie

I'm sitting at the kitchen table surrounded by a great forest of wine bottles. I'm halfway through bottling my 4 gallons of blackberry, 4 gallons of elderberry plus 5 gallons of plum, with a carboy with about 12 gallons of apple wine awaiting its finings. Smells like a brewery. Aren't bottles <u>nice</u> things ?! Just been looking at them. (Nicer when full of something of course !) The plum wine is such a lovely pale pink, the other two rich burgundy. Why everybody doesn't make their own wine beats me. I really prefer it now to the 'real' stuff.

I do wish you lived a bit closer - physically that is. I've always felt very close the real way. It would be so nice to be able to call on each other and talk instead of all this scribbling, and perhaps just as important, to be able to join in things together with mutual friends. All the people I know here are crazy and 'odd' in their own ways/relationships, all mutually dependent, almost daily, for sorting each other out and coping with crises. I wonder sometimes what sort of social life you have these days and whether you are a bit isolated - you do sound so. It helps so much to see yourself as part of a collection of individuals all thrown together and all enjoying and suffering and all laughing and crying, at different times and with different intensities; all going through the same hell/heaven together. It helps so much to know that you are never on your own and that there's always someone worse off than you financially, emotionally, relationship-wise and so on, so you can only turn back to your own life with all its upsets and problems and still count all the outpoured blessings day by day. I'm sure you do that anyway with your lovely children and home comforts - which can of course make all the 'unnecessary' unhappiness etc. seem all the more sad and stupid. It's so important to open up the old soul now and again - there are bits of my soul splattered all over the place ! - bedrooms and pubs and books and letters and over sad, dark, winter countrysides. We have to pour it all out and I can say to myself AND Jodi how much I love you and have often wanted you without feeling guilty or disloyal. It's human nature and the real problems only arise when we indulge our loves or lustings and behave greedily and uncaringly and selfishly. We all need each other all the time - "God uses us to help each other so, lending our minds out" said Browning and then there's John Donne's "No man is an island."

I have to interrupt Chris here with a note of explanation. He was absolutely right about my being isolated, even though like a lot of women with small children, I had acquired a very supportive local network of other mums. We babysat for each other, shared clothes, toys and child-rearing paraphernalia and generally helped each other out in meeting the demands of our common experience. Our focus was our children. Who WE were as individuals was a rather more private matter, although we may never have realised

64

this limitation in our contact. For me, there were three main reasons for this.

Years previously, when I had first met Zarek and his position as a stateless person in this country had made him feel incredibly vulnerable, he had insisted on absolute secrecy about our affair. The second reason was that with a wife and child left behind in Poland, he was frightened that he would have difficulty in obtaining a divorce and when it finally came about, he did a belt and braces job, getting divorced via both English and Polish law, just to make sure. During the time that we worked in the same hospital, our conduct in front of our colleagues was always professional. We never talked about activities or outings we had shared at the weekends, or acknowledged our relationship in any way. As far as anyone else was concerned, neither of us had a private life. In a small hospital rife with intrigue, this was of course a total giveaway but the habit of reticence became firmly entrenched.

The final reason was to do with status. As a hospital Consultant, Zarek saw himself as a little above the common man so as his consort, I was also required to maintain this distance. I cannot in all honesty pass the entire responsibility for this on to him. At that time, it suited me to feel a bit superior - I was proud of his status and his achievements which marked him out as someone different.

Back to Chris's comments about us all needing supportive networks:

You know all this Lizzie, so please don't feel guilty or disloyal when you dare to express it, though frankly I do wonder if a little spot of disloyalty wouldn't be a good idea for your situation. I wouldn't normally recommend it - very irresponsible and all that but it just might work wonders slashing at some of the nasty and soul destroying chauvinism that seems to be swamping your life with Zarek. You sound in need of a good dollop of T.L.C. - a nice tender, handsome, tall dark stranger who's familiar with one or two cosy restaurants and a warm shady pad and soft music to take you back to ….. I'd be pleased to offer my humble services but we'd probably spend all night TALKING ! - not the object of the exercise …..

And I'm absolutely certain that the outbursts you describe, screaming back etc. are more than adequately compensated for by a background of constant care and loving and thoughtfulness and tenderness. Your love for the children shines out above all else Lizzie. Please don't worry for them. They too like all of us, have to know about the dark side of life, and who better to learn it from than parents, and where safer to learn it than the background of a secure home. Because my father died when I was a baby, I didn't experience parental rows and for years I couldn't cope with 'scenes'. I thought people who rowed were unnatural and shouldn't have married. All so naïve and simplistic. Goodness I've learnt that lesson now, to the tune of mugs thrown through windows and actually BEATING Jodi till parts of her were blue with bruises - isn't that awful ?! And then the rest of the time I creep around oozing concern and involvement, hoping that everyone will think, "ah, what a nice, tender, thoughtful man !" Yuk !

And we all constantly need feedback in very different ways. We all have different fears, needs, aspirations, hopes, disappointments, frustrations......but they are all holes in the dam that need more than the fingers each of us alone possesses, poked in to them to stop the flood of tears and despair. Kind friends' fingers poked in, in letters and talk over pots of tea. Goodness Lizzie, it's the very stuff of life and living.

LIFE GOES ON - I think you've told me that. The very fact that we keep going somehow, kicking and screaming maybe but alive to others and their needs, friends, children, partners, whatever, that's what matters. Life IS an awful mess but so's my back garden just now, with dead leaves and slushy grass and frozen cat shits, but in six months' time (God willing) we'll be sitting out there in our knickers, sipping cold drinks and snoozing in the sunshine. So's the house - dusty with jeans and jerseys cast around like a jumble sale, splodges of red wine on the lino, empty bottles everywhere, papers, books, letters, bills, but all evidence that life is going on here. When things, people, places are at their messiest, then, like a crocus in spring, up pops the evidence, tiny and frail as it might be, that the world is still spinning with us on it. For you, an innocent but heart-twisting word from Greg or Daisy and I'm sure you know it's all worthwhile.

We have so much to try and be content with, but it's easier said than done. For instance, I know, I just know how easy so much of life would be with you Lizzie. I know how we communicate, like a warm knife going through butter. I know by now your values and interests and attitudes and how they would key so immediately with mine. I do have to struggle to communicate with Jodi and so often we miss by miles. I sigh inside, feeling 'older' and more experienced and responsible and protective and patient when so much of the time I desperately want to lean. A moment's leaning keeps me going for days. I've always wanted to lean, but fate says time and time again, NO - you must give and give. And I've thought so often how I could lean on you - indeed have, frequently, in letters down the years, with all my desperate emotional ups and downs. I could follow that train of thought and feel bitter that fate didn't provide me with an Elizabeth Mayhew to share all of ME. I sometimes think that I have a potential that I'm too weak to realise on my own, and that given the right woman........

You know that you, in your marriage are the "bigger" partner, despite all Zarek's books and professional life and hence, despite his wage earning capacity, you are in reality more, far more in a position of responsibility. For some reason, I too have always been in this position towards others, and how dearly I would have shed it, over and over. But I'm lumbered with it, and so are you - it's a privilege, like all responsibilities, isn't it. Ah. So that's why I've never had my own Lizzie Mayhew - we'd have turned inwards and possibly not been available, as we must be, to others. "...... as more exposed to suffering and distress thence also, more alive to tenderness."

Less than two weeks to blast off to America. I can't believe it. And it won't be a reality unless some of the buggers settle my overdue invoices pretty smartly. Must also get out and jog a little and try and get some early nights to appear fairly fit and acceptable when I arrive on the doorstep of my next *in-laws. Yesterday I took the plunge and went to see the Registrar to book our wedding day - 14th February, St. Valentine's Day which I thought would be appropriate. Jodi telephoned her parents last night and broke the news but it's a bit tricky all round, trying to explain things over 3,000 miles of telephone cable. I think her parents don't quite know what to expect. They know I'm a lot older, and Jodi has a strange emotional hang-up with her mother. I feel just a little like a football. All I want is a quiet life and to help Jodi and to have happy days, which we do have. Problems only arise when we <u>examine</u> our relationship, as I'm a little short of the romance these days, together with all its trappings and have constantly to remind myself that although it's third time round for me, it's Jodi's first time and of course she expects a little more enthusiasm and excitement on my part, even though I tell her I'm looking forward to it.*

My next job, after finishing this letter, is to write to Vanessa. I've been putting it off but it's her birthday next week and if I don't write now, she won't get it in time. Even so, it'll be a sort of farewell cum explanation/justification, "it really wouldn't have worked anyway and you can't live backwards" sort of birthday card, carefully and kindly worded, which is why I've been putting it off. It's sad though because you leave a chunk of yourself with everybody you've ever been really close to, so writing this letter to her, I know is going to hurt me too.

Ah well - the teapot's empty, the toast all eaten and the day presses. Must rush but, oh joy, another cheque arrived. Back into the black at the bank and I can now order the yellow wellies Jodi wants for Christmas. And I think I just glimpsed the sunshine. Doesn't this cold weather make you pee a lot !

So, a big hug Lizzie - don't ever stop writing, will you. Thinking of you, love and hugs, Chris.

Back to our garden where one Sunday afternoon, Greg wanted to do something to help me so I entrusted him with the secateurs and said he could go and dead-head the last of the year's roses - one of his favourite jobs. I was washing-up and intended to go and work in the garden myself but it must have been a good half hour before I actually got there. Greg was nowhere to be seen, all was silent and it was a while before I saw him standing very still and quiet by the front garden wall, apparently watching the passing cars. When I reached him, he gingerly turned his head to reveal a tragic, tear-stained little face.

"I'm stuck," he wailed. And looking down, I saw that one branch of the rosebush he'd been working on had passed across his bottom with several huge thorns disappearing into the seat of his track suit. I managed to extricate them, not without getting impaled once or twice myself and had a productive afternoon in the garden, with Greg's help.

Later on, my right thumb began to feel sore. A small dark dot was barely visible but obviously I'd got something in it so I found a needle and went to Zarek who was watching sport on the television.

"Can you get this out of my thumb please ?"

"What ?"

"I've got a minute thorn in my thumb from gardening this afternoon."

"Come here."

The poke that he gave it with the needle felt vicious so I remonstrated and we repaired reluctantly to the kitchen where the light was better. He poked around so hard this time that I practically wet myself. Then he pronounced, "There is no splinter." Incredible. He couldn't find it therefore he denied its existence, in spite of what I could feel. Later I managed to remove the splinter myself. It existed.

December 1980

My dearest Liz

It's now two months since Hugh put that unbelievable 'Dear Jane' letter into my suitcase as I was setting off for England. Will I ever find it in me to feel one shred of forgiveness for such a cowardly act ? Will I ever ? Yes, of course I will. I forgive him every day and mourn.

I can't read this poem without bursting into tears but I want to share it with you - you know how I feel, much love, Hilda.

<u>*Sonnet*</u> *- by Edna St. Vincent Millay.*

Time does not bring relief; you all have lied

Who told me time would ease me of my pain !

I miss him in the weeping of the rain;

I want him at the shrinking of the tide;

The old snows melt from every mountain-side,

And last year's leaves are smoke in every lane;

But last year's bitter loving must remain

Heaped on my heart, and my old thoughts abide.

There are a hundred places where I fear

To go, - so with his memory they brim.

And entering with relief some quiet place

Where never fell his feet nor shone his face

I say, "There is no memory of him here !"

And so stand stricken, so remembering him.

7. A proposition

I found that poem heart-rending. Hilda had paid a flying visit one weekend when Zarek was away, when we were able to weep and hug and talk, which is all you can do when something really searing has happened. In truth I felt as though she had helped me much more than I her. "Of course he's quite mad" she said of Zarek at one point and with that came the realisation that trying to reconcile life with my dotty husband and most other people's reality was tearing me in two. It must have been clearly written across my face because even five year old Greg noticed, "Mummy, why d'you often have mudguards above your eyes ?"

So why try ? I felt that I had to keep going for the sake of the children, that well-worn phrase, but that if I could sustain some kind of emotional independence, I might be able to manage. Things were a bit better after this although it may have been Zarek's appetite suppressant which he had started taking again, that sweetened his mood. He used to take Tenuate and although there's no medical evidence to suggest it's a mood enhancer, he was definitely much nicer to know when he was on it. Maybe it was an extension of the control thing. Having control over his weight made him more benign ? And wowee - we even spent an hour planning a summer holiday – a cottage in the north somewhere so that we could visit far-flung friends in Northumberland.

Then we were nearly overwhelmed by a progression of illnesses. First mumps - Daisy, mild; then gastric flu - Greg, quite severe and off school for a week. Another gastric flu - Zarek, and in his own overstated words, torrential; then impetigo - Greg, you know, one of those conditions associated with deprivation and squalid living. Then I got mumps - awful - couldn't even open my mouth and felt so ill. Zarek was foul, never even offering to make me a cup of tea. The most he did was to take Greg to the school bus, twice. Thank goodness for kindly friends who helped with shopping and school runs. It was a bit like having the plague as they didn't want to catch it, so they came and delivered children and food rather hastily on the doorstep. Then poor little Alice who'd had no appetite and been off colour all the time I was ill, woke up one day looking like a hamster - she'd got mumps too. All we needed by then was head lice to keep things interesting.

One really positive event that autumn was that Zarek SOLD THE BOAT ! Apart from a few odd bits of nautical clutter, the only item left in the garage was the liferaft which seemed oddly appropriate. He'd finally recognised how incompatible sailing was, with our attempts at family life with three small children, and had hardly sailed at all during the preceding summer. The thought of all the maintenance work and expense of getting it out of the water yet again for the winter, was wearisome so, though niggardly in relation to its value, he snapped at the offer made by a sailing club pal like a shark after a swimmer's leg !

Chris was still havering over whether to marry Jodi or not. 'Typical Piscean dilemma' he said. His trip to New York to meet her mother sounded very unsettling. She and her mother had been arguing all the time, hammer and tongs, with him feeling like a pig-in-the-middle, fearful of the lonely prospect of being without her, fearful of the responsibilities of being loved by her and another marriage. I wrote to him in an attempt to help him unpack his feelings and get closer to understanding why he was confused. I even sent him a jokey Valentine card but I'm not sure any of it was a good idea. He was very appreciative and wrote to tell me that as soon as they got back from the States, he'd cancelled their wedding plans for Valentine's day. Ever the Piscean, he was still dithering and there had been arguments between them about what I'd said, with him claiming I'd tried to be objective (which I had) and her saying I couldn't know her feelings or how difficult he could be (which I didn't).

I'm not sure about any of this. My twice married, long-standing friend writes to me about problems he's having with his American girlfriend who clearly loves him but is holding a pistol to his head because her visa enabling her to stay in this country is about to expire. Marriage is the obvious solution, but with his past experience, no wonder he is cautious. However, is there another dimension to all this - our exchange of 'fun' Valentine cards (yes, he'd sent me one too but then he always had, every year since I'd known him), his suggestion not three months previously that he would see me as a very desirable partner with the justification that it's alright to say it as long as one doesn't do it, and even that whiff of suggested infidelity to ease my own marital discomfort ? Was I, were we, really being objective ? I had written, questioning the wisdom of this third marriage and Jodi was right to say that I knew neither her feelings, nor about Chris being 'difficult'. What I did know about were many of the doubts and uncertainties that he was expressing, but stirred into this were some other covert messages between us, which I now think compromised my objectivity. I was unaware of it at the time but now I wonder if this was when a small seed started to germinate ……..

By April 1981, Jodi had returned to the USA so Chris was on his own again. Knowing that he would be lonely, of course, I wrote to him. This triggered a whole stream of letters, bustling back and forth between us ………..

April 1981 Hampshire

Dear Old Friend

I'd thought at first that I wouldn't write to you now - that somehow it would be better to let you crawl away into your hole licking your wounds to emerge, yet another Chris, bloody but unbowed by his experience. Or how one sometimes feels when someone has been bereaved - you don't know what to say that will bring any comfort so it may be better not to say anything at all. I think that all too often the one thing we really want to do is pour it all out to anyone that will listen.

But then I thought, if ever you need not to feel lonely, it must be now, so here's another letter. It doesn't have to be replied to or given any further consideration, just a perfunctory read - although as I haven't written it yet, I don't know that it will even justify that !

I cannot think how you and Jodi could have passed those final few hours together without feeling 'sod this' and rushing off to the nearest Registry Office for a special licence. I'd guess that the most painful aspect of such an ambivalent relationship must be that it's the good feelings that we hang on to so that one is left with the hope that it <u>could</u> work if given another chance. And yet we know that things don't change and what has been good and bad in a relationship will still be there no matter how many times we pick it up and put it down again.

I suspect you might both have found yourselves making too many compromises for comfort and in any case, there's no point in continuing to thrash around - SURVIVAL is the name of the game right now.

So how about a bit of light relief ? I'd bought a pair of stretchy denims, ideal for middle-aged mothers of three as they're like a long-legged corset. Greg was open-mouthed in his admiration of my trimmer back-side and said, "Mummy, when you're dead can I have your jeans ?" Of course my son, of course !

We've got a dozen tadpoles in a tank in the garden and I'd thought that chopping up worms might be high on his list of preferred holiday activity, but not a bit of it. I'm the one that has to hold a morning massacre while Greg is watching Lassie on television !

Zarek is in a distinctly humpy frame of mind at the moment. We're at long last getting our kitchen rebuilt, or at least, we've had the wall between the kitchen and the living room knocked down and we're busy planning the resulting space.

Mind you, this is virtually impossible as when we <u>are</u> speaking to each other, our tastes and ideas are utterly different. Added to which, despite his excellent earning capacity, Zarek can hardly bear the thought of spending so much money.

We went today to look at kitchen furniture. I was holding Alice and desperately trying to absorb the high-powered sales talk being fired at us. Zarek sat passively by, while the other two children ran riot, up and down stairs, opening and closing cupboards, lying on the floor, laughing and shrieking to the obvious annoyance of both staff and customers. I went to restrain them and was myself physically held back by Zarek who said they were just expressing themselves, at everyone else's expense it seemed to me. Could this be his way of showing his disapproval of the new kitchen I wondered ? Then when we got back to the village, I'd jumped out of the car to get some shopping and he just drove off leaving me to carry ten ton ten month Alice and the shopping, the half mile back home.

There's also the evening litany, regular as clockwork - "Have you salted the potatoes ?" Aaaaargh !

It's just struck me Chris, that even if you're feeling very fragile and alone and disorientated at the moment, you'd better make the most of your solitude and really relish it as I can't see you ever having uncomplicated situations to deal with - it's in the nature of the beast ! Perhaps you should start writing it all down instead of writing letters to me, and turn it into a bodice-ripping novel !

Can't think of any more bons mots - there's nothing I can write which would make any difference to what you have to bear, as you well know, so have a piece of Polish Easter cake instead - I hope it survives its journey. It's called Mazurek and is made with egg white and ground almonds. Here are some mung beans too. They are great if you germinate them for a few days and then add them to salad but watch who you share them with as they can have a pretty explosive effect on the gut !

Hope you aren't feeling too awful Chris - I mean in general rather than because of the cake or beans - I think of you a lot, lots of love, Lizzie.

May 1981 Suffolk

Dear Lizzie

What a lovely letter - not to mention Polish Easter cake and mung beans. Thus both body and soul catered for - many thanks, once again. You advise against sharing the mung beans but the only bed companions I have right now are Jodi's two cats who come and wake me for their breakfast at 6.30 a.m. Isolde, the lady cat has a habit of farting in my face (not to mention occasionally shitting all around the house) so, bunged with mungs, I will now be able to retaliate and hold her head under the duvet while I do so. That'll teach her !

Hope your new jeans don't squash your bum in too much - ladies bums are nice and shouldn't be restricted. We have a 'glamorous' young mum at the Dramatic Society who lashed herself into the tightest of jeans during both pregnancies

79

and drooled every time someone said "Ooh Ros, but you don't look at all pregnant." She has absolutely no arse at all - tits not bad but inevitably make her look top heavy and disproportionate. She drips around in these bloody stupid 'fashion' jeans and knee boots, deep in the conceit that she's the absolute dog's dinner, when in fact she's totally unfeminine and looks for all the world like some weird insect. Jodi had such a lovely bottom but was forever complaining thereby taking all the fun out of it and reducing sex appeal - so Lizzie, just WATCH it !

How's the kitchen going ? I've decided to revamp my dull /grotty bathroom, swapping bath for a four foot tub (like a geriatric hospital bath but without the seat - DON'T LAUGH !). This will exactly fit across the end of my tiny bathroom - an instant shower unit, matching wash basin, thick fluffy carpet and exchanging the disgusting blanket that has served as a door for the last ten years with a really thick patchwork curtain. All very sexy, I hope ! As it's the only room I use apart from the bedroom now I'm alone, I think it's worth treating myself. Also got an offer of a Raeburn solid fuel stove for £45 which I can't yet believe. It would make such a difference in the kitchen if it's OK and I can get it......

I've been involved in so many activities since Jodi left. Amnesty International had a super Chilean Folk Group for a concert and there have been films, cycle rides, walks, supper out with friends and yesterday helping to launch and berth 'Curtsy' a 32 foot sailing boat at Woodbridge - there's just no end to distractions.

I strongly suspect that everyone here has got bets on just how soon there'll be another woman moving in with me. No go. I am enormously relieved to be without the emotional turmoil of the last three months with Jodi although I do worry that I may have thrown out the baby with the bathwater. She was special - loved me so much with loads of guts and get-up-and-go. She was a silly old softie to boot, always leaving me little presents and thoughtfulnesses. On the other hand, it's nice to have it quiet here, to get up early and make tea and write like this, not having to be accountable all the time. Poor Jodi - she was such a sorry sight as she dashed for the plane with too much hand luggage including a special talking dolly called "shrinking Violet". There wasn't time for fond farewells and she kept dropping everything in the rush, tears behind dark glasses, brave smile - oh dear, Lizzie, when I think of those bits I want her here now to hug and make it all better. I've had one or two letters but she's very disorientated and not at all sure what she is going to do for a job but I've no way of knowing how she is inside.......

A great chunk of me wants to hear that she really does want to come back eventually. But this separation hasn't hurt as much as other times. I am enjoying solitude rather than loneliness except that it is lonely when you can't turn and swap notes on the little things that used to make life such fun together - people and friends and tele, books, newspapers, films.......but if she does find I'm not the be all and end all of existence, find other men and lovers and satisfaction in work in the USA, then perhaps sadly and regretfully, I will know we did the right thing.

Ten o'clock has just clanged on the kitchen clock, so must terminate communication herewith and pack kiln before I leap out and collect my allocation of Christian Aid envelopes and start planning a solitary walking holiday on Rhum, way up in the Hebrides. D'you want to 'c(h)um' ?! Thanks again for your letters. Here, sprinkle some of this space dust on your tongue and lo, you have a mouthful of the galaxy !

Keep truckin' as they say. Lots of love Liz, Chris.

May 1981 Hampshire

Dear Chris,

Your lovely letter arrived just when I needed it, making your news all the more cheering. I must say, the all-pervasive feeling, whether you intended it or not, was one of relief that all the emotional hassle of the last few months was over.

I'm feeling pretty ragged and hoarse after the end of the Easter holiday and the Bank holiday today. For reasons best known to himself, Zarek has recently tended to opt out of family life so I've had to implement a pretty energetic programme of activity to keep everyone happy and out of mischief. I love taking the children out and have one or two good friends locally (who aren't so encumbered) who will come with me on the more adventurous expeditions.

Our most strenuous outing this holiday was a trip to Blackgang Chine on the other side of the Isle of Wight. We drove to Southsea, then took a boat, then a train, then a bus, then another bus and three hours later arrived at this marvellous adventure playpark for children. The nicest thing about it was that it was incredibly compact and although a bit twee, I have never seen so many ecstatic little faces and busy legs and bodies as they scrambled on and off dinosaurs, stage coaches, covered wagons, fairy castles, giant mushrooms, spaceships, pirate galleons, crazy houses, lions, tigers etc. etc. and that's not to mention the maze and the water garden - a real children's paradise. Pity the restaurant only had two dry scones and three pies left by three in the afternoon ! We staggered home at 7.30 with poor little Alice still wide awake and wondering what had hit her. She has coped incredibly well with a variety of holiday assaults - tadpoling (doing nicely thank you but no legs yet), kite flying, even a trip to see the Popeye film. She wriggled and chortled the whole time but it hardly mattered as the cinema was so empty. We all loved it, especially Olive Oyl, and Daisy and Greg thought the giant octopus at the end was out of this world – when I was worried they might be frightened silly !

When are you going to Rhum ? And yes, I'd love to c(h)um but I think three children and a ton of disposable nappies would rather cramp my style. In fact we'd planned to go to Scotland, starting with a week in a cottage in Yorkshire and then on and up to Fife where we have friends but I doubt if it will happen. At the moment it's going to be a fortnight in Holland-on-Sea with my parents at the beginning of August - could be worse!

Lots of love, Lizzie.

June 1981 Hampshire

Dear Chris

Will the sunshine never come ? Every morning when I get up, I look out of the window longing NOT to see the wet, black shine on the road surface or the branches of our garden shrubs so constantly weighed down by water. I am tired of compromise clothing, warm enough but not too heavy. I long to see Alice's little legs, bare and brown, and the children to be able to trot backwards and forwards in the garden without always the warning admonition for them to "stay away from the soggy patch at the bottom." And it's June, flaming June !

An odd season altogether. Half term for some strange reason came four weeks after the start of the summer term and I spent my time rushing backwards and forwards to the swimming baths with Greg who was on a crash swimming course, at the end of which he had proudly achieved two metres dog paddle ! Daisy is now in a water babies class in which the mums also take part. "Now children, we're going to push our mummies' heads under the water. That's it, RIGHT under !" How we love it. Alice is our most natural water baby of all. She bobs around in her orange arm bands with great delight and not a hint of anxiety which is amazing considering we normally go on Sunday mornings when there is a maximum of one cubic metre of water per person and the noise level is horrendous.

A topsy turvy time. Zarek is now speaking to me (a long angry silence has lasted since February) but in a rather perfunctory fashion. My close friends say they don't know how I can stand it, but I don't know how I cannot. Are things really that bad ? No, they can't be. We go on existing. We love our children. We eat food, drink, evacuate. We say "pass the marmalade please." We manage the basic transactions fairly normally. But we don't communicate, either verbally, emotionally or physically. It feels so cold. We went to an Art Exhibition yesterday (rare for us to be anywhere together). "What did you think of it ?" I asked, wondering if somehow I could get a reaction. "It doesn't make it better to talk about it," was his reply. Silence. "I have the impression you set so little store by what I have to say, you can't be bothered to tell me." "You could be right."

So I shut up for a bit longer. If I do say anything now, it becomes challenging simply by virtue of all the non-saying that has gone before. I wonder how long it can last - no wonder the world feels a bit unreal. While Popes and Presidents are shot, Irish political prisoners starve themselves to death for their principles and my husband doesn't speak to me for two months, I am propositioned by the husband of my best friend. My only reason for declining was out of respect for her and her family, not my own. The phone call that heralded it was totally unexpected and did wonders for my morale, sending shivers up my spine and butterflies a-flutter in my tummy. But how wrong that I should seek or need such an escape. Funny really with Zarek setting himself up as a marital counsellor and running sex clinics etc.

I feel frozen in a sort of impasse situation - not wanting to move in any direction for fear of making things worse or for fear of having to accept that I can't make them different. The option of being able to improve them doesn't seem to exist – are they really that bad ? Maybe I should find a therapist rather than spilling my worries all over the place, although I don't truly feel worried, just resigned.

Alice keeps waking at 5.00 a.m. wanting breakfast which, since I'm rarely in bed before midnight or sometimes 1.00 a.m. is another reason for feeling unreal. It's amazing how much one can do at that crisp time of the day except that by 7.00 p.m. I'm usually feeling like a floppy lettuce !

The gutting of our kitchen progresses and should look stunning when it's finished. At least if we aren't deliriously happy about our lives, we can be miserable in comfort. I'm not feeling miserable though - just very much my own person!

Lots of love, Lizzie.

I see this as a seminal moment in the story. There's delight and loving warmth in everything to do with the children contrasted with icy detachment from their father. As for the proposition, perhaps I should have gone straight to my friend and told her that her husband was up to no good but there was a feeling of suppressed excitement that something that had been missing for so long in my life, the feeling of being valued, might be revived. On the other hand, you might think it an opportunistic approach of a man to use a woman made vulnerable by the oppression of another man, but the story must continue ………

June 1981 Hampshire

Hello Chris !

Well now. Thanks for the space dust. Isn't it odd how it feels as though it's right up inside your head ? Or perhaps there really IS nothing between my ears ! And going into further details about my anatomy, my bum is alive and well and steadfastly denying all my half-hearted attempts to control it ! Actually I've lost some weight recently which is lovely - makes me feel much less matronly and lumpy - perhaps that's why I was propositioned.......

I'm glad that life is being involved and fun for you, despite the poverty. It reminds me of how the patients used to comment when we ran socials for them in the Day Hospital where I worked. "Good heavens. I actually enjoyed myself without having a drink !" Being high, getting something out of life - fun, excitement, reassurance, stimulation is much more dependent on what we have in us than artificial stimulants. Even the soddish times can be relished as confirmation that we are alive and thinking, feeling, caring, loving, sensitive people. I feel dreadfully sad for Zarek who seems determined not to enjoy anything or like anyone except for the children. I'm pretty involved with the family scene in the village - money-making efforts, expeditions, social gatherings etc. and OK, so it's not wildly stimulating, doesn't make heavy demands of the intellect, but it's fun and people are decent and intelligent. Zarek always acts so bloody superior, thereby depriving himself of so many pleasurable opportunities. I admit that they aren't profoundly intellectual but when he does get involved in a discussion, it becomes an argument because he never wants to consider anyone else's point of view so I don't know why he bothers. The other day I suggested some people came round after the gymkhana which is being arranged in the village, for a barbecue. "Why ?" he asked. "Because it would be fun," I replied, admittedly rather challengingly. "Who wants fun , " he said. Subject closed.

So, I'm almost a one-parent family now. I do as much as I can with the children as they're easier to cope with if we plan something definite. I try to involve and include him as much as possible but all he wants to do is practise his violin, read the paper or fall asleep in front of the television. Christ.

I felt guilty about betraying the deficiencies of our marriage but somehow, I couldn't help myself. I realised that although he adored the children, his work left him nothing, absolutely nothing in reserve so that any spare time or holiday had to be spent making up the deficit of emotional exhaustion which had accrued over a prolonged working period. I wished I could show more concern. I would have done <u>anything</u> for him when we were first together but felt that this love had been eroded over the years. And stupidly we didn't talk about it, it was as much as we could do to stay together and talking about it would have piled on the agony. But I felt I ought to try. Felt tough but sad, very sad, and mostly determined that the children shouldn't miss out, either on family life as best we could manage it, or FUN ! But one evening, whilst returning from a baby-sitting session for a friend, a sadly desperate feeling welled from the depths of my sub-conscious to the surface - "My God, please somebody get me out of all this."

8. Proposition accepted

Chris' response to the proposition I'd received and this final cri-de-coeur was predictable. "How dare anyone proposition you before me. I'm first in the queue" he'd said.

Even so, we were chatting on the phone one evening when he happened to mention lovely 'Jessica' who apparently had masses of Wurzel Gummidge hair and was down from University and had called in on him, wanting to go for a drink. He'd told her he already had a date for that evening ie me on the phone, but that he'd see her at the weekend. So he was first in *my* queue but was I necessarily first in *his* ? His openness about this was reassuring. "I don't have much income but people flood my days like tides, leaving a high water mark of stories, laughs, experiences, travels, all to be beachcombed and picked over, long after they have gone," but I did find myself wondering……… ?

June 1981 Suffolk

My Very Dear Lizzie

D'you know whenever I start writing to you, I want to tell you so much that I know would always interest you. I could write for days……..

I've opened one cut of clay to stiffen up for tomorrow's pots, brought in the washing - lovely clear sunshine and, well, yes, the sun actually came today - 'came' being the operative word, like a much needed orgasm. It's been so dull, on and on, and I don't often complain about our weather - love our seasons and enjoy rain but there are limits, especially when it affects people driving out to craft shops at weekends and buying up my pots which they patently haven't been doing these last six months or more. I wore shorts yesterday when cycling round our lovely Suffolk lanes with a buddy, and came home frozen stiff and that was midsummer's bloody day.

I've fed the cats (Jodi's two orphans), stirred the elderflower wine, bubble, bubble, fizz, pop........put on my standard meal to cook - ½ lb. new potatoes with two eggs to hardboil at the same time and baked beans with tomato sauce to liven them up, and some herbs (Jodi's trick). I've also started another pint of homemade yoghurt which I eat by the half pint per sitting, drained the dregs of the weekends wine bottles into a glass, capitulated after two days without fags - and here I sit at the garden table with a nice rose, a cloud of gnats and droopy eyes - a mixture of wine on an empty stomach and no sleep last night. No fag this evening - your letter instead - you should feel honoured as I usually puff while writing. Pollen making me sneezy. Pause while I check spuds. Done, so I'm eating them while I write, fork in one hand, pen in t'other. Watch out for splodges of salad dressing on letter........ pinkening sky now and birds saying goodnight to each other. Magic.

Down goes egg no. 2 - chewy and satisfying, followed by a forkful of salad, watercress slopping dressing down my chin - thank God I'm eating alone ! You don't matter - I know you wouldn't object to my pig-manners. Now it's time to dollop a great spoonful of Jodi's strawberry jam into creamy yoghurt

- I always add lashings of powdered milk when making it so that it brews all thick and gooey. Oh Liz, I wish you could see the sunset. It's one long rose coloured streak, spotlighting the back of the house all pink. If only it wasn't so bloody cold ! I'll either have to go in or get another jersey and light the candles. The latter I think. It's so nice out here with the swifts screaming over the gardens. D'you know Liz, either side of me the gardens are immaculate. I bash away at mine in spare moments, bulldozing the grass into a vaguely flattish mat with the lawn-mower, tear out the ground elder that threatens to engulf everything - but still it's more like a nature reserve than a suburban garden. And on either side, they never use their gardens, never sit in them, or eat in them - crazy. Nine o'clock strikes in the church tower. Tiddler, the small male (well, he was once) cat, dozes and eyes the gnat cloud above him........

Enough. Supposing, just supposing, you and I had married, I wonder how long it would have lasted/been firm/creative/fulfilling ? How long before we screwed each other up ? Watkin said the other night that he didn't know anyone that marriage had been good for - 'benefitted' was his actual word, I recall. I said, "Should you expect 'benefit' from marriage ?" You should though, shouldn't you ? I'm so scared of trying it again although I do miss Jodi a lot, she provided such GRIT - think that's the word. But do I always want what's gone, what I can no longer reach ? Have I poured out the baby with the bathwater ? It's dreadful when I'm on my own, down, scared, missing Jodi and not sleeping. But I'm not here to write about me, but to try and comfort you, yet what can I say after all the loving support your letters have given me over the years ? You are always so wise in your words, so careful in your consideration and advice.

Oh dear Liz. I feel I'm not being much use - I bounce around as ever, but each bounce seems more frantic than the last. A lot of it has to do with lack of money coming in although I'm owed £400 for pots. But I wish I had Jodi's hand to hold right now - she was always so positive and plucky. I've a list of 25 London shops to blitz in the next few weeks so maybe I'd better get off my whinging arse and get stuck in. And I must say a firm NO to all the delightful distractions - like pretty nineteen year old Jessica I mentioned, who comes round now and again to read poetry in bed with me .... We met at the Amnesty 'do' and clicked immediately so have stayed in touch. She's a bit crazy, wears daft hats, loves poetry which has stimulated me to read more ...... no, we don't just read poetry, though we did start that way and the rest just came naturally, though with no commitments on either side as she's at University where it seems the men are queuing up for her. So it's a very pleasant summery dalliance with no hurt likely on either side, save that it does distract me from pots and letter writing ! Hm. Playing the perpetual Peter Pan can get boring but at least it keeps you alive.

Indoors now. Couldn't see edge of paper.

Above all your situation is such a waste, - a waste of Zarek I'm sure, but most certainly a waste of you and all you have to give. Thank God you can talk about it - it's not a let-down or betrayal, just a must for all of us from time to time. Do please write as often as you like. Goodness knows I owe you a few wet shoulders ! You know you'd be more than welcome to stay here with the children for a couple of days - heaps of room. And for all my seeming bravado, I'd be much too nervous to stammer out anything in the way of a 'proposition' to you, so I give you my word I have no ulterior motive. It would just be nice to try and arrange a bit of fun for all of us and leave the games in the mind and the fantasies, where they give undoubted pleasure from time to time, but can do absolutely no harm !

Well, dear Lizzie, it's 11.30 and I've just been upstairs and switched on the electric blanket - in flaming June ! So, goodnight, sleep tight - see you in the morning's bright. Chrisx.

P.S. - Bliss, perfect bliss ! Slept from 12.30 until 7.00 to wake to sunshine and bird twitter and Tiddler asking for his breakfast outside the bedroom door. He pats at the doorknobs and windows - well, he can't miaow like a proper cat - no balls, but squeaks which is why I sometimes call him Squeaker, tho' his proper name is Othello. Natalie of the smart garden next door is very proper and always calls him Othello even though he shits all round her rose bushes. But it's wonderful to have a good sleep - I feel like a new person, and there's a doormat full of post - this morning I could eat the world !

Lots of love and God bless from Chris xx

July 1981 Suffolk

Dear Lizzie,

Having potted like mad for two days, I feel free to scrawl for a day - to you and also to Jodi and her parents. I haven't written to them since we got back from the USA in January, not even to say thank you - isn't that awful, and there are numerous other odds and ends of letters that I wake up in the night thinking about. So, having set myself up with a mug of tea and a whopping great cheese wad, liberally larded with mango pickle, here goes.

Zarek. Being as objective and unbiased as I can, and knowing there's always the other person's point of view, nevertheless it's a sorry tale of woe and he sounds absolutely <u>impossible</u>. And after all your passion and striving in the early days - <u>what</u> a waste/pity. I just can't understand how a man who professes to help/cure/advise the ailing of this world can behave so impossibly himself. <u>Why</u> the arrogance ? <u>Why</u> the intellectualizing ? He must be in a state of utter misery himself surely ? Can <u>he</u> go on indefinitely like this ? From what does he derive <u>his</u> pleasure/happiness/relaxation/belly laughs ? How can he reckon to be "intellectual" when all he seems to do is snooze in front of the television ? You say he, like you, loves the children yet abandons the meal table and shares little with you, doesn't connect. Yet perhaps he's never really 'broken through' to the realities of life - fun, colours, swapping thoughts, sharing the simplest things ....

As for the possibility of an affair - all I can say is that if there's <u>any</u> way of indulging yourself <u>without</u> hurt to your admirer's wife, the innocent party in the foursome, then for goodness sake, go ahead - burn it up in you both - satiate yourself - you owe it to yourself and so does Zarek, for God's *sake. Seems straightforward to me - if Zarek doesn't want to make love to you and denies the old conjugals, after perhaps a hint from you of what his denial could result in, and time for him to mend his ways and make courtly effort - then go ahead elsewhere with discretion, if only to keep yourself sane and with some self-confidence still glowing.*

In the meantime, enjoy your fantasies Liz and anything else positive that might result from them ! At least your lustings (like pain), prove that you are ALIVE - more than Zarek seems to be these days. Write as much and as often as you have times for. It's always good to hear from you, whatever the content. Keep your pecker up (and hopefully some other lucky guy's too !) - lots of love, as ever, Cxxx

July 1981 Hampshire

Dear Hilda, dear Friend and Confidante,

Where are you now when I have so much to tell you ?
Nothing has happened and yet I'm in a different world.
Here's how.

God, I don't know where to start it's so exciting, devastating, worrying. And irresistible. You remember the phone call from the husband of one of my good friends here in the village ? THE phone call. Then some more, just chats. Then the playschool barbecue attended by most of the families I know in the village and Zarek coming in for an hour and being his usual aloof self - all a bit beneath him but he'd come for the sake of the children. So I stayed until the end and was rewarded with a stolen kiss and quick grapple in the road which made me feel I'd like a great deal more.

Would you believe it, when we met en famille the next day, I even found the smell of his nicotine chewing gum erotic !

More phone calls - an arrangement to meet. A bright sunshiny day with Alice in the pushchair and me feeling slim and sexy. (Lost a lot of weight recently - feels lovely.) And honestly, when he put his hand on my neck and "drew me to him", as in all the best women's novelettes, I felt as though I'd been struck by lightning. I had recently realised how much I had missed the intimacy associated with a close relationship. Zarek deplores small talk which he dismisses as idle chatter and because of our long physical dissociation, there has been no contact of any sort between us. Almost as though we live in separate worlds - we touch each other neither with our minds and voices nor our hands or bodies.

I had thought I could do without it, that it was unnecessary but I now realise how wrong I was. Apart from the delicious feeling of having another body close to mine, I had forgotten, may even never have known in this way, the joy of looking into another person's face and seeing loving interest, concern and caring there. My problem was always that I wanted to love rather than be loved so that inevitably, I fell for people I could idolise. Zarek has raised his own pedestal so high that I'm fed up with the struggle to peep over the edge and now, to have some really ordinary, nice bloke looking at me longingly and lovingly is quite delightful.

Another intimacy I realise I missed, were the endearments which may be difficult for a foreigner (like swearing in another language), but Zarek never said anything without it being part of a long psychoanalytical discussion. All of which could lead you to believe that I'm on a very dangerous slippery slope from which it seems impossible to escape

So now I'm being much less mature about it. Pete rings me nearly every day and I don't care what he says, it's just so good to hear his voice. Have you ever had those silent sort of conversations where you only need to feel that the other person is at the end of the telephone line ? We've met once more, in the Church where I was practising on the organ (!) and it's perfectly obvious that another meeting, circumstances permitting, will commit us beyond recall. I suspect that he's quite besotted in a way that many boyfriends I chose to ignore were; they seemed too ordinary. Now I've had the exotic and this kindly, considerate, nice kind of guy seems infinitely more attractive. Isolated from our individual environments, it's delightful. However, there are many more good reasons why we shouldn't indulge ourselves. I feel <u>dreadful</u> about his wife who is probably the person I know and like best in the village. He doesn't. Says that the sexual side of things has lost its excitement but that his relationship with her is quite separate. He doesn't see an affair as making one jot of difference to this and I can quite believe him. The funny thing is that knowing his wife as I do, I'm quite certain she would say you can do anything as long as you don't get found out.

Is there anyone who hasn't been challenged by this age-old deception dilemma and the way it confronts one's conscience ? Taking a bus ride without paying the fare may be one thing as one deprives what is in effect a faceless organisation, of a small amount of money, but potentially undermining the stability of a family unit ? Ooh er.

But what chance do we stand. Although there are a few brief opportunities to meet in the daytime, there are always children around and it would seem unlikely that we'd ever get more than the odd hour or so together. And one does want more and more. I want more. My sexual freeze-up has undergone a remarkable change in that I'm utterly choked with desire and feel that it must be written all over me for the whole world to see. I hardly dare look the milkman in the eye ! But for Zarek I feel nothing. Isn't it sad. I have tried to create opportunities to talk, open things up in a way that is neither aggressive nor provocative and all I get is a great irrational tirade. "I've given you home and children, what more do you want."

I vacillate between feeling I'm an employee or a one-parent family. But deception would be both difficult and wicked. And delicious ! I keep thinking perhaps when the kitchen is finished things will be better. Perhaps after we've had friends to stay and Zarek will <u>have</u> to sleep in our bed, things will be better. Perhaps after we've been on holiday etc. etc. but I don't want them to be. I enjoy the easy relaxation I feel with this other man (to whom I wouldn't want to be married) - in fact an ideal candidate for an affair as he's happy with his wife and family. Why do most men manage without something extra though ? Have I led this one on, have I possibly set up the situation unwittingly……..? No, I can honestly say that I have never thought of other women's husbands, it has never occurred to me. Oh dear. What a dilemma. I've been avoiding the more obvious opportunities for another meeting in the hope of receiving some SIGN or other but feel that the inevitable will surely happen. Ugh. Can you bear all this ? Do ring me as soon as you're back in *this country in September and for goodness sake, SAY NOTHING to anyone. Paranoia about how things can seep out, seeps in to one's thinking.*

Do so wish you were here to talk to. Much love, lust-full Lizzie x

Postcard September 1981 Hampshire

Dear Hilda - wrote you a long electrifying letter recently but decided it had too much detail, more soul than I dared expose in writing so it was relegated to the bin. My briar patch has become an erotic dream-world, a secret garden with fruits more delicious than anything I have yet tasted. And perhaps more deadly ……… I don't know …….. Apologies for not writing more but there is just too much to say……….love Liz.

There's a bit of me that experienced both shock and shame at what I was letting myself in for. Though my own unbearable situation could justify action of some sort, I felt as though I was abdicating any sense of responsibility for the implications of this particular route. Someone was being 'nice' to me, so was my accumulated misery, desperation, frustration, anger such that I could close my eyes to the potential pain and damage that my response could inflict on others ? I guess the answer to that has to be, yes, it was, and I did.

Awfulnesses ie justifications at home continued. This, early one morning:

1.30 a.m. - I get up because Alice is demanding a drink.

2.30 a.m - She wants another drink.

5.00 a.m - Breakfast for Alice as she couldn't/wouldn't sleep.

6.00 a.m - All the children up and around, I'd returned to bed to try and get some overdue sleep.

7.15 a.m - Zarek storms in - *"Get up. You think of yourself as a single person. You should be up attending to the needs of your children."* Then a row about Alice feeding herself. I should sit down in front of her like a proper mother and put the spoon in her mouth as she's only a 16 month old baby, despite the fact that she has been objecting vociferously to my attempts to feed her. And of course, after he'd gone, she stopped yelling and gave herself her food. Only the previous week, he'd been bragging about how clever she was to feed herself.

Two days later, I took the children to the Natural History Museum in London as Greg was desperate to see the dinosaurs. Quite a marathon really, on my own with three children aged six, five and one and a bit, with bad traffic on the outward journey and torrential rain for the dark drive home. I was woken by Zarek at 6.20 the next morning in tones of advanced irritation. *"Get up. Alice wants feeding. I've made her breakfast."* I didn't stir, I was just too tired and anyway, if he'd made it, why couldn't he give it to her ?

Ten minutes later he returned firing Gregs' cap gun. *"Didn't you hear me ? You have to get up. I haven't time, the mornings are too precious and I have to practise my violin and read the newspapers."*

Oh God …………………..

October 1981 Hampshire

Dear Chris,

Normally I expect my pen to glide across the paper effortlessly releasing yet another string of literary pearls (ha!) but today it's like digging into anthracite on account of the fact that some over-curious child has yet again dropped it on its nose and bent it. Damn.

Talking of digging, I had the odd experience on Sunday of having the fork handle snap in two as I heaved on it. As usual Zarek attributed it to my stupidity, incompetence etc. Maybe, but it <u>was</u> funny !

I live a life of extremes right now. The one is a sort of creeping inertia which permits me nothing more than the basic maintenance of routines - feeding and clothing the children and getting them to school. I've given up on attempts at creativity. Don't know if this is due to life being fully taken up with the family or that Zarek has expected me to be so utterly a slave to them all that I've lost the energy to express myself in <u>my</u> way. For once, I'd cooked a proper meal yesterday (which after all, is sort of creative) ie, not the usual collection of tins, packets and freezer food. Apart from Zarek's absence until the very last minute, which meant that I had to clear away the morning's residual mess, lay the table, keep Alice happy, serve the food, respond to demands,

demands, demands - apart from all that, guess who was the chief orchestrator of the stream of complaints and dissatisfactions throughout and about the meal ? And that's what the children learn as normal ? Ugh.

The other extreme, when I dare to allow myself to experience it, has me sleepless with excitement. It's the briefest and most tantalising glimpse - of freedom. That if I left Zarek, I might for once be able to express myself in _my_ way. Today for example, I suddenly realised with an intensity that reduced me to tears, that I could never be what _Zarek_ wanted. He's already declared I'm a failure as a mother and I know that this is how he's setting me up. His own mother set him impossibly high standards and now he's doing to me what she did to him, possibly to get his own back. I am in the position of attempting to fulfil the most fundamental role available to me, as a woman in relation to a man, and he simply cannot tolerate my succeeding. Perhaps instead of saying, "No, I'm not a failure," - say it ? - I bloody scream it at him, - perhaps I should calmly respond, "but that's how you see it, not how it is for me." Shouldn't I have a right to expect some coincidence of attitudes ? I cannot go on sharing my existence and that of my children with someone who considers me to be worthless. Everything I've done in our marriage has been an attempt to prove my competence to Zarek (even having a third child), without realising how heavily the odds were stacked against me.

We _have_ to part, but I've really no idea how. I'm waiting to see a Marriage Guidance Counsellor who might be able to help but the alarmingly matter-of-fact book on divorce which I got from the library scares me silly. What's *'unreasonable' - and how can you put down any one thing in the last six months as an example when the whole situation is dotty ? Does a meal-time mutiny count or the continued illogicality of argument or what ? And must it really happen ? Must that heart-breaking word DIVORCE take shape and assume meaning in all our lives ? Can't we somehow run the film backwards until we reach a bearable bit and start again ? Where things are sort of OK even though right now they feel impossible ?*

Sorry about this doom and gloom. Sorry, Lizzie.

November 1981 Suffolk

Down in my cellar, gas heater popping and fluttering comfortingly - otherwise, lovely peace and quiet. 11.00 a.m. - pot of tea, wads of jam butties and a fag, even though I shouldn't. Smoked so much over the last two weeks I've even got a cough. Pots to make that will have to wait .... get the scene ?

My very dear Lizzie, you need more than dear Liz after your last letter -

Where do I start .... oh goodness, so much I want to say to you - to thank you, cheer you, console you, sympathise, reason, amuse, hug, laugh, cry, put two fingers up to Madam Fate and Dame Fortune .... what a letter. That's the craziest, saddest, all-revealing sentence you've ever written to me - "things are OK even though right now they feel impossible." Says it all, doesn't it. And your last letter's summary of the hopelessness of the situation is masterly. But so sad.

Such a funny, sad letter. Wish I'd been there when the garden fork broke. I'd have laughed my head off - called it a day in the garden and suggested tea and hot crumpets by the fire (perhaps with more hot crumpet to follow later in bed !).

You don't need to worry about making demands on me Liz. It's all my own fault for cultivating it down the years, to the detriment of 'finding myself' - whatever that means. I've avoided myself in losing myself in other people, and now its facing me rather scarily for the first time ever - here I am approaching 50 with nothing to show for it, no marriage, no partnership, no children, no real work or profession and the future an absolute blank. The second-hand Raeburn which arrived six months ago, is still sitting out in the garden rusting gently away and all the bathroom stuff, bath, handbasin, lovely Instamatic shower and fluffy white, very sexy rug are still in their plastic and cardboard wrappings. I work from 7 'til 7, jog, have a fag and beer supper at eightish in my local. If I'm feeling really energetic, I cook spuds, carrots and parsnips all together in one pot, mash them into a hash and crawl into electric blanketed bed at 9.30 p.m. to watch whatever tele happens to be on. Then fret every other night away in fears and anxieties about the future and desperate remorse about all I could/should/ought to have been to Jodi and her overwhelming loving that I just threw away.

I've drifted the whole of my life - into college, teaching, potting - just waiting for things to come to me, so really deserve to have ended up where I am. Not so for you - bloody hard family life for years and now virtually without *reward - indeed, having to fight for your <u>self</u>-existence, the real you. God, ain't life unjust.*

I'd like to tell Zarek what a fucking idiot he is, denigrating such an incredible wife (I'd like to say that to half the husbands I meet) but then, who am I to accuse with my track record ? And the awful prospect of dismantling your marriage .... oh Lizzie - can't you shock him into appreciation ? Leave him and take the children with you so that he realises what he'll be losing ? If you begin to make moves, might he see the light ?

A mish-mash of a letter Liz, for what it's worth. If you're ever really desperate for a bolt-hole, you could always come here - then wouldn't the burghers of Suffolk have something to talk about ! Meanwhile, press on dear girl, keep in touch, don't worry. <u>I</u> think you're lovely. XXXXC

November 1981 Hampshire

Dearest Chris

Lacey violet cami-knickers of the utmost delicacy ?

Givenchy III talcum powder ?

And John Lennon's 'Woman' ?

Could this be a sort of mail-order love affair - innocent of the fearful complications of consummation and therefore free from anxiety ? Honestly Chris, I couldn't quite believe my birthday parcel so full of loving, touching, sensual significances. I sit now in front of the sitting-room fire with my customary whisky, wishing that I could unravel my mind

105

for you to see and understand all the loving appreciation I'm feeling. Perhaps I should have written the instant I opened it or perhaps I should have telephoned, or perhaps I should have jumped in my car clad only in talc and camiknicks in a madcap dash to Suffolk, forsaking all, to thank you in the most appropriate way possible.

But no. Here I sit, warm and quiet by the fire, secretly savouring the pleasure of it all. Thank you Chris.

The children were lovely. At 6.45 I was awoken by lots of whispering and rustling and then a rousing chorus of 'Happy Birthday.' Greg presented me with a much-loved piece of quartz he'd found six months ago and Daisy had decorated one of her little baskets with ribbon and flower petals and little marbles of rolled up tinfoil. There were constant birthday references throughout the day with cake and candles at teatime. Stella and Pete from down the road came to supper in the evening and as her fortieth is only a week after mine, we really pushed the boat out with lots of good food and champagne. As usual, Zarek was conspicuous by his absence. And then, finally at 2.00 a.m. sitting quietly staring into the firelight, wondering what the other half of my life could possibly bring ....

Thank you Chris for enhancing my dreams with that most perfect of presents. Thank you for all the loving and sharing we've had so innocently for years and thank you for all that we shall be able to share in the future. All this for you Chris. Lizzie.

P.S. If the kiss you say you planted in the camiknickers is where I think it is, I shall keep it very warm and cosy !

My dear Lizzie

It's incredible - I opened your letter down here in the cellar before starting on the pots and now the whole atmosphere is swamped with the Givenchy III that you must have sprinkled inside. I have to admit the smell is closely associated in my mind with very carnal evenings (long ago I hasten to add) in front of the log fire with heaps of very pretty underclothes everywhere and the air heavy with the scent of lust and sweat. The moment I smelt it again, plus the thought of your white skin and violet lace, I experienced the most delightful throbbings that I haven't felt for ages - I mean real hairy ones. I made love a couple of times in the last month and honestly it was hardly worth the effort, but I had to press on to the end if only out of good manners. In fact I felt more sexual excitement receiving your letter and accompanying whiff than I actually did in bed recently. How about that ! I'm so glad that you liked it all - I told you, and I meant it, that I had tremendous excitement buying it and wrapping it for you. I <u>do</u> have a strong and tasteful I hope, underclothes fetish - NOT all nylon lace and black suspenders - though they can be nice - but <u>pretty</u>, delicate and feminine ones - thin white cotton being the biggest turn-on (virginity too !!). So I indulged <u>myself</u> as well as you, have no fear. Plus the excitement of <u>not</u> knowing your body - anticipation being nine tenths of the pleasure etc. - not that the remaining one tenth wouldn't be just as delicious, of that I'm absolutely certain!

Right now the Jodi business has left me feeling very un-physical even though it's getting on for a year since she left. I feel the need for cuddling and close contact, almost a sort of mothering. But even so, it wouldn't take too much effort and persuasion for Willie to rear his excitable head given the right person and circumstances - hint hint - just in case you happen to find you've run out of petrol right by the front door one dark and stormy night - nice thought.

Yes Liz, you're quite right (as usual) about the 'mail order' loving ! Very clever. With the added bonus that it's harmless, guiltless (virtually) and endless - although I think, given the opportunity, I'd risk all of those for a crack at consummation ! It's so lovely to have it just to contemplate - over and over (and over) - hence the delectable throbbings !

Did you know that the RAF pilots often took an 'intimate' article of their girlfriend's clothing with them when they went to do battle, for good luck ? So, sometime, I'll borrow back your/my camiknickers, smelling lusciously of you of course, to stuff down my boots when I know the sortie is going to be a tough one. This is not an oblique request for them back after you've worn them for a week. Who knows, I might just one day take them gently off you, or even more excitingly, pull them gently, oh so very gently to one side ! I think they were designed for making love in ! - oops - throbs again .... love you. Chrisx

P.S. My kisses have a habit of moving around - in case you feel tickling !

December 1981 Suffolk

It's past midnight, Wednesday ? No, I s'pose it's Thursday morning and I'm just back from seeing The French Lieutenant's Woman - with so many luscious associations with you and Meryl Streep and I'm bloody tired and bloody hungry and I've endless dishes to finish tomorrow but I had to read your letter through again and realised that I'd read too hastily and written too lustily .... so dawdled over it again and its delicate eroticism with firelight and whisky and tender thoughts leading to touchings and kissings in secret places .... right now I could just sink in to you to sleep and shelter and escape from the night as you make me feel so safe. So safe Liz .... I wonder if it would work with you and me ? I'd be almost too frightened to put it to the test in case it destroyed all we do have in these pages of written thoughts over the years and that would be too awful to contemplate. D'you realise if we lived together, all this scrawling would stop - though we could always write in different rooms and poke letters under each other's doors !

Sat today right through a rainstorm, out on my bike, seeing it coming, solid grey in front, double rainbow behind. Just sat there to let it all happen around and over me - watched it come and go, heedless of soaked clothes .... so many precious moments ....

Thus to bed with my cheese on toast and intermingling thoughts of F. L. Woman and you in my bed in first talcum and camiknickers and then just talcum on your pale skin and touching and muddling arms and legs and sleeping like that for ever and never waking up ....

And now I'm laughing at myself and my indulgence and the mess of life, secure in the knowledge that love and friendship outlasts and outshines <u>everything</u> …….. thank God I've known that - so many people don't, you know. God bless and sweet dreams dear Lizzie. XC

Oh my goodness. This was all getting a bit steamy. Next missive to arrive from Chris was a postcard of the Matterhorn, looking magnificent but impregnable. It made me think of what it would be like if I was leading a climb and I'd got my ice-axe wedged firmly into the side of the mountain (of life) but it had got frozen in. So there I'd be, dangling in my violet camiknickers, worrying about the lovely view Chris would have from below !

December 1981 Hampshire

Dearest Chris

On Saturday night I drove Greg to a party through the most beautiful sunset I have ever seen and quite honestly, I felt I could simply, at that moment in time, have dissolved away from existence. Then, back to reality when I got home because our boiler had sprung a leak and I spent the whole evening mopping up the mess and acclimatising myself to the resulting drop in temperature.

Odd isn't it, that we both seem to have so much love we want to share and yet we've both made such a cock-up of the distribution process. We've been programmed to feel that it shouldn't <u>just</u> be screwing but the establishment of something permanent, mutually supportive and 'meaningful', so why are we never satisfied ? I have a sort of *tingly, flesh-creepy feeling that makes me want to stretch out 150 mile long arms to you, and yet is that just the screwing bit or is it the fact that we seem to share and understand so many things in the same sort of way ?*

Like possibly even sharing the same rainstorm as it dipped across the country - you alone and soaking, me with a carload of little girls I'd collected from school, totally wrapped up in their children's chatter and with only a passing interest in my constant exhortations to look at the rainbows arching one after the other transcendentally across the grey concrete motorway.

But if paper were made flesh, would I find it in my heart to welcome Jodi back should she return tomorrow ? I can <u>write</u> that I'd be truly happy for you both to have a chance to try again. In my fantasies, I would be envious but not jealous that she should claim you. I would purge my letters of their passion and anticipate another twenty years of innocent but knowing friendship, knitting clothes for your inevitable babies and welcoming you all to my home. Could I do that I wonder ?

Part of me longs for Zarek and me to be able to rediscover each other, but now I find myself wondering if we ever really knew each other in the first place. Initially he wooed me extravagantly with flowers, wine and compliments but sexually, I don't think we ever had 'fun'. I loved him. Yes, but he always dictated the terms so there was always an imbalance.

I don't understand myself. I have a husband for whom I feel nothing. And I have had a lover. I have you and our letters.

With Pete, everything started with an eruption of unbridled passion which became significant self-discovery. In being loved, I discovered that I was lovable. But now that I know it can go nowhere and has such destructive potential for him and his family, my heart is no longer in it and I've avoided having anything to do with him. Tricky as his wife is one of my best friends in the village …….. feel as though I'm on a road to nowhere ……..

Having said all that, I must confess that without the actual need for expurgation, this well of passion goes on bubbling away and there's no knowing what could follow if you and I got the chance to meet. Dammit, of course we both know what would follow ! I feel like a firework, just waiting, longing to have its blue touch paper lit ! Love you Chris, but what can we do about it ?! Lizziexxx

December 1981 Suffolk

Ooh Liz - up at 7.30 and straight into housework which I tackle as if I'm on an archaeological dig with every bit of dust potentially precious - to be wiped up assiduously. I move the bog brush as if it's a priceless relic, scrub scum off the washbasin as if I'm about to reveal a Leonardo. Sounds frightfully obsessional but at least it gets it done and a fresh bedroom with clean duvet cover and pillow slips has the same delight as yanking on clean jeans after a good bath. If only it would <u>stay</u> bloody well done ! Shall leave downstairs until tomorrow as I've got to glaze four sets of dishes for all the families who've fed me since Jodi went. And I must attend to Christmas tree lights for the fir tree outside which *really cheers up this dull corner of the town. There goes yet another ambulance - somebody else copped it on the ice !?*

<u>Awful</u> last Sunday when I got home from my sister's just before a blizzard. I leapt down into the cellar and unpacked the kiln and then repacked it solid with dishes already glazed and waiting. Then I noticed a burnt out element near the base of the kiln. AAAARGH ! - Had to unpack the lot, battle with two busted elements, replace damaged brickwork, repack dishes and finally get it going by 11.00 p.m. Only way to cope with that was to pretend cellar was a sunken submarine and I had just two hours to repair the damage before 250 men suffocated to death ! Walter Mitty's got nothing on me !

Anyway, dodged the snowdrifts and massive gritting lorry on its side in a ditch, like a dead dinosaur, not to mention Jaguar with its nose deep in a hedge/snowdrift, to take last of £500 dish order to station to send up to Glasgow. Feel very superior driving a Mini in those conditions, even if it <u>is</u> rotting all down one side like it's been machine-gunned. (Bloody Luftwaffe again !)

Have a lovely Chrissymus, dear Lizzie - of course I'll think of you, you're never far away. God bless you all, especially Zarek !

Lots of love as ever, Cx

9. Impasse

Christmas had felt like a bit of a charade, so much food, so many presents, so little love, except for the children. Once it was over, it was back to the world of school runs, washing and ironing, messy mealtimes, sticky fingers, domestic shopping, paying bills, baby-sitting for friends. It might have been bearable if only some of it had been shared, but after six weeks of non-communication which started in mid-December, the new year brought one of those grim talking sessions which left me filled with total despair. The one thing we agreed on was that our relationship was barren - non-existent. Keeping things going 'for the sake of the children' was the only option that Zarek was prepared to countenance. He said I could leave if I wanted to, but the children would stay with him and there would be no compromises, so what kind of mother could consider that, especially knowing the working realities of maintaining domestic continuity for three young children ? He wouldn't be able to do it. His argument for staying together, possibly with some awareness of the need for a cook, cleaner, chauffeur, child-minder, laundress etc. etc. was that it would be worth putting up with the negative aspects, just to keep things going for them, which it might well have been if I wasn't feeling such utter dislike, distaste, revulsion for him. It felt as though he was wanting to punish me for all the things that had gone wrong and the only mistake he'd acknowledge was having married me in the first place. He saw his behaviour as exemplary whilst for me, I felt I'd tolerated so much that wasn't over the years, because I'd believed in the existence of our relationship, believed that you had to take the downs with the ups, believed we were survivors.

Getting a job might have been one temporary way out for me, but there was no way I could consider that until Alice started school and that was three and a half years away. So at the start of 1982 there was 1983, 1984 and half of 1985 before any possibility of liberation.

Liberation. Well, the clandestine correspondence that Chris and I had been conducting helped, but we found ourselves wondering how Zarek seemed to be totally unaware of the fat envelopes that were plopping on to the doormat most mornings, and my late evening rendez-vous, once domestic chores were completed and the children in bed, with my writing pad and pen. In fact there was little that was clandestine about it as I was usually perfectly visible in the same place at the kitchen table, scribbling like fury. My eagerness to retrieve whatever the postman might deliver, could be said to render letters invisible as I always got to the front door first but Zarek was so intent on being above bread and butter issues that any attempts to chat or exchange news whether it came by word of mouth or letter, were greeted with an impatient and disdainful, "what are you trying to tell me ?" So I stopped.

Chris and I made new year's resolutions, his to make some money and mine to be a better wife and mother. His was easier. For example being a children's party entertainer could provide some useful back-pocket cash as could Art School modelling (imagine the surge of interest in the Life

Class). We also wondered about bits of himself that he could sell. Kidneys or blood are both a bit dodgy unless you live quite a long way east and with short, curly hair, selling it would be a long-term project especially as the preference is for the long, straight, Eurasian variety. However, there's always sperm which led to private giggles about the possibility of lopping bits off here and there, activating the glands, encouraging the orifices to exude, all for cash.

Some of Zarek's nastiness was also beginning to rub off on the children. A typical tirade one lunch-time, came not from him but Greg when I'd accidentally given him a dirty cup. "Why d'you give me a dirty cup ? Can't you even wash it properly ?" he demanded with Zarek backing him up, "Yes, it's called technology," which was a snide reference to the inefficient dish-washer which Zarek considered to be an unnecessary luxury. It felt as though they were both intent on humiliating me. We seemed to be so much at odds, there was no way of reclaiming any of the common ground we had once shared. Instead of hoping that if I kept quiet, things would settle down, I found myself measuring every challenge with a mental yardstick that was leading me time and again to the conclusion that I had to somehow escape. I felt guilty not for not loving Zarek any more, but for not wanting to even try. So much for new year resolutions.

February 1982 Hampshire

Dear Chris

You are still alive aren't you ? I've just got myself fixed up with a large mug of black coffee, half a tumblerful of whisky and some fags - suggest you do likewise or else get yourself

116

a big pot of tea and some peanut butter and toast if it's more that time of day. I've been experiencing misery with a big M recently - so much of it that I couldn't even write, just wallow. And I'm not even sure right now whether writing is what I really want to do, so don't be surprised if I stop. Just like that.

I suppose it all boils down to the grim realisation that I can't really change my life at all. And even just writing that makes me want to weep. Again. I've shed enough salty tears to bathe in over the last couple of days. Just misery. Ugh.

And that's what started it. I've just had another appointment with my Marriage Guidance Counsellor. I'd tried to fix it ages ago but there seemed to be a very long queue so I've had to wait for a vacancy. She's been an enormous help even in the few sessions we've already had. With gentle persistence she kept on coming back to why I had opted to be the family doormat. She was searching for family precedents that I might be copying, but could find nothing and I found myself apologising for not being able to help when inside, I felt angry because I knew that I hadn't chosen to be a doormat but it was where I had been put by Zarek. And driving home, I was crying and thinking, "Am I really so wet ?" And I knew because it was affecting me so intensely, that yes, I must be. And it really hurt. Then I started to wonder why I'd apologised for not being able to help her find what she was looking for, and suddenly I realised that my apology was a sort of cover-up for anger, anger at Zarek, because he wanted to control me so much in areas that I neither wanted nor needed to be controlled. Then I realised that my emotional mainspring was in fact a fear of my own anger, and that I'd married Zarek because of his hugely controlling strength. Perhaps he could manage my anger for me. But instead, he'd ended up controlling everything I didn't feel needed it. So I get even more angry. Then I grovel because that's the only way I know how to deal with it. That's me.

It was such a relief to get to the bottom of all this - it really feels right to me - but then, what to do with it ? I felt lost for a couple of days and then thought I should share it with Zarek, even though I hadn't told him about seeing the Marriage Guidance Counsellor because when I'd suggested it ages ago, he'd poo pooed the whole idea. For once, I managed to pick the right time and say the right things - he was amazed and didn't talk down to me or play the usual patronising psychiatrist. He still doesn't know about the MGC but that doesn't matter, the insight does. He's been incredibly kindly and solicitous ever since - has tried to be more co-operative in all respects, including with the children and not just with practical help but actually endorsing my decisions with them so that I no longer <u>need</u> to be a doormat. Our mutual co-existence has again become a viable reality which ought to make me happy. BUT.

Because of my involvement with Pete, I've experienced a different sort of partnership, a different sort of role model. There has never been any struggle, never any need for negotiation, no challenging, no constant questioning, no competing. I <u>cannot</u> just revert to where we were before. For example, this is what happened a couple of nights ago. Alice wouldn't settle, screamed and screamed and just wanted cuddles all evening. I was about to give her a spoonful of a *mild aspirin based sedative when Zarek swept in, insisted that she must have a very powerful broad spectrum antibiotic, and completely took over. Two days later, I discovered that it was a new tooth that had been troubling her and that my remedy would have been perfectly appropriate. His was like dropping an atom bomb to quell a guerrilla attack. These examples abound. I understand it, I understand that he's well meaning, that he wants to do what is best but I just can't swallow it any more. I can't love him either emotionally or physically.*

Perhaps I should just resign myself; make the most of such fleeting opportunities for pleasure which come my way and put aside the dissatisfactions, not mind about the daily differences we experience, ignore the messes he makes, and especially the contradictions and counter-commands given to the children, the BIG I am. But I do mind. I want to be somewhere else, with someone else. And I have to be here. Do I .... ?

Lonesome Lizzie.

Chris's response to this was to send me an invitation to his birthday party. This arrived in the form of an old fashioned and entirely genuine British Rail Reserved Seat ticket. Quite where he got them from, I cannot imagine but it showed the time and date of the train/party, the fact that it was for a first class seat, facing the engine and that there was a reservation fee of one shilling to pay ! My excitement at this possibility was hard to contain, especially when I discovered that Zarek had already arranged to go away on a weekend music course. My parents lived an hour's drive away from

Chris' home and were happy to look after the children that Saturday evening. So, failing blizzards, outbreaks of measles, mumps, chicken pox, Scarlet Fever, bubonic plague, punctures, pile-ups or pestilences, I could launch myself into the reality of Chris' life untrammelled. It seemed like a dream come true. This was his response:

February 1982 Suffolk

Fantastic ! I can't believe it ! Pinch me to tell me it's true. The booking office thanks you for your 1/- reservation fee, (out of 60 /70 people you're the only one to have the sense of imagination/humour to take the ticket seriously and return 10p ie a shilling in old money) and assures you that I'm duly booked, hook line and sinker.

There are unlikely to be any other dossers, assuming there won't be too many heart attacks, or drunkards, collapsing in various corners - so dear Liz, you can have the pick of three bedroom floors, one single or two double beds and I leave you to guess whose will be sprinkled with Givenchy, not to mention cosied with an electric blanket ! Perhaps you'd care to sample each one in turn, like Goldilocks, so for goodness sake, don't hamper yourself with a duvet, just bring a nightie or something to sleep in - we do observe certain proprieties here in Suffolk don'tcher know ! Oh, and a toothbrush - unless you'd like to share that too ! And you will be the very first lady to christen my new shower - what an honour ! I suspect you might just need one, the morning after the night before .... I mean the dancing of course !!

I'm so glad Liz - the Gods seem to be on our side - drive carefully - tally ho ! Chris.

Shortly after this another British Rail Reserved Seat ticket arrived but this time the SEAT bit had been deleted and exchanged for Couchette, dated 'Anytime' and on a train 'Anywhere'. This one was also first class but instead of saying FACING or BACK, it said 'Both FACING' and the reservation fee had been crossed out to be replaced by COMPLIMENTARY.

Co-respondents 1982 - 1983

10. Confusion

The party was all that I had hoped for. It was more, but not all of it. It felt odd when I first arrived, taking my bag up to Chris' bedroom, noticing his duvet cover with its pattern of huge green chestnut leaves, on the bed that we were eventually to share. Noticing the little bunch of violets on my side of the bed, the waiting candlestick and matches on his, the scene perfectly set for romantic seduction.

Chris had a way with parties, and his friends knew it, so they came in droves. For a start his sitting room was huge and alive with vibrant colours and shapes – definitely '60s Art School' rather than dated Festival of Britain 'Contemporary'. An open staircase without bannisters went up at one end and on the adjacent wall, he'd encouraged anyone who could write large and legibly with a fat felt-tip pen to put their favourite quotations/bon mots, a mixture of Spike Milligan and pop philosophy with a whiff of Patience Strong. At the other end of the room, he'd turned an old-fashioned fireplace into an open brick hearth for burning logs, raised several sets of bricks above floor level. It certainly generated a warm and cosy atmosphere, even if most of the heat went up the chimney. Beside the fire, a huge upholstered basket chair, a family heirloom, beckoned invitingly and the combination of colour, warmth, music, food, drink of course, and especially the right lighting, guaranteed a party that would be long remembered.

As host, Chris was inevitably busy with his guests and although I knew no-one apart from his sister, who I'd met many years previously in London, I soon found that people wanted to meet me. Tight black corduroy trousers, black chiffon shirt, topped by velvety patchwork waistcoat probably helped and had they known about the violet camiknickers underneath, it might have helped even more but they were for Chris alone. He told me afterwards that I had been seen as the elegant, mystery woman of the occasion. Martin, a near neighbour plied me with whisky which was very much to the advantage of Ron, with whom I shared rapturously seductive dances inspired by the music of the Electric Light Orchestra. Meanwhile, Chris was nowhere to be seen.

Around 3.00 in the morning, we got to bed but in truth, my memory was numbed by too much excitement, too much alcohol. We made love, of course we did, but more vivid in my mind were Chris' anguished sobs as he relived the conversation he'd had with Jodi who'd phoned from America in the middle of the evening, hence his absence. A first sexual encounter punctuated by remorse at the loss of a previous partner, wouldn't seem like a promising start for a new relationship but our letters continued, the first from Chris containing a tape of the party music and the little bunch of violets, delicately wrapped in pink tissue paper, which had been on the bedside table, that first time.

March 1982 Hampshire

My Sweet,

Oh dear - I've had a very watery sort of morning and there's no-one here to help me mop it up/talk to. But don't spend time replying - make pots. That's REALITY, bread and butter etc. etc. First of all it was watery because I started to think supposing I never heard from you again because you'd killed yourself because of losing Jodi. And I thought my way all through your funeral , and back at your house and lots of daffodils everywhere, and that was very watery indeed. And you're probably doubled up with laughter but it hurt me dreadfully. Then your package with its tape of party music arrived and I cried some more just for remembering the almost unbearable richness and intensity of it, the sheer pleasure, delight, comfort, relaxation and all the love. Maybe for me it was easier - to waft in as if from another planet with no connections or responsibilities to anyone there except for yourself. It's easy to be an attractively enigmatic figure when no-one knows anything about you.

Now, it's really hard to come back here as if everything is normal when I'm floating several feet above this particular world, shedding tears like rain and feeling so unreal. It's as though I've suddenly woken up to all the sensual delights which were emerging in my twenties but were then subjugated to the intellectual satisfactions of my association with Zarek. I suppose there must come a time when one starts to feel that time is running out, that one has reached one's Indian summer but not yet, not yet please. I delight in being lithe and sexy, in dancing, even doing exercises to those special songs …….. the poignancy of that little bunch of bedside violets …….. the thrill of the telephone bell with its promise of your voice, the taste of salty sweat, the warm softness of my children's skin when I cuddle them up in a towel after their bath, of tears and laughter. What's life without it ?

I feel estranged from Zarek and his intellectualised world, feel it can only be a matter of time before I say goodbye to it. And yet it cannot be like that. There's school uniform to buy for the children, the garden to be dug, so many jobs which I ought to feel compelled to do - but don't. Maybe Zarek has been right to keep me on a short rein all these years. Now I've made it longer, I don't want to go back. And yet if I keep on pulling away, I hardly know what I want or expect to find if I do manage to escape. Maybe it's all just a last fling before I settle down and become menopausal. Oh God. But they are so boring. Other parties where people stand around being proper and exchanging polite conversation. D'you know, one of the things that I noticed at your party was that <u>nobody</u> spent their time talking about domestic issues, the comparative costs of double glazing, the latest exciting recipe for porridge with bananas and cinnamon, the cost of a pair of children's shoes - which frankly doesn't matter two pins to most of the people who live round here anyway. And yet the people for whom it might matter don't talk about it at parties - they just want to enjoy themselves …….. funny.

But is it part of the human condition to want that which we can't have or haven't got ? Why can't we look around and

128

say "this much is good. I <u>must</u> be satisfied with it". D'you know anyone like that ? I'd like to meet them.

Licks this time, not kisses.

Everywhere.

Lizzie.

Oh Chris. <u>Must</u> go. Wish you were here. No. Wish I was there.

March 1982 Suffolk

Wotcha !

Just stopped a very sluggish afternoon's potting to have a cup of tea and a slice of the gorgeous chocolate birthday cake you brought me. Yum yum. Also to paint a pair of old shoes bright red - very therapeutic - I recommend it.

Your letter was golden - sad yes, but so FULL of warmth and loving and tenderness and comfort - made me GLOW inside Liz (which is assuming that Zarek isn't glowing inside with rage, having intercepted my replies ?) which is just what I needed. That phone call during the party really unnerved me, plunged me back into all the mixed up feelings I'd had before Jodi left and worst of all, the guilt at not really appreciating all that she meant to me. I know that I have to live the rest of my life with my horrors unless I can change course radically. There's a lot of talent I waste and all this self-examination is despicable and pathetic with two thirds of the world not knowing where their next meal is coming from. Maybe I'll just rot in my own self-pity.

And bear in mind that it's not always, not often party time here. You'd be sure to find things that bore you here as much as where you are now. But I know you'd bring to the house so much that it is lacking, above all your presence and constancy, your companionship and talk, instead of this deadly daylong silence, apart from the wind. Both Vanessa and Jodi wanted to move away but I can understand that as it's very much my house with my stamp on it - naturally they wanted to at least help to create their own home environment, away from all the past associations but that doesn't seem to matter to you. I'm glad. Now at least, I have the comfort of your written words by my bedside. (Not to mention the marks of tiny puddles that spot the sheets - sweet remembrance of delicious couplings all over the bed ....)

Love to you, in haste. C XXX.

March 1982 Hampshire

Chris, one half of you is like Miss Havisham in Great Expectations, sitting in her tattered wedding finery watching her wedding cake turn to dust and the other is the exact opposite, positive and bouncy and full of creativity - a Jekyll and Hyde personality. You keep on telling me about your anxieties and deficiencies - don't you think I can't see them for myself ? But when you are happy, it simply floods out of you like sunshine, warming everyone around you.

You say you've never had a partner as physically and emotionally dependable as yourself although I might question the emotional dependability bit given how quickly you can plunge to the depths of despair. Well mate, you've *met your match in me, which is maybe what's worrying you - I might just show <u>you</u> up ! But I don't want to because I accept you as you are, warts and all, and I can see that we could form an incredibly potent partnership. I don't want to take <u>from</u> you, I want to share <u>with</u> you - what you have and what I have, whether it's in your home, my home or anywhere else for that matter.. And I don't give a toss for your ghosts, ghosts of failure with Vanessa and Jodi and countless others. I feel sure enough of myself to know my worth which is why I have fought so hard against Zarek's constant denigration. I care about you and the effect your ghosts have on you but you're like a patient who won't allow a festering wound to be touched because it will hurt too much. Well, I don't know how long you intend to fester for, but it isn't good for your general health so you'd better get a doctor, quick.*

What I'm thinking about a lot now, is how not to sink into the same sort of situation and become yet another ghost. How to prevent you from repeating the same old pattern again. I could simply say "that's it". Would you feel relieved that I'd removed an impending burden of responsibility from your shoulders ? Would you ?

Last weekend was a real crisis time, even though it might not have sounded like it when we talked on the phone - being all matter of fact and oh, it's nothing really. Like heck. It was something alright. Everything. Zarek thumping the table so hard I thought he'd break his fingers, declaring that even if before a jury of my peers I was judged to be an adequate mother, to him I wasn't. Knowing that I can never convert this apparent failure into success in his eyes because so much of it has to do with his own upbringing. Standing there, quivering with rage in the hall in my coat, just telling myself to walk out there and then. But somehow staying yet feeling a frightening sense of detachment from the whole situation.

Caring for the children but not giving a damn about anything else. Oh God. Why is it that the people we once felt could so completely meet our needs, can subsequently fail us so completely ? At twenty-five, I needed a strong powerful father-figure, to take control of my anger in a way that my own father couldn't, to lead me into a larger more mature person than I could have achieved with anyone else I'd met until then. But now I'm sort of there, I don't need this paternalistic control anymore and it's positively detrimental to my own development and functioning as a mother. I'm still choked with anger and feel as though the wheel has turned full circle. All this came out when James, one of our psychiatrist friends was visiting, talking long into the night. You came into the conversation briefly, how both you and James as apparently strong, powerful people, tended to attract dependent females, the little cuddly sort who are unable to satisfy your/his own dependency needs. At one point James asked Zarek about your present involvements and he said "Oh, there's always someone's wife who's ready to warm his bed." Ah hem !

Away from all this, we've had a nice day today. There was a children's concert in Bournemouth with Johnny Morris narrating Peter and the Wolf. He gave it his own inimitable touch and was much appreciated by the packed house. It reminded me of Saturday morning pictures ! Master Greg

132

added his own range of rude noises and unwelcome interjections of "it's boring" whenever the music went quiet. Another child who was with us said brightly after they had played the National Anthem, "I know that piece" !

Then this afternoon, we purchased three goldfish (one each), duly christened Superfish, Catty (a nice touch that, by Daisy) and Booboo - by Alice who can't say anything else. It wasn't until much later that I discovered Greg had cleaned out the fishtank with a container full of bubble bath - no wonder the fish were looking a little peaky and purged !

Memories of your party are still so vivid - more real than reality. What a pity we can't invent a mental video to retain accurate details of our lives instead of having to depend on unreliable memories - such an incredibly RICH experience but at least I have the music on tape. I've played it so much, Greg and Daisy keep saying to me, "Mummy, why do you keep singing those tunes ?" I know it's not all parties chez Christoph - I'd also like to hear the wind whistling around your house, to admire the first snowdrops in the garden, even to clean out the loo or commiserate over the latest batch of bills, and clean out the hearth the morning after the night before.

D'you know, if Zarek opened practically any cupboard in this house, there's be a positive avalanche of your letters. And I'm comforted by the fact that even if he did take it upon himself to read them, he'd soon give up as he's hopeless with anything hand written. Isn't it odd that he's so concerned with news and what's going on in the world at large, but can't see what's happening under his nose. It

133

makes me feel sad for him really, despite all our dissatisfactions.

Take care Chris - remember me to anyone who might cherish the memory .... why do I want to come back so much .... ? Love Lizzie

Oh Liz - what an awful weekend you had - I can just picture it . I've banged fists, head against the wall, thump thump to try and make a point get through to Jodi. And I did the same with Vanessa - once hit myself on the head with a poker - sheer frustration at trying to convince her that it was her I loved and wanted and no-one else. Knowing this, why couldn't she relax and be happy. Sounds funny I know but it hurt my head and there was blood everywhere and she got hysterical - oh yes, Liz, I do know, I do sympathise - I've had some !

Invitation today from Nancy - local bank manager's daughter working in advertising, whatever that means. Lives in Henley-on-Thames - 25ish - always calls to see me when she's in Suffolk. Very pretty and intelligent although maybe unsure of herself sexually even though she did the rounds at Oxford. She's keen for me to go and visit for a weekend which would be nice and quiet and interesting and different.

What a lot we'll have to mull over as we sit in our bath chairs, blankets over our knees in the sunshine when we are 75 ! God bless. Cx

Coming so soon after our lovely consummation, I'd begun to wonder if Chris' regular references to other ladies, whether they were former wives or girl-friends, were a covert signal not to see him as my personal property. Were all his loving words as sincere as he would have liked me to believe or was he simply being open and realistic about his needs and aware of the time and effort I would need to extricate myself from my marriage? Only then would we be able to consider whether there was a future for us together and so much could happen in-between. Even so, his letters were peppered with references that included me, for example redecorating a bedroom so that when we had a row *"you could decamp to that bedroom and I could have the exciting pleasure of creeping in and seducing you all over again."* What was I supposed to think ?

Sessions with my Marriage Guidance Counsellor only increased my awareness of the terrible freedom I could be confronting. At one point, she asked me what I was going to do with my realisation that Zarek's pedestal no longer existed for me, but we both felt the need for his contribution to this discussion and so far, he'd refused to come. He'd always rejected the idea that we should seek help but I knew that if at this stage he would not co-operate, then I could say without fear, that I would definitely leave him since there would be no other way of escaping from our existential knot.

All of this was terrifying. Terrifying that he wouldn't share with me the real responsibilities for our partnership, terrifying that he might. Our main problem with living together was our shared duties and obligations, especially in relation to the children. The trouble was that I no longer liked him and had no wish to share a family life with someone that I could now see was old-fashioned, bossy, assertive, demanding and positively snake-like in his ability to argue that black was white. Could this change ? I thought not.

But at least with this 'terrible freedom', I knew that if I had to go, then I would, knowing that I had explored every possibility, notwithstanding my failure to engage Zarek in the debate. And it wouldn't be an escape into the arms of a Pete or a Chris or any other bloke for that matter. It would be because I had found myself at last, not looking to others for definition, not leaning on my role as wife and mother for identity, but becoming an integrated adult. Was it possible ? It had to be, but a cynic might ask how I could be so confident in my own ability to change whilst denying that same opportunity and quality in my husband.

11. Another visit

My life was one of contrasts, the delight of being with the children and the distaste of being with Zarek whose constant criticisms I found crushing. It felt as though I could do nothing right and my role, at first proudly maintained, as wife and then mother, was being pummelled out of existence and me with it. If ever Zarek and I attempted a family outing, the strain of getting everybody organised was compounded by his earlier inertia, sitting in the chair all morning with the newspaper and then deciding he has 50 million things to do before we leave. In the meantime, I will have been trying to muster the brood, find gloves, shoes, hats etc. which then disperses, gets hungry/dissatisfied. Then there was the tension generated while he wanted to buy or at least consider umpteen purchases we didn't remotely need like pyjamas for Daisy who had plenty, or buns for the children when they were up to their sticky eyebrows in crisps, chocolates, sweets he'd insisted on bringing with us as essential provisions for the journey, probably barely ten minutes down the road. Then he'd vanish completely and I'd eventually discover him doing Daisy's hair in the middle of the car park so I ended up feeling generally frayed because we weren't pursuing the same objectives. And it was usually mine that were sacrificed. It felt as though I was occupying a different reality with the children precariously balanced between the two.

Nevertheless, there were a few small pleasing satisfactions that we enjoyed, even if they meant nothing to Zarek. For example that Easter, although Greg had watched practically every cartoon on television, he'd also achieved an unbelievably high Space Invaders score and the high spot for Daisy was her trip to the dentist, who not only filled her aching tooth but gave her a tissue and pink water to spit into a funnel, and drew a horse on her thumbnail with his drill. She was most indignant when this was decapitated at nail-cutting time.

Pets featured too. I was showing off to a friend. "You wouldn't believe it" says I, "but I can tell you the names of each of these identical fish. That's Superfish, that's Catty and that's ……. oh, but where's Booboo ?" And truly, the third fish had VANISHED. Then out of the corner of my eye, I spotted a limp, motionless, gold object, some distance away and perilously close to the recently boiled kettle. In its excitement at my having changed the water and having filled the tank rather fuller than usual, Booboo had obviously made a foolish leap for freedom, possibly aiming for the kettle but nearly committing piscean Hara Kiri. When I thought of the hundreds of fish I have gutted and cleaned without a qualm, it's funny that I actually reached for a spoon, rather than pick up the fish with my fingers !

The newly-acquired rabbit, following Alice's birth, was rather more demanding. Greg had let it out of its hutch one afternoon and hadn't bothered to put it back. We looked for it unsuccessfully around teatime but then at 8.15, in the middle of a Rupert Bear story, there was great hilarity from next door where they were still rabbit chasing. With, I

138

suspect, a telepathic awareness of my increasing appetite for rabbit stew, the little beast took refuge in an eight inch gap between the utility room and the garden fence. And refused to budge. One and a half hours later we gave up because it was dark but rabbit was eventually shown clemency and reprieved from his ordeal by stewpot when he agreed to return to his hutch, in the early hours of the morning.

I negotiated another visit to see Chris, a weekday visit when Greg and Daisy would be at school and I could take Alice with me under the pretext of visiting an old school friend. Deception and duplicity are inevitable bed-fellows but I hated the enormity of my deceit, even if I felt it was justified. I could convince myself that I had little to lose but how could I know until I no longer had it ? I felt like Burns' 'wee sleekit, cow'rin, tim'rous beastie', the smallest, most insignificant and vulnerable field mouse, cowering under a dock leaf and hoping that if I kept very still and very quiet and didn't even wiggle my whiskers, then all the gigantic horrors of the world ie. Zarek, would safely pass me by and not notice what I was up to. On the practical side, I was worried about what Chris' neighbours might think when they saw me arriving at his house lumbered with baby paraphernalia, cot and push-chair but his reaction appeared in a letter and was unequivocal:

'The thought of your visit sends, no, not shivers down my spine - but butterflies and bloody great hairy moths, not fluttering in my stomach, but battering right low down, somewhere behind my pubic hairs, trying to get out. That in turn made a mutual friend raise his ugly head, well, I don't

think pricks are very pretty - or balls either compared with the gloriously smooth lines women have from whatever angle. Your body is beautiful. I've relived that party night over and over and can't wait. We'll have a log fire and start making love there - sort of explore what we have in store. I want to undress you, very very slowly - not even that to begin with, just disarrange you and look at your pretty wrapping papers and feel the present underneath. Sorry to be so crude about it Lizzie, but rest assured that my carnal cravings are all mixed up with knowing you - all the millions of words that have travelled to and fro over the years, trusting you, feeling safe with you, knowing we share so much instinctively without words, knowing when we look at something, we are seeing it with the same eyes. Knowing in our different ways that we've both been through the mill and want to help and please and delight each other - remembering that as a young man I often wanted you, and often since, imagined being your lover. Honest dear, it's not just your delicious body I'm after !'

I too was experiencing the female equivalent of the fluttering moths and butterflies. And for me the anticipation was like hugging the softest, warmest blanket really close, or more realistically, clinging to a Mae West, to keep me afloat. This was all very well, but in the quiet of the evening when the children were in bed, Zarek asleep in front of the television and the light gradually fading in diagonal stripes across the sky with solitary birds gossiping to each other before finally settling, I had time to think. I knew that I could not expect anyone to take me on with three children and that the most I could hope for would be independence and perhaps the occasional comfort and support of good friends. Even at this early stage, I felt that my relationship with Chris was an intense friendship rather than an affair, which begins with quivering sexual curiosity and passion, but which has to fade. What I looked forward to, which was so lacking in the life that I had, was domestic companionship and I could see that despite Chris' apparent gregariousness, he needed autonomy and not to be depended upon. For me, having three dependent children was enough; I needed autonomy too.

I could see three distinct courses of action. The first was to stay put and carry on as I was - a grabby and grubby way of life, taking from Zarek without him realising what he was giving, snatching pleasure where I could find it to compensate for other deficiencies and hoping not to be found out. Fun, but I thought I should behave better.

Secondly, I could have left immediately, feeling perfectly justified, but what about the children, what was to become of them ? And finally, the hardest of all, switch off all the diversions and try and invest in what I already had. The disadvantage of this was that I felt I had already been doing it for too long. Before Greg had been born I had tried, had been utterly devoted to my marriage but since having the children, the whole show had got lousier and lousier. None of these possibilities felt workable to me at that time. But the anticipation of another visit to see Chris, was too distracting to give more than the briefest consideration to the real issues.

So Alice and I set off, late one evening after Greg and Daisy were in bed. I knew she would sleep in the car and that it would be easy to pop her into her cot once we had arrived. I was almost holding my breath until the minute after we departed. I could hear an owl hooting as we drove away, probably making the most of the inky darkness. The moon was like a skinny fingernail - not quite as hazardous for fieldmice as when it's full, I thought.......

That visit was a total joy and exceeded all my expectations. It was like finding the pot of gold at the end of the rainbow but that was because I had detached myself from the reality of my three options or any others which might enable me to escape from my unsuccessful marriage, and was living purely for the moment. Inevitably, there had to be a downside and this came with a realisation of what a victim I'd made Zarek. OK so he pursued me initially, but I'd followed it through with a tenacity and determination against which he could have done nothing, even if he'd wanted to. At one point in the early days when I was in London and he'd been struggling to requalify and was living in Belfast, he'd written to tell me that he couldn't cope with pressure from me as well as his studies, so it was over. What did I do but jump on the first plane in order to persuade him to change his mind, which he did. Having had enough, I was the one who was breaking things up and planning on destroying all that he had worked to achieve. He couldn't help who or what he was. I was the one who was stupid for not seeing it in the first place.

12. Unravelling

It had to happen, sooner or later. It was inevitable. It was not a stark moment of truth but a gradual unravelling of our web of deceit, a gradual realisation that Chris and I were no longer alone together with our shared thoughts; Zarek, like the proverbial elephant, had entered the room.

I'd received a letter from Chris and had written but not posted my reply. Both letters were supposedly 'hidden' in a plastic carrier with all my writing clutter, in a cupboard in our bedroom. When I went to the bag one lunchtime in May, both letters were nowhere to be seen. At first I thought I might have got it wrong, misremembered where I had put them, so turned the whole house upside down, Alice screaming for food, me shaking with fear and apprehension and yet almost relieved that it might all be out in the open at last. Quaked all afternoon and then when Zarek came home, he said he'd gone to the bag for some stationery (suspicious – he has his own and never touches mine, besides it was supposedly hidden), found my letter to you and so had posted it. He said. And how were you he wanted to know, and what had happened to your American girlfriend, and weren't you coming to visit us some time ? I plucked up courage to ask where your letter to me was, but he said he didn't know and when I went and looked in the bag, there it was sandwiched between pages of my notepad although I'd swear it hadn't been there when I'd looked earlier. What to do ? Sit tight ? See what happens ? Could I be wrong………?

NO ! Of course I wasn't. Though Zarek continued for a few days to be unbelievably correct in his behaviour, offering to sleep in the spare bedroom although we effectively slept apart anyway, there was a quietly deafening intensity everywhere which seemed to presage more than just the lull before the storm. At one point he put his arms round me as if to say, don't let this happen to us, but I simply felt trapped as though a metal cage was falling around me. Neither of us said anything, maybe both wondering where to start and what to say or do. And the weekend was almost pleasant with lovely late spring sunshine and corners of the garden ablaze with colour, deep pink hydrangeas, darling little bright blue grape hyacinths and the first golden yellow rose from our Golden Shower climber. More flowers too in Cookham where the children and I visited friend Hilda, lilac, laburnum and magnificent Horse Chestnut trees, undulating in the breeze like huge jellyfish. We walked along the river and saw dinghys skilfully weaving in and out as though they were plaiting a watery maypole.

I had an unexpected school run to do that Monday morning after Greg's normal lift had ground to a halt with an alarming cloud of smoke inside the other mum's car so I had to pack three hefty teenagers plus Greg and Alice into my uncomplaining little Beetle and was about to set off when one of them said "but what about Alistair's euphonium ?" so that came too and we made it, uneventfully. I went to bed that evening feeling all sorts of agonies about what was happening but awoke the next day full of lightness and pleasurable anticipation. Yes, I'd find somewhere to live in Suffolk where the children could go to school and I'd find a job but then it hit me. I must be crazy to think that this spirit of freedom could survive untrammelled. One glance back and like Lot's wife I would instantly become a pillar of salt or worse.

That evening my worst fears were confirmed. How naïve I had been to think that my letter had mysteriously jumped out of the plastic bag and then back in again. It couldn't have done because Zarek had indeed taken it and the quiet of the previous few days had been him formulating his plan. I was to keep house indefinitely. Zarek would pay all necessary expenses and would give me £4 a week pin money (his expression) for my services as housekeeper. He made it clear that he considered it my duty to stay but if I chose to go or to fight, he would spare me nothing and would make it as difficult and as unpleasant as possible.

I couldn't imagine living for any length of time under his conditions; extreme difficulty and unpleasantness were what I was in for but the shock of that realisation, the knowledge of the strength and power with which he would fight, made the likelihood of becoming a pillar of salt, almost attractive. I dashed off a quick letter to Chris, aware that his own emotional vulnerability and the delicacy of our precious tender feelings for each other, would be unlikely to withstand the maelstrom to come.

I was rewarded with a phone call offering love and sympathy and support but accompanied by a confession. Chris told me how about the fights he'd had with Jodi, his American girlfriend, and how unkind he'd been to her, shouting, throwing water at her, hitting, bruising her, slamming the phone down when she'd been pleading with him, even snatching a little gold heart from her throat that he'd given her in lieu of a wedding ring. All this in an attempt to persuade me to give Zarek time, to give him a chance to understand what he was doing because eventually he might, like Chris, live to regret his decision. So did this mean that it might suit Chris for me to remain with Zarek and that I might have to revise my own thinking ? It all seemed a hopeless muddle, but also an intolerable one.

This was followed by two letters, one full of abject misery, depression and regret about losing Jodi, the other delighting in the work that he was doing as a supply teacher at a local school. *'....taking kids all over the place to look at Victorian details on our school. Used to be the old Grammar School, built in 1857. Then painting scenery with them - old Dylan Thomas type fishing village, cut out houses and pubs with windows missing to let the concealed light out - paint and kids everywhere, cutting out fishes of every shape and size to stick on backdrop, incredible fun, and I'm getting PAID for it ! Chats and sweeties for the children always about me to comfort, cheer, encourage when they need it. It's going to be such an anti-climax when I have to leave - supply teaching is better than no teaching but oh for a permanent job. Your presence would make things complete......... How can Zarek on his enormous Consultant's salary, with all his supposed intelligence, be so stupid as to say "she's never loved me", after those five endless years of you patiently waiting for him to get settled in this country. He just wants to WIN, to be right, to come out on top. So what of KINDNESS, PATIENCE, TOLERANCE, UNDERSTANDING and HIS bloody LOVE ? He needs a damned good punch, right on the end of his ego. And if I was there, I'd do just that, then put you and your kids astride my white charger and gallop back here where we'd all play games and feed the ducks and water the radishes and wander through the market and picnic before putting the kids to bed and getting a baby sitter so that we could go out to the pub for a pint before coming home and touching gently and teasing and tickling and making deep love. Then to sleep in one lovely loose-limbed tangle, how about that ? Lizzie dear, bear up and have as happy a weekend as you can. The cats send their furry, purry love. So do I. And a painty, sweaty, gluey, happy kiss. And a big sticky HUG. God bless, C.'*

May 1982 Hampshire

Dear Sweet Chris - I feel so much better, knowing you are there, if only on paper. I'm babysitting for a friend now so that unless her babes awaken, there's no fear of interruption or Zarek breathing down my neck. With any luck, you'll get a 'letter' rather than one of my recent incoherent scrawls. Your own letters exude so much warmth, love and compassion. I'd guess that in spite of all your awfulness to Jodi, probably the hardest thing for you has been not to be forgiven. You've sort of crucified yourself emotionally to try and atone for what you did to her and couldn't give her. And maybe you need more emotional space than she was able to give you.

Last night was truly terrible. We really talked for the first time for years; it's left me feeling utterly drained emotionally and certain that I have to leave despite everything he says. So many words. I can barely remember them, only the feelings they aroused, and above it all, a sort of icy detachment. I'm so calm on the surface but underneath I feel raw and frightened. Zarek is now falling over himself to be kind and helpful. He's being super-loving to the children which makes me want to run away. He's supporting my judgments and decisions - a sort of 'yes dear, you can do whatever you like dear' attitude which I find unconvincing and patronising. Why couldn't he have been like this all along ? He knows what he is likely to lose and yet still says, "Any judge would say you are out of your mind to break up this family" .... I'm not am I ? And he's certain that he'll have the children. He talked about how hard he'd tried to raise me up to his level, about how I'd always disappointed him in love-making - and he's the one who always has his back to me in bed and is either already snoring or else dozing with the earphones and Radio Free Europe on. Not exactly a sexual turn-on. He talked about how important it was to give the children a loving, secure family background - even if he and I found it impossible to make decisions and never spoke to each other. This isn't my idea of family life. Should I try to show him some sort of affection when I feel nothing, knowing that all the love that I poured out in the past was either crushed or went unnoticed ? I just cannot do it Chris. I cannot accept his present artificial efforts either, because they are only a cover for his underlying attitudes, which remain the same. I'm not good enough and I never shall be.

When I think of all the awfulness over the years, the ghastly rows, the gradually deteriorating level of communication , the lousy holidays, the misunderstandings .... it doesn't have to be like that, does it Chris ? Even with small children who are stressful to live with, it doesn't have to be like that ?

Even with his difficult and demanding job, does it have to be like that ? I feel such sorrow that all this has to happen but I'm also quite sure of what I have to do. Please don't feel that you have precipitated any of this - you may have been a catalyst, but something would have happened to trigger it. I'm terrified of what the future may hold but I'm longing to be honest with myself and the rest of the world.

So that little rainbow sticker you gave me that I've put on the windscreen of my car is a real help. It has brought a whole family of fuzzy mini-rainbows with it which dance about my car in the sunshine and up my arms as I drive along. It gives me so much pleasure .... I need it, especially when scarey things are happening. Today Alice removed the pondweed from the fishtank and substituted two beautiful, big, golden polyanthus heads from a vase of flowers nearby. So touchingly pretty ..... there are still joys to be had, if only one can see them.......

My love for you Sweetheart, Elizabeth.

13. Firm plans, wobbly intentions

Zarek had smartly closed our joint bank account and my own meagre Building Society account would never support the costs of a divorce, let alone a mortgage, even if I knew how much it would all cost. A handy book on divorce drew my attention to the possibility of legal aid and with that, I took courage in both hands and found myself a solicitor. Taking ownership of a solicitor, as in "I'm going to see 'my' solicitor" – is a clear indication of serious intention and terrifying though it felt, this was a necessary step. I imagined that we might be able to avoid confrontation and reach an agreement that our ways should part, acknowledging practical and emotional needs especially for the children, via compromises rather than battles.

Zarek meanwhile, had presented HIS PLAN which at first filled me with a sort of euphoria until I grasped the realities of its implications. My £4 a week pay was like being a student again. Writing paper, stamps, tights, tampax, toiletries, entertainment, fuel for the car all had to come out of this miniscule sum. For this, he was getting cook, cleaner, chauffeur, child-minder, baby-sitter, gardener, launderer, housekeeper, secretary, receptionist etc. etc. But not lover. Even when I was thoroughly sloshed on whisky, I didn't feel the faintest glimmer of desire, and feeling nothing for him, made me completely sure of everything else I was feeling. Without wishing him any sort of bad luck or mishap, I simply hoped he'd vanish out of my life. I dreaded the sound of his returning car each evening and longed for his departure each morning, all of which made me very tetchy.

He purchased two brand new single beds for our bedroom, having moved our saggy old double bed into the guest room where he'd taken up residence. No great loss to me as I'd been moaning for years about the mattress which was like sleeping on a wet sponge. With Zarek's weight and bulk occupying most of it, I'd often rolled into the middle but more recently had acquired a fakir-like ability to manage very nicely on an eighteen inch strip down the far side. To sleep alone in a single bed was a positive luxury.

Zarek looked awful, wasn't eating much and instead of falling asleep in front of the television every night, took to his bed early. He was dreadfully concerned about losing face and keeping up appearances to the rest of the world, especially the children, who were curious about the change in our sleeping arrangements. He even rang a very close local friend of mine, whom I respected and loved dearly, to give her his side of the story. To her immense credit, she refused to listen, telling me later that she didn't want to be drawn into our conflict or take sides as she was my friend, not his and felt entirely loyal to me. That made me feel very undeserving, or that perhaps I wasn't half what people seemed to think I was.

Originally with Zarek, I had accepted all that he stood for, probably too readily, seduced by his position, his intellect, his mysterious 'foreign-ness', his allure, fuelled by his perception of me as a worthwhile conquest. But since the births of our children, he had consistently bludgeoned me with his attitudes and finally had said after all this "you're not good enough, get out of my space." I knew that in reality, I <u>was</u> good enough, but I didn't want to share his space any more. Chris, like Zarek, was another controlling person, but one who would have administered it with unfailing consideration and kindness - and for this, he would have had my complete support. His limited earning capacity in comparison with what I had been used to didn't matter. And I'd even at 40+ have been prepared to have another child if that would have provided the centre that he had so often felt was lacking in his life. But, if he had felt the cold hand of fear clutching at his heart, that the game wouldn't have been worth the candle, then that would have been alright too.

We both knew that we cared enough, that it could be good, that it might work, but his deep-seated insecurities and my three children didn't make for a very compatible combination. However, I didn't feel I needed security from Chris, as I was confident of what I had in myself, providing I was sure of his love and respect. I thought I could live with his insecurities without them being a threat to my autonomy. As for the children, I could not tell how I would feel if I was deprived of them for great chunks of time, but if I left Zarek, I knew he'd fight to hang on to them and that, should it come to a confrontation, he would be prepared to paint me as black as possible in order to win. There were no compromises with Zarek when a fight was involved so really what I was having to decide was whether I dared to take the risk. And my guts reaction to that, whether Chris was involved or not, was yes, I had to.

If my way ahead was clear, Chris' letters expressed ambivalence at every turn.

"I'm convinced you and I would get on very well together, but the thought of three children and being in the middle of another bust-up makes me panic - could I cope ? Does that sound unkind or cowardly ? The very last thing it means is that your feelings aren't reciprocated - I assure you they are and you know that. But I fear that I'm too selfish and that I'd want you in all ways all the time. If I had children, I'd like them to be mine but I know I'm too old for that now and am probably condemning myself to a lonely and bitter old age. Suicide still frequently beckons like a soft warm bed and endless deep, deep sleep. Feel I've wasted life, like my old school reports - 'could do better if he tried.'"

"Want to share so much with you Liz, to experience life together. I know we'd have such a CIVILIZED life style - all the ordinary things plus special ones too - music, plays, books - and gentle degenerate loving and lusting with shyness used, rather than a barrier."

"Needless to say, I'm concerned that your preoccupation with me (that I've certainly encouraged – or not discouraged, to say the least) turns you away from Zarek, even though you say it would have happened anyway. You are special Liz, special, special, special."

"My way of life and my personality are such wobbly indefinite things, in spite of all the fun and arty-farty satisfactions that it brings. Although I look for every chance to support and help out whenever I can, I guess it's my ego pushing me on, wanting to be liked and loved and well

thought of. I'm deeply moved that you see such a strong possibility of life with me, without the reservations that I have. Please understand that they are largely to do with me, especially in relation to the children. It's such a commitment, day long, night long, week long, life long and I get scratchy and bad-tempered when they interrupt things I want to say, do or get on with. It frightens me, as well as the worry of money. OK I can just about cope, but five of us ? I don't know.

14. Plan B

As far as the children were concerned, the basic routine of their lives was unchanged. Zarek continued to be forever grumpy in the mornings with the usual harangue at me because they were up at 5.45 and I wasn't. More than once, I'd seen the door of my room quietly open and then close again as though he *wanted* me to oversleep. By 6.45, he often had them up, dressed, breakfasted and thoroughly over-stimulated by sums and reading sessions. My inclination would have been to tell them to be quiet and go back to bed because we needed more rest but perhaps the disparity in our bedtimes and my compulsive nocturnal scribbling sessions caused my inertia and opt-out. If he wanted to get them up at crack of dawn, then he could deal with looking after them.

There were often arguments about the clothes they should wear. For example, once when Daisy's favourite dress had missed the daily wash and I'd tried to persuade her to accept a substitute, Zarek made a big fuss, washed it, dried it with the hair-dryer and then ironed it ready for her to wear again to school that day. I suppose I should have been appreciative and said "there, what a kind Daddy," but my guts told me he was doing it to demonstrate what an unkind Mummy she had.

Then there was the business of the christening, fuelled by Daisy who desperately wanted the beautiful white dress she thought should go with it. Greg was baptised as a baby but declaring a Catholic faith at that time for anyone Polish was more of a political statement than a religious one, to consolidate Polishness rather than for any religious beliefs. Off we had gone to the Polish Church in London where we stood in complete ignorance of the proceedings as it was all mumbo-jumbo in a mixture of Polish and latin. Quite what the Godparents signed up to I don't know. Many of our friends raised an eyebrow (or even two) having heard Zarek's serpentine polemic on the uselessness of religious faith and the organised church, but we were sure it was what we wanted for Greg. Needless to say, none of us had set foot in a Catholic Church since then and, given my own baptism and upbringing as a very conventional Protestant, if there were to be baptisms, then that is what they should have been. Zarek was making a big thing of it to gratify Daisy when he hadn't bothered a scrap until then.

The poor old rabbit had a struggle for survival too. One evening, glancing out of the kitchen window, I was surprised to see how frolicsome he was being. I then realised that he was not alone and the reason for his frenzied cavortings in mid-air was that he had been joined by ……. A RAT ! A rat ? Yes, HUGE, as big as Rabbit ….. well, nearly. Dashed out to frighten it off but was rather horrified to see it dive behind the coal bunker by the back door where it probably went to alert all its ratty friends that there were great delicacies available if they were patient ….. rabbits, babies etc.

The contrast between life with Zarek and my experiences on the very rare occasions when I was able to visit Chris, was marked. We'd been cutting the grass in his garden prior to going out to a party. With Zarek, not only would he have given me a lecture on how to do it, in spite of it being one of my routine jobs, he'd have worked on much too late and I'd have felt either resentful at being obliged to do the same, or else guilty if I'd stopped while he was still carrying on - a no-win situation. As it was, I was thinking while raking Chris' grass up "oh crikey, I'd really like to stop, otherwise I'll never be ready in time," when he insisted that we both went indoors for precisely that reason. Mind reader. And he was genuinely grateful that I wanted to help when with Zarek, I'd become used to hearing grumbles, complaints and criticism; gratitude was the last thing I expected.

A couple of uncomfortable months had passed since the day of discovery during which time both Zarek and I were individually reassessing the reality of his plan and for once were coming to the same conclusion, that it was impossible. His Plan B took us to a new and previously unthinkable realm. This was that as the Scarlet Woman, I should leave home and the children should stay with him.

I found this idea overwhelming; that I should have been so stupid as to get myself into this situation, that as a mother I could even contemplate relinquishing responsibility for my children. It felt unthinkable.

But there it was and once I had taken hold of it, initially I almost felt relieved. Alternatives would have created so much unpleasantness, so much distress for the children that if we managed to work something sensible out, it mightn't be that bad. I imagined everything remaining the same except that I would waft in and out like a ghost, all-seeing, all-knowing. Being there but not there. And as a friend pointed out, I would be much better able to cope with and make use of a generous access arrangement whereas if I had the children, he would be forever in my hair and trying to control things from the sidelines. Zarek, with both job and income well-established, saw himself as being able to provide stability for the children so I would be the one to take the leap into the unknown and bear the brunt of the change and upset. After all, he had been the exemplary provider, I the sinner. His plan was that I should leave alone, without my children.

Without my children. Without seven year old Greg, Daisy aged five and Alice barely two who would be left in the care of a child-minder when I <u>knew</u> she should be with me. These darling children who had been my life for all those years ? Indeed it was unthinkable.

Sharing this impossible thought with Chris, he responded with a tangled reflection of his own uncertainties.

'What are you most afraid of - actually leaving, or leaving the children ? I can see that. I was so seduced by the idea of 'freedom' ie other women, when Vanessa, wife no. 2, said she would go, that I jumped at it - foolishly. I'm a little scared that your two nice weekends here might over-ride your caring as a mother. You said in a recent letter how you had to get the children away from Zarek and all his dotty attitudes, and then phoned the next day with the opposite alternative - leaving the children with him. You've got to live with it don't forget. Freedom and instant gratification at the expense of loving and caring for your children ? Even so, you mustn't blame yourself entirely, or say you are stupid for

being in this situation. It's just as much his doing as yours - indeed more so.

And then you ask if I need 'a relationship' or a relationship with <u>you</u>. I think what I need most of all, is to repair somehow, to heal inside and I certainly need folk around me. No, I never get bored with anyone, or life here - it's just this constant wearing deep dissatisfaction and lack of faith in myself. It's so ingrained now that I seriously wonder if I'll ever be free of it. I can't imagine life without your company and your letters, and you yourself when you are able to make it. But just as much, I need space and time and perhaps a routine of work and a centre to life, which a teaching job might just provide. I'd like to be <u>strong</u>, and almost a loner, to avoid even the possibility of any more distress and upset, so that I could then come back from that solitary strength <u>to</u> people and loving, but I doubt if I'll ever achieve that. I'm too weak and self-indulgent. I'd love, for you, to be able to say "Lizzie, move in right now, lock, stock and barrel," but I wouldn't believe myself. It would be repeating the pattern of so often before - leaping straight at the easy way, into your arms/support, straight out of somebody else's. (And I feel Jodi to be still that close, you see, however unrealistic I might be.) There's got to be space and balance in my life, head, heart, to be subjective about my future, d'you see? I desperately hope this isn't hurting you Liz, but you know I say it all in love and kindness and with years of our friendship behind us. I've got to feel I'm GOOD for somebody - I don't satisfy <u>me</u> yet. Will I ever ? I do feel fatalistic these days. I've had times and opportunities over and over, but spoilt them. And maybe I'm spoiling this chance with you - but we <u>do</u> have time, don't we Liz ?

Why didn't it work with Jodi ? Why was I so afraid of the responsibility of marrying her when, despite fearful rows, I was kind and helpful and never ever the ogre that you make Zarek sound. Why haven't I got a fraction of his masculine self-assuredness and confidence ? I see so many thoughtless men around me who never seem to judge themselves and go demandingly on through marriage and have children as a matter of course. If you lose a leg in an accident, you have to learn to live a different sort of life without it. Perhaps I have always to live now with remorse, doubts, fears, memories that have possibly rendered me for all time an emotional cripple.

You see my weakness Liz ? This attraction that stops short of commitment. I encourage women, know I attract them, then put the brakes on. Liz, d'you feel that I'm doing that with you ? I'd feel <u>terrible</u>, absolutely terrible if I'd made you feel I'd let you down, or had used you, or had given you hopes that I am now betraying, after all your kindness and love towards me. Is the old pattern repeating itself with you now at the centre of my spidery web ?'

At this stage, we were both confused, allowing ourselves to be swept along by a tsunami of passion and imagining a life together, while he was still yearning for Jodi and worried about involvement with me and my children, and I was thinking of renouncing that which ought to have been a million times more precious to me - my maternal role. It wasn't that I was worried what other people might think of me for doing it, more that I didn't know how I would feel about myself if I did. Zarek had deprived me of maternal responsibility for so long, that I didn't feel that I'd ever really

160

had it, particularly in relation to Greg and from that point of view, it might have seemed almost like leaving a job. But would it, and would I torture myself for ever if I <u>didn't</u> put up a fight ? Would I feel vulnerable, like a crab without its shell ?

As for Chris' Jodi hang-up. I was convinced that it was guilt rather than love that was perpetuating her memory. In fact it seemed to me that if he couldn't love her while she was with him, then it would continue to be impossible if she came back even though that was what he thought he wanted. Under those circumstances, I could see his guilt turning to anger that she had trapped him. I wondered too about his dissatisfaction with himself and why he couldn't accept other people's opinion of whether he was 'good enough'. He certainly felt good enough to me.

15. Plan C

If Plan B was that I should leave without the children, then Plan C had to be that I should leave with them. With both Chris, my parents and several old friends living in East Anglia, that seemed like a possible destination but having barely got my head round the idea of leaving all that was familiar in Hampshire, it was a step too far to start considering at that stage, how I should make it happen. How people manage to 'throw their husbands out' or 'pack their bags and leave overnight' defeated me and in any case were actions driven by extreme and sudden rage. Acting in haste and repenting at leisure wasn't what I had in mind. My departure, whatever the circumstances, needed time to plan and prepare if it was really going to work and my moments of rage were slow-burning rather than volcanic eruptions. In the meantime, there were still school runs to be undertaken, meals to be prepared, children to be placated or comforted, all the daily routines of keeping family life going.

Their birthdays too, came and went. Alice's first birthday party was fun. We decorated a pear tree in the garden with streamers, held crawling races for all the children and had a sort of paper chase with little bits of coloured tissue paper scattered all over the garden which then had to be collected up again. The following summer of 1982 when she was two, she was treated to a butterfly birthday cake with wings comprising four smaller cakes, bejewelled with silver balls and tiny diamond bits of jelly. Greg's cake that year was a rocket made out of an ice-cream cone on a meringue moon landscape with a marzipan space-man, two liquorice comfits on his back for oxygen cylinders. I loved creating these cakes, a sort of transitory art-form and a happy distraction from everything else that was going on. Zarek meanwhile noticed none of this, none of the effort I put into making things nice or fun for the children. As far as he was concerned, it was my whim and nothing to do with any contribution to family life.

Pete, my earlier paramour, was often lurking in the background, contributing to the strangeness of my life. His family home was less than half a mile from where we lived so it was impossible to avoid bumping in to him now and again, though I tried very hard not to. Without our daily telephone conversations and occasional assignations, his life must have seemed very dull although I had no doubt that he would soon be pursuing someone else's wife - he was like that. "Meat and two veg. is alright" he'd once said, "but it's the sauce that goes with it that gives it the flavour." I think he valued the fact that I chose not to break up his marriage when, had I been more determined (or truly loved him), I could have done. He certainly triggered my detachment from Zarek and contributed to the thought that I needed an escape route even though I wasn't searching for an affair; it was a generalised feeling of desperation and despair.

Guilt ? No, I didn't feel guilty about breaking up my family although put so bluntly, it's surprising. If anything, I felt guilty about not having the courage to do it on my own. And it wasn't just men who had helped me to make sense of my circumstances; there was my lifetime's friend Hilda, who was constantly supportive and helpful in assessing the situation as was Annabel, architect friend from school days and my Marriage Guidance Counsellor.

Plan C was followed by several more, Plan D and even a Plan E. These all comprised various permutations of the children staying with me or their father. One minute I'd consider Greg staying with his father and taking the two girls with me, the next I'd feel it better to leave them all behind. Then the reality of being parted from my little Alice would hit me and I'd consider relinquishing the older two but not her. Then the impossibility of being without any of them would strike even more forcefully and I'd know that I had to fight to the death to keep them all. These plans represented the many aspects of the dilemma I was facing and the awfulness of it was that the only way I could see of escaping from this crushing relationship was to use my children as bargaining chips. Of this I was deeply ashamed. My husband may have been tyrannical but my confused desperation was no less culpable in terms of what I was prepared to do to effect an escape. What I had failed to grasp when I'd tried to find out if there was any room for manoeuvre, was that as far as he was concerned, he had all the chips and I had none. His bald intention was to punish me in any way he could and that I should leave the house with nothing. He felt that a nanny would be better for Alice than me and his only concession was to offer to buy me a microwave whenever I remarried.

I kept returning to my 'Which' divorce book in the hope of finding some comfort but the section on contested custody cases was absolutely clear. To stand any chance of success, one had to present a detailed plan of all one's arrangements for the children to a judge in court and s/he would be the final arbiter of which parent eventually provided a home for them. I could see that all of this was going to take time and wondered how long I could stand it for. On the surface, Zarek was benign and efficient but underneath it there was cold steely hatred and a ghastly determination to make me suffer. At this stage, my parents had no idea of what lay ahead but in honesty, my own understanding was pretty limited.

As a distraction, Chris and I were continuing our literary love affair often describing erotic fantasies for want of actual opportunities to indulge them.

July 1982

Lizzie dear - you just <u>overwhelm</u> me ! Goodness where do I start ?! I've just been eating the chocolates you sent me with one hand, making love to you with the other, listening to the tape of bawdy songs that accompanied the chocs <u>and</u> reading all your letters through for the third time. And I should explain, just in case you find my love-making not quite up to scratch, I'm laying a carpet, putting two weeks wash out before the rain comes, weeding, paper-hanging, painting woodwork, racking off wine, syphoning beer. Thank God the bread was baked on Thursday so <u>that's</u> out of the way (wouldn't I make somebody a <u>lovely</u> wife!) . Actually it's descending my GULLET this very moment choke choke, liberally larded with peanut butter. Oh yes, and I've rebuilt the garden table <u>and</u> been out three nights rehearsing the theatre's revue, all dressed up in gangster kit - striped pants, 'ice cream' jacket, waistcoat with gun poking out of pocket,

Fedora, little pointy patent leather shoes and moustache on upper lip. And everybody keeps saying how handsome I look, which has to be because they only ever see me in shorts ! And in the middle of all this, <u>you</u> write about dragging me out for a great long lovely walk, stuffing me with a stone of delicious food having attempted to rape me in the shower and then proceeding to writhe all over the bed in total abandonment and screw me inside out and back again. Whew ! Liz, I can't keep up - in more ways than one. <u>Please</u> let's have a rest!

I must be a looney not to say to you, let's team up <u>immediately</u> - all that cooking and lovemaking. Wow ! Poor poor Zarek. All those lovely cakes you make for the children .... Doesn't he notice <u>anything</u> ?!

Love and hugs, Chris.

July 1982 Hampshire

No of course he doesn't Chris, not even the pretty posy of roses picked by Daisy for Alice's birthday table - all rather tiny and different colours. Here's a petal from each - I hope they don't fade too much before they reach you.

The children made the most of Alice being two, although as usual the inevitable misunderstandings with Zarek created equally inevitable tensions over the birthday meal - there has never been one without them. This time, when he saw six children sitting down to lunch (quite a modest gathering) he decided he'd thought we were to have our lunch separately so wouldn't sit at the place that was laid for him with the children or help me cope with their non-stop demands, or encourage them to eat what I'd prepared. It makes such a difference if the adult attitude to a situation is consistent and I've never had that - always this feeling of pulling in opposite directions, not apparently seeing the need to _read_ a situation and see how and where you can help, but wanting to impose control. Half of it boils down to basic lack of communication.

His half or my half I wonder ? I also wonder about the 'pulling in opposite directions'. If one person is actively pulling, then the other has to either give in completely so that they both travel in the same direction, or stand still. But by doing this, they are creating resistance, which thus becomes an active component. In other words, I cannot plead passivity in this situation, I was actively _not_ wanting to go in his direction.

Zarek has never shown any interest in the planning of these events so I get on and do it in a way which I hope will be fun and the children will enjoy but invariably he barges in and wants to change everything. If only he'd leave us completely alone it would be OK but no, he has to wade in so that while the ice cream is melting on the table and the children are waiting for the candles to be lit, waiting to sing Happy Birthday, waiting for their slice of cake, then he decides he'll take a photo. But of course, the camera has no film in it, the flash won't work, and the setting takes ages so that the whole situation goes flump and one is left desperately trying to sustain the magic of it for them. Timing is _so_ important but for him it means nothing - or rather, he owns time and therefore demands the right to use it as he wishes, regardless of anything else that is going on.

Exasperation ? Ugh. And then he tells me off for reprimanding Greg who is always wicked at the other children's parties, when I'm desperately trying to hold things together. Scream? I feel murderous.

I still feel low after our last discussion. I frequently used to feel he was trying to crush me but now I feel it's total annihilation, no less. He is obviously determined to <u>punish</u> me - you cannot imagine how truly terrible his apparent omnipotence is. Yes, the marriage has broken down but he holds me totally responsible and despises me. In recent years, he has often behaved as though he thought me pretty worthless - now I've lived up/down to his expectations he no longer needs to conceal it any more. He is determined to play the whole thing with heavy-handed Victorian melodrama and I am to leave the house, totally dispossessed, clutching my few poor effects in a bundle under my arm. A close friend once described his attitude to me and marriage as 'pre-Tolstoy' - all this just proves the point.

I am sorry to go on so, but grateful at least to have an address at which to direct this verbal torment. Tenderest love Chris, and so many thanks for your closeness. Lizziex

My sense of isolation and unreality was becoming very taxing, particularly because there seemed to be nothing I could do to resolve my anxiety. It sat on my shoulders like a heavy wet overcoat. Phone calls from Chris helped, and our letters, but there was a constant cat and mouse game going on with Zarek, each of us trying to conceal from the other, what we were up to. At one point he started asking about

Pete, lover number one. "There's an ugly rumour ," he'd said, odd thought I because no-one was talking to him, " that Pete has been putting himself about in the village." Then I remembered that there had been some mention of him in one of Chris's letters, or at least some fairly open talk of extra-marital relationships which must, had he read it, have had him jumping to conclusions. I was sure he couldn't be sure and felt he was trying to put the frighteners on me, to make me get out quickly and leave everything. "Everyone will know what you have done and you will carry it with you for the rest of your life." This felt like emotional blackmail, with him offering me nothing and made me all the more determined to stay and fight for everything.

I wanted to check on what he knew and asked Chris if he could find my letter alluding to Pete and send it back to me, which he did. I'd taken it straight from the doormat after it had dropped through the letterbox but Zarek later pinched it from my handbag and I realised when he was briefly absent that evening, that he'd dashed back to the local hospital where he worked, to photocopy it.

A couple of days later, I'd started another letter to Chris and had hidden it so that I could carry on writing at the weekend. I don't know what made me think of it but quite by chance when I was getting ready to write more on the Sunday evening, I discovered Zarek's car was unlocked, late at night and still in the drive, and this was really unusual. Thought I'd do the decent thing so took his keys from his bedroom table where he was sound asleep and snoring. I'd actually tried to waken him but he hadn't responded. Went to put the car away and lock it up when something suddenly reminded me that he often put personal papers or anything confidential, under the carpet in the boot of the car. And BINGO. The jackpot. Found photocopies of all sorts of things including a scrawl I'd written last summer - "I really wonder if the world is going mad. While Popes and Presidents are shot, men starve themselves to death for their principles, my husband doesn't speak to me for two months, I am propositioned by the husband of my best friend - and the baby cries on." More significantly, a copy of a letter I'd written to Chris last January which mentioned Pete and Stella, not exactly incriminatingly but enough to arouse curiosity.

There were copies of umpteen other letters to all sorts of people and a notebook with jottings of his plan of campaign - deprive me of my car, install a coin phone, paternity test for Alice etc. etc. But most unbelievable of all was a photocopy of the letter to Chris that I was still in the middle of writing ! Made me feel as though he was copying things that I hadn't yet committed to paper ! I was tempted to put it all back, pretend I didn't know, but thought that if it was the only evidence he'd got, I'd be daft to leave it there.

Next day, he asked if I'd thought about his proposal to leave everything and go, and when I said he couldn't do that, he implied that he'd attempt to drag Pete and his family into it. My useful divorce book said that you had to have very concrete evidence before anything would hold up in court but I'd assumed that it would be Chris who would be named as co-respondent - much less damaging than Pete. Oh dear.

Zarek's determination to punish me said more about him than what I'd done. It amazed me that the law, which often lagged behind public opinion and indeed public behaviour, simply accepted adultery as a symptom of marital collapse without any reference to the surrounding circumstances. Zarek's attitude was quite incredibly old-fashioned but so apparently at that time, was the prevailing legal approach.

16. Pit, pendulum and Slough of Despond

It's hardly surprising that Edgar Alan Poe's terrifying story about the pit and the pendulum came to mind at this time, the pit closing in on me and the pendulum guillotine swinging only a hair's breadth away, ever closer to my throat. That's how I was beginning to feel, living with Zarek's increasingly threatening behaviour and the knowledge that I might soon have to deal with his exposure of my relationship with the husband of my best friend. I hadn't told Pete that he was to be named in the petition but I knew I would have to. Which set me wondering whether I might as well go the whole hog and tell his wife as well ? I could do it. I could tell her knowing that I would certainly lose a well-respected friend and much worse, she might lose her marriage, but should I ? Maybe it could all happen without her being involved and Pete could go on pretending he was the loyal and faithful husband he clearly wasn't. Maybe if we hung on to our anxiety and didn't spread it around, it would be ok ? Zarek quite definitely intended to drag both Pete and Stella through the dirt and I'd guess the only reason Pete had been fairly decent about it was that he was trying to hold on to a bit of me – insurance against a rainy day in case Stella threw him out. All Zarek had to do to ensure that Stella found out, was to have the divorce papers sent to their home. What wife wouldn't have been curious about an envelope addressed to her husband emblazoned 'Lord High Chancellor's Division' ? I discovered from my solicitor that all the legal beagles were horrified that a man in Zarek's position could contemplate such a crudely vengeful act but it came as no surprise to me. How did I know all this ? Well, it seemed that the local 'huddle' of solicitors were all hand in glove and mine, who was also acting for Pete, had contacted Zarek's and suggested that any papers for Pete should be sent to his office and not to their home address. All very frightening. Much later on I had drafted a letter to Stella but I never had the courage to send it. There could be no justification for infidelity and even though I was in danger of being crushed out of existence, my escape should not have been made at the expense of another family with young children that functioned efficiently and apparently harmoniously.

With hindsight, I found it difficult to understand my naivety in believing what I was told by Pete about his feelings for his family that enabled him to speak of loving devotion and yet permitted sexual betrayal. They were near neighbours with our children growing up together and our two families had always remained in contact in spite of geographical moves over the years. Many years later, this seemingly secure marriage had deteriorated and Stella herself had revived a love interest from the past, rendezvousing in hotels where she and her lover would spend a few precious hours. In making these arrangements, one of the hotels had sent an acknowledgement addressed to Mr. and Mrs. Clarke which Pete had opened. Cat out of bag. His reaction was to file for divorce which included, on account of what he claimed to be his whiter than driven snow reputation, a demand to receive a goodly chunk of her substantial salary and also part of her pension. In the small village where we all had lived, his extra-marital dalliances had not gone unnoticed but his propositions had mostly been rebuffed so although rumours had reached Stella, there was no concrete evidence of anyone who might have succumbed. Until she phoned me.

My heart didn't exactly stop for a moment, but for ten seconds I remained silent, desperately trying to think what I should say. I was cautious and evasive but arranged to meet her that afternoon at a motorway service station equidistant from where we both lived, knowing that I would spill the beans and knowing that this might be the end of our friendship.

As a result, Pete's cover was blown and I was cited in her divorce. All of which seemed like poetic justice. There was no loss of friendship - Stella and I have remained sisters under the skin ever since.

Seeing both Pete and Chris listed as co-respondents in my divorce was in itself un-nerving. In black and white, it made me feel like an utter trollope, whereas doing it, being unfaithful to my husband, firstly with one lover, then closely followed by another, had felt like an inevitability, something I had been driven to. And having recognised the reality that there was no longer any future in my present home, I started to feel distinctly bored. There was very little I could do, very little I wanted to do. For Zarek it was exactly the opposite. His contribution to our domestic life had previously been absolutely minimal but suddenly he was transformed, beavering away in the garden and actually mending things, like the punctures in the children's bicycle wheels which he'd never touched in the past.

In our village, there had been a steady recycling of children's bikes once they were outgrown, but not ours, they were usually too battered and rusty to appeal to any but the poorest and most desperate of children. When I was young, I can remember treating my first new bike with devoted reverence, regularly cleaning it, even down to the wheel rims, between every single spoke, and always putting it away in our shed. I was eager to pass this habit on to my own children when they were of a cycling age but it was all too much for me especially as Zarek's solution, when a bike was outgrown or unrideable, was to go and buy another one. Consequently, Greg, Daisy and Alice's bikes were left outside regardless of the weather and abandoned completely if anything went mechanically wrong with them.

Social isolation was another consequence of my situation. I had many friends in the village as you do when your children are at school and you regularly meet other Mums and share experiences - how to deal with the latest plague of head lice, what to do about the old boy who hangs around the local playground watching the little girls on the swings, who was having the next coffee morning etc. etc. I noticed at our village fair where I was trailing around with the children, that most of the other mums and dads were either actively involved with running the show, or else affiliated to the various village organisations represented. I felt spare. Spare to the family set-up at home and spare to the community. And yet if Chris had been there for goodness sake, he'd have been running a coconut shy, doing a one-man band and having wet sponges thrown at him all at the same time. Zarek of course was nowhere to be seen.

My dentist laughed when I told him I thought I was suffering from psychosomatic toothache. He'd found the holes; but my teeth had always ached when I was in trouble or facing a stressful situation. And there were so many things to worry about apart from the Stella/Pete situation. Should I have disturbed the children's equilibrium, their apparently contented and stable childhood ? Would I feel lonely when or if I was on my own ? Would I be given the cold shoulder by other wives who feared the roving eye of the emotionally detached woman when actually what I needed were supportive friends ? And how on earth did Zarek think he could cope with his demanding job AND three children ? He made constant references to the future as he saw it and all the things he'd do when I was out of the way and the children were with him, what he'd do to the house and garden, changes he'd make to their education. It felt as though he'd embarked on a deliberate offensive to undermine my confidence and even annihilate me and it was beginning to work. There were times when I felt utterly wretched and couldn't stop crying but if Zarek saw me in a state, he would know he was winning and I was determined not to let him have that satisfaction. My only outlet was in the letters I wrote, this one for example, to my friend Hilda:

Dear Hilda,

I'm not exactly wavering in my resolve but I am feeling utterly wretched, mostly because of the children. It's the whole business of disturbing their equilibrium that makes me feel anxious and there's no-one to talk to although a session with my Marriage Guidance Counsellor tomorrow should help. If Zarek and I 'talk' it's totally one-sided - him saying how the children mustn't be separated, that their home is here with all their familiar things (except as far as he's concerned, their Mum) and friends, and that their education mustn't be disturbed either. I went to Greg's school on Monday and heard what an affable chap they seem to think him and then read Daisy's mostly very positive school report today. It makes me feel AWFUL about the likely tussle we are exposing them to. It's easy to understand Zarek's feelings - I don't want to be without the children either but it's the dirty determination that he's applying to the battle which is so scary. For me, if the worst came to the worst, I'd be prepared to accept compromise, I <u>could</u> accept that Daisy and Greg should stay here for all the reasons that he's given, if I could take only Alice. If he would give that little bit, then I'd be prepared to relinquish them rather than embark on the awful confrontation that a custody contest would surely create but he'll never compromise - it's total annihilation or nothing. I'll bet you never anticipated all this when you said "you've got to do it now, Wong" !

I'd guess that part of Zarek's problem is that he simply can't conceptualise any alternative kind of existence. As long as he can keep everything going more or less as it is, he could manage but to create a new home environment would be too much for him, whilst for me, it's what I long to do. For Zarek, it would be a very neat solution if I was prepared to wave goodbye to the children and my Hampshire life and move in with Chris, who doesn't want me with three sprogs in the shadows, and I understand why, even though I'd prefer not to have to. If I chose not to fight for the children and just walked out of their lives, then it might be a possibility to live with him but I COULD NOT do that. As for the chance of taking the children with me, I simply cannot put that sort of pressure on Chris - he's never lived with children (although he's marvellous with them) and couldn't be subjected to the financial and emotional burdens which an instant family would create. And he still basically wants Jodi, his American girlfriend, to return. All of this is in spite of agreeing about our compatibility and knowing that we could have a good, understanding life together. As he said in one of his letters - "three children ? oo-er".

The worst thing is that it all takes so long. All the agro here has burnt itself out so that Zarek and I are only involved with each other through the children. I guess he's as lonely as I am since we both occasionally open up with snippets of our private lives, how he's lost a stone in weight or about the deer he ran into on his way home from playing in a concert. It would be easy to be lulled into a false sense of security, to think that if it could be like this all the time, it could be alright, but then I have a sane, sensible 'outside' conversation, for example with my solicitor, or Chris on the *phone, or my friend Annabel and I <u>know</u> which world I want to be in. The basic trust that's essential for the stability of a marriage has gone. I'm sure he's still searching for letters and he gave a very sarcastic "oh, are you" when I told him I was going up to Greg's school for an open evening, as though I was off on some secret assignation. I feel continued irritation about so many silly little things and I can't <u>bear</u> for him to touch me - so it's not on, is it. I'm beginning to wish I could just vanish from this particular scene, be magicked elsewhere, rather than tolerate all that I know is to come. It's taking SO LONG ....*

So Hilda, dear supportive friend, that's where I'm at, the nadir, the lowest ebb, the bottom of the pit. Zarek raided my handbag again the other evening, almost under my nose and I actually caught him at it, emerging from the downstairs loo with one of Chris's brown envelopes sticking out of his pocket. I couldn't quite believe what I was seeing so went to look for the letter that had arrived that morning which of course wasn't in my bag, by which time he and his car had disappeared. He returned fifteen minutes later, presumably having gone to the hospital photocopier. I asked him for it back and he actually said "I haven't finished with it yet" but gave it to me. Then he sat watching football on the television for an hour with a blank unseeing gaze and consuming large quantities of whisky. I suddenly had a sense of his absolute desperation and sadness, trying so hard to pin something on me. Perhaps I should offer him this letter. Here you are Zarek, come on, read it like you have all my other letters. See what you are doing. Gloat.

17. Distractions

My only real solace at this time was in the kitchen, comfort cooking. I made chocolate fudge shortbread, Bakewell tart and dark treacly gingerbread all of which was rapidly demolished by the children. More risky, given their preference for fish fingers and Noodle Doodles, was my piece de resistance, a puff pastry plait filled with fish and cheese sauce, parsley and hard boiled eggs, which to my surprise also met with their approval. Polish cooking also featured and I had learnt much from Zarek even though I was scullery maid rather than sous chef. This meant that any pleasure derived from the delicacies that eventually emerged from the kitchen was dissipated by the energy and time required to clean up the mountains of pots and pans that had been used, not to mention the emotional exhaustion of working under Zarek's direction.

Once or twice, we had actually laughed over something to do with the children and I could just remember what it was like when I was unquestioningly committed to our future as a family. It seemed so stupid to be searching for nastiness in order to win a battle when we ought (he ought) to be able to accept that there had to be compromises. I felt nothing for him, no sexual arousal (rather, shudders), little interest in his opinions, irritation at countless little behavioural details, cool detachment from him as a person, but we still both had commitment to our children and therein lay the problem. He must have known I wasn't evil but he was determined to tar and feather me even though it diminished him in the process. He'd said that the whole world would know of my affairs but frankly I didn't give a shit for the world I didn't know and half of the rest had made it very clear that it wasn't surprised, and supported me regardless of anything I might have done. I just about clung to my self-esteem but identified with that judgment of Solomon I've mentioned, when the true mother of a child would rather it lived than be sacrificed when a false claim to its maternity was made. Only problem for me, there were three of them.

Daily routine continued. Delivering children to school, cleaning shoes, washing, ironing, shopping, admiring their paintings and sticking them to the kitchen cupboards that is, when I could find the sellotape. Daisy had a habit of squirelling away scissors, sellotape and felt tips when she was busy writing some of her admittedly very sweet little letters. "Dear Mummy, I love you, love Daisy" was the usual message. And – practising the piano. Playing the piano with my friend Bronwen was a happy diversion. Firstly, she was lovely sympathetic company and appreciated the benefit to me of having a pleasing distraction, and secondly she was a really good pianist. It was a bit like playing tennis with someone better than oneself, it somehow upped the game so that together, we played well.

Then there was the long-promised chicken farm visit where Zarek knew the farmer. We saw not only 2,000 two day old chicks but calves being suckled, a very friendly horse and some tiny kittens, still with unopened eyes, one of which Zarek earmarked as 'ours'. His denial of the future was incredible. It was as though he was trying to create a feeling of continuity and yet for me it was far too late. By then I was finding his every word and gesture irritating beyond belief and although I could see the tragedy in it all, I couldn't find it in me to want the tiniest bit of him - I just wanted to get away.

The chicken farm was interesting. It must be very cosy to be a two day old chick but not much of a life thereafter. One end of an enormous shed had been curtained off with polythene and the floor covered with a thick carpet of wood shavings. In the middle of this was an area the size of a circus ring, fenced off and warmed by overhead gas heaters. At any sudden sound, such as the children shouting, the chicks would all instantly freeze and then start undulating in huge yellow waves, with one or two isolated fluffy balls separating from the mass and then coming together again. The sound was odd too - a sort of muffled clattering like thousands of false teeth chattering or little bones being rattled together.

These were welcome diversions against a backdrop of suspicion and hostility from which I longed to escape. Having relinquished myself and my legal problem to a solicitor, I was obliged to conform to his timetable but with the long school holiday rapidly approaching, a temporary escape at least, was possible. I planned to take myself and the children to stay with my parents in East Anglia which also created the opportunity for me to see Chris who lived fairly close to them. Zarek of course had a different plan which was that I should take myself away alone, wherever I wanted so that he could see how he could manage, looking after the children on his own. Yet again he had reiterated the importance of them staying in their familiar environment, best for me to leave everything behind and start again as soon as possible, but never any mention of *him* moving out. He was convinced that Chris and I intended to get together and although I could sense his desperation, could feel that he might just respond if I apologised and said OK, let's try carrying on together despite everything, I couldn't do it. I felt that he had gained more from me than ever he deserved and I no longer wanted to be part of his life, nor him a part of mine. I wanted something different and it wouldn't have been sincere if I had apologised. It would have been me making things come right once again for the sake of carrying on and this time I didn't want to.

You can only feel truly 'sorry' if you understand the nature of the offence that has been caused. It's easy if you've trodden on someone's toe, but if it is to do with differing perceptions and sensitivities that are a deep-seated parts of one's psyche, understanding exactly why or how one has caused offence, emotional pain or upset can become a great deal more complicated. First of all, we need to be aware that we've done or said something the other person is unhappy about and time becomes a factor in this. Leave it too late and an immediate hurt or offending remark, something we've done or haven't done, even a look on our faces, becomes a festering dissatisfaction.

We only have our perceptions of what might cause *us* offence to give us clues about what might hurt other people. So do we ever really 'know' another person well enough, even a dearly loved partner, for 'sorry' to have integrity ? I don't know. As a pretty tyrannical teenager, the one person I felt understood me and accepted my apologies, was my father who I knew really loved me. Is that rare and profound love, a necessary condition for the acceptance of an unconditional apology ? I've certainly found since my father is no longer alive so nothing to say sorry for, that sincerely intended apologies to other people (which would have satisfied him) have sometimes misfired or not been acceptable and I've then felt lost, knowing there was a need to say sorry somehow or other but not knowing how to put it in terms that had meaning for the person I had upset.

I doubt very much whether my failure to see anything to apologise for to Zarek made any difference although it suggests very different perceptions of what each of us felt we were contributing to our relationship. I'm inclined here to say 'supposed relationship' as I'm unsure now whether such a thing ever existed.

This could explain why I never seemed to talk openly with Zarek about the problems we were having even though I saw myself as a straight sort of person, liking to have things clearly defined. There had been too many years when he was uninterested in what I had to say, the implication being that it was beneath his notice, and if I did say anything, it was contradicted, distorted or reorganised to suit his ends. Or else he had just grunted and said he was too tired, or wanted to hear the news. And although he would try any means of manipulating to get his way, I didn't want to give him any chances. I couldn't outwit him, he was too clever but by being as reactionless and informationless as possible, he had to play his game in the dark. There was no point in 'coming clean' with him in the same way that an apology was meaningless, sincere or not. He didn't play by those rules. My earnest intention was to get away to the REAL world where those <u>were</u> the real rules. My Achilles heel of course was my terrible compulsion to commit everything to paper, particularly my feelings for Chris. Once Zarek had unearthed this source of information, it became an open sesame to everything that I was thinking, feeling and planning. All he had to do was find it.

Facing reality - 1982

18. Waiting wobbles

My solicitor rang that July to say that Zarek was going ahead with divorce proceedings and did I want to contest the arrangements for the children, which were that they should all stay with him. It was at this point that the reality of what I was embarking on really hit me. It was no longer a question of us reaching some sort of agreement, any decisions about the children's future would be made by a court, not us. This would be based on whatever arguments we produced to support our case, so there was going to be a fight. This was when I really got the wobbles and started to feel small when I needed to feel strong.

And I was so tired of the eternal waiting. Already it had been a year since the realisation that our marriage was dead. How much longer would it be before I could get away, before things would be different, before I could relate to people in a normal, ordinary, friendly way without this odd-ball husband lurking in the background, always having to make allowances for him, being the bit of elastic between him and the rest of the world ? I knew that escaping into another relationship was a bad idea, it would be too easy and that with so much negative baggage I wouldn't be any use to anyone else, no matter how much I thought I loved them. Chris had been my lifeline to the real world but what would happen if I cast myself adrift, could I survive ? And my poor darling children, what about them ? My mind churned away at all the supposed variables, keeping, relinquishing one two or three of them. But once the question had been posed, did I want to contest Zarek's arrangements, then the question about which of them I should fight for evaporated completely. Of course I would fight for them all, tooth and nail.

Zarek meanwhile was being nauseatingly correct and reasonable and decent. I thought of two opposing reasons for this. One was that he had written me off as beneath contempt and therefore not even worthy of his manipulations. The other could have been that he knew I was more likely to get custody of the children and was attempting to butter me up so that I might not contest his claim. If this was the case, he was completely wrong. For me, there was absolutely no choice.

About this time, I received an interesting interpretation of events from a psychologist friend who both Zarek and I had worked with in our early days at the Day Hospital.

I'm sorry to hear from you, that things have now reached the stage of a legal battle. So disappointing that there couldn't have been some negotiation and opportunity for understanding of the best way of ensuring the needs particularly of the children. I can't think that law courts can really sort such matters out, but divorce counselling may be an appropriate way to work out some of the issues. I don't pretend to understand the complexity of the inter/intrapersonal dynamics - but the continued dispute as to the mothering seems to me to be about attribution of guilt - a bad mother had to be found. So it'll be important for you to fight for your rights and a just solution and not continue to absorb such guilt. Part of that may mean giving up your belief in an invincible father/husband/psychiatrist, which is already happening and which is a means of belief in a non-guilty part of yourself - that all the competence doesn't have to be projected out to someone else.

It's all the more sad and crazy because the children clearly demonstrate that there need be no guilt at all. They're doing very well and in my opinion are unimpaired, undamaged, just delightful.

I do however think it an irreconcilable position to be in the business of treating/working with crazy people and not to attend to one's own craziness. The madness has to appear somewhere and contaminate someone, inevitably the loved ones, as well as being projected on to the mad patients.

Nevertheless, I do feel very sad for you and Zarek. As you know, if at any time I may be able to help then please ask.

This sort of response from someone who had known us throughout all the years of our relationship, even the early days, when Zarek had felt it necessary to be discreet to the point of complete embargo, was comforting and stabilising. Support also continued to pour in from Chris as our exchanges of letters continued, regardless of Zarek's constant snooping and my constant attempts to frustrate his efforts by finding new hiding places.

Dearest Lizzie,

Today is catching up day for all the many jobs I've neglected to do before going away. So many that I don't stand a chance but it's amazing what you can achieve if you really bash on. There are two things in life I'm <u>really</u> fussy about - tea and jeans ! OK, so tea's no problem - hot pot hotting and so on, but I gave up on jeans years ago when I saw James (6'6") Coburn in "The Magnificent Seven." 5'6 ½" runts like me just don't have enough LEG for the long lean look. Nevertheless, I have a bash now and again and borrow a hand-driven (ger-jugga, ger-jugga) sewing machine. Like last night/this morning - three pairs of mediocre-fit jeans undergoing the third degree - turn 'em inside out and bash up the inside legs. The more wine I had on an empty tum, the less I could get it right. First shot they came out like tights - with a ballooning arse - can't do the crutch bit d'you see. Got them off just before my legs went gangrenous. Second shot, back to where we started, third shot and so on until they looked like an aerial view of Clapham Junction or plan of World War I trenches - sort of machine-gunned, riddled with stitching, bust threads, frayed denim ....

Eventually the needle went "b-o-i-n-g" and snapped. Good job as it was supper cum bedtime. Next day went into sewing-machine shop and asked for needle for 'old fashioned hand-type machine' - out came incredible stream of technological questions as to <u>which</u> machine needle (I'd of course forgotten to take the two broken bits I'd carefully stuck to sellotape). "Oh, I don't suppose it matters. Any old *needle. Sort of thicker at one end than the other ?" Ghastly silence. Furrowed brows from gent and lady shopkeeper who sank down into respective seats. And I suddenly realised that with one thoughtless sentence, I'd demolished their total raison d'etre. Anyway, here I am again, the sewing machine thrashing away like a bren gun in full spate. Also bought a pair of plimsolls - tennis shoes? trainers? sneakers? that seemed to fit in the shop but after a day's wear pinched at the toe. They too have been subjected to a night of terrifying torture. I jammed a hammer into one and a screwdriver in t'other and stuck them on top of the hot kiln, all stretched and taut like on the dreaded rack in the bowels of the Tower. I maybe imagined it, but <u>think</u> I heard them screaming in the night as the kiln hotted up.*

Oh dear, how this self-indulgent scribbling eats into old man time - my only real enemy. It would take pages and pages to tell you why and how you matter to me and I'd tell you over and over again when we cook together, listen to music and walk the fields this coming holiday if/when you manage to get here. I'll repeat it with every thrust of my body into yours and afterwards, when we lie sweating and panting and oozing over the sheets. I'll tell you what a very special and wonderful woman you are and always have been (and always <u>will</u> be). Please, despite your good nature and gentleness, start sticking up for yourself now Liz. The cards are down for good and Zarek has chosen to be an absolute bastard. He is to be pitied but not at the expense of your self-esteem and beastly attacks on your lovely character and personality. Ignore him for a while and then turn to him and say "Look Buster, you're on your own, so cut it out, you're wasting your time, breath ...." Tell him what you've told me about no-one wanting to work with him, how the whole community is backing you with sympathy and understanding. Ask him where all _his_ friends are. It may be bitter and unkind but he's asking for it, for your _own_ good. Stop pulling your punches. He's like the Wizard of Oz - all strings and cardboard, piss and wind. _Tell_ him so.

OK Kiddo. Back to the machine gun post and those dreaded jeans - and then the garden. I can't leave it all to you when you're here, besides, you'd lose the children in it, the grass is so long. I have to swish the Flymo above the top of it, like a mine detector and slowly lower it, otherwise it jams to a halt and blows the fuse.

Your letters are always so full and interesting .... I _do do do_ enjoy them, as much as your lovely body. Heh. Do you have any pyjamas I could feel you through, by any chance ? Or maybe a nightie I could pull up - _slowly_ !

Love you. Ger-jugga, ger-jugga, ger-jugga.

19. School holiday

We had a babysitting network in the village which meant that even though Zarek and I never went out together in the evenings so hardly used its services, I was regularly called upon to look after other people's children. A Cinderella role, never going to the party that everyone else seemed to be at, which only served to heighten my feelings of detachment from our immediate community. Some children slept, enabling me to pursue my letter-writing obsession uninterrupted. Others were more bother particularly one family with a four year old daughter and two boys aged ten and fourteen. On one occasion, the little girl had gone to bed happily but her brothers had been joined by four of their mates, all playing a lovely game chucking mud pies out of their bedroom window, so I had to get nasty. I finally bribed the younger son into bed with the sandwiches that had been left for me but the eldest son disappeared altogether, muttering a phone number as he departed and as far as I was concerned was never seen again. Their mother was one of those seemingly sweet, nice, kind, gentle people, but she didn't FOOL ME ! She was neurotic beyond belief - no wonder her kids were tricky.

By early August we were well into the school holiday but my plan to travel with the children to East Anglia to see my parents and Chris was thwarted by a blast from Zarek forbidding me to take them away. Yes I could go on my own but I had to leave them behind so that he could see if he was able to cope. He might also have been frightened that I would disappear completely with them. To me that seemed a short sighted idea but I also couldn't bear the prospect of not having some kind of break from the barely tolerable conditions at home. I felt guilty about my desperate need to briefly escape but the death throes of our relationship had been so prolonged, my need for relief was acute. One reason Zarek gave me for not taking the children away was that Chris's influence might 'contaminate' them and after he had said this, he gave me a copy of The Lady so that I could 'look through it and choose my successor'. I pointed out that as he'd just given me a massive no-confidence vote about my choice of friends, I was hardly the right person to be involved but he seemed to comprehend neither my reasoning, nor the joke.

He had also made me the most amazingly magnanimous offer, "When this is all over and I'm no longer in a marital/emotional relationship with you, I would be very pleased to help you with your problems."

Christ, I nearly hit the roof. "When I am no longer in a marital/emotional relationship with you, I will have no problems."

For some strange reason best known to himself, one lunchtime, Zarek had decided to taunt me. We'd managed to be quite civil to each other for a short while prior to this so maybe it was the strain beginning to tell, or his large whisky before lunch and the beer during it. First of all he was watching me very closely and then having private jokes with himself which had the children curious.

"Why are you laughing Daddy ?"

"Oh nothing 'ha ha' just something amusing."

So they all have a good laugh with Daddy. "It's funny isn't it Alice" he said to his two year old daughter, giving her a tickle to make sure he elicited the right response. Then he really started. "Seen much of Pete lately ?" he asked. "And how's Stella ?" etc. etc. needling me to try and get a reaction. But failing. Then he started on the analytical bit. "Would you like your children to be like you ?" he asked. "Some parts yes, some parts no" was my guarded reply. And he then went on about how he once valued and esteemed me and how I'd let him down. So I challenged him. "Yes, but am I really a failure as a mother ?"

And he played his usual serpentine trick of wriggling away from the question and attacking from another quarter. In summary, he regarded himself as blameless and me as contemptible, a fallen woman. His was a scarey sort of madness and the derision with which he regarded me made me feel as though physical violence would be no more to him than squashing a mosquito. The power of his hatred as I experienced it, was truly awful. No wonder when I looked in the mirror, I saw this pale, beige, haggard, tense, unhappy face staring back at me. That desperate look in my eyes was to remain for a long time yet.

In spite of all this, being holiday time, it was essential to somehow keep things going for the children. To my amazement, on one occasion when I'd suggested a trip to see the Mary Rose, the historical English battleship, recently lifted from the seabed, Zarek had offered to come and was content to distract Alice while Greg, Daisy and I took a closer look at the exhibition. Although I had no doubts about my decision for the future, it made me very sad that he couldn't have seen the value of these family expeditions before. It made such a difference having someone else there and although the reason he went walk about with Alice was because he wasn't very interested, it did mean that I could get a closer look at things and talk to Daisy and Greg about them instead of having to cope with wriggly excitable Alice all the time. Finding the wreck on the sea floor must have been fascinating and it was amazing to see leather shoes and jerkins which were actually on people's bodies as she sank - the shoes looked like a pair of anybody's old slippers. And the jerkin had the shape of a comb impressed on to it where it had been stuffed into a pocket.

Greg was really excited by the models of the machinery used for bringing the Mary Rose up from the sea floor and in the souvenir shop, he decided to buy an up-to-date booklet of all the Navy's ships. Not normally my sort of thing, but actually fascinating. We were able to look up the type and class of several vessels that other children's fathers had served on in the Falklands, including their armaments and the number of people on board. I stupidly hadn't realised, because all the publicity had been about our ships being hit by Exocet missiles, that of course we were carrying them too, and using them. The sitting room carpet became the scene of a fierce battle between English and Germans with all Greg's soldiers neatly lined up in opposition with the full back-up of as many field guns, tanks, ambulances etc. as he could muster.

Another time during the holiday, Zarek turned up with four hens, completely unannounced - no discussion, no consideration of what you needed to do to look after them – he and they just appeared. He then spent the whole evening when I was out babysitting, searching the neighbours' gardens for three that had flown away. I had tentatively suggested they should have their wings clipped and after he'd retrieved them all for the nth time, he said as he didn't know how, that I should do it. I didn't either, but acting on the instructions of a friend and no other experience, I took the kitchen scissors and chopped off the flight feathers from one wing of each bird. Nothing awful about it - no worse than cutting the children's toenails or Daisy's hair. Then he had the nerve to say to Stella, "……. And you should have seen the expression on her face as she did it." This to imply that I was giving vent to what he interpreted as my poorly concealed castrative impulses ! Anyway, the hens seemed happy enough, pecking and scratching, as hens do. In due course they produced eggs, but without the necessity of having their bottoms kissed. Which is what Zarek had told Greg he had to do before they would begin to lay.

After paying my £4 weekly 'salary', he had started to check over all the household bills and supermarket receipts. However, I'd discovered that if I left them lying in the sun on the kitchen window ledge, all the writing and figures faded to incomprehensibility so that things like writing paper and tights and Tampax which I'd purchased from the supermarket, got merged into the weekly shop. Even so, I hated the duplicity of what I was doing and hated the fact that I'd been put in that position. Hated the dishonesty, hated the disloyalty. Despised myself and him all at the same time. Doubted if I could emerge with <u>any</u> integrity at the end of it all.

This self-doubt had overflowed into my letters to Chris but once again, his response was unequivocal:

August 1982 Suffolk

Dearest Lizzie - you've no idea how worried I get when days go by without the plop of your fat letter on the doormat. I start wondering what I said to you in my last letter or on the phone. Or I start wondering if Zarek has really stuck the breadknife into you, or more subtly, cruelly, your tender heart and thoughtful mind have finally exploded out of existence. I've known/admired/been impressed/amused/ fascinated/HELPED/encouraged by you for years and years. You are one of my oldest friends and we've always been honest and straight which is why I can be involved with you and your problems. You have given me <u>so</u> much; of course I want to help you. It <u>is</u> going to be good for you. You're living in total unreality now which makes it impossible to believe that there will be anything more than grind and worry if you have the children with you. But you will be FREE and away from Zarek's perpetual diminishing. I can't tell you how sad I am to see how he's sapped the incredible vigour and creativeness I've always associated with you - and relied on too, over the years. I anticipate watching you flower again in whichever community you eventually fetch up in - <u>and</u> to taking my place in the long line of lovers queuing at your hot steamy bedside, unkempt from tossings and tumblings and streaked with the sweat and flow of couplings and *mountings and full of spent knickers and damp tissues ! How's that for a vision of the future ? Keep it pinned in the top of your mind Lizzie. Or let it slide silkily down your camiknickers and get stuck in your suspender belt.*

God bless Lovely Liz - phone if you're really stuck. No, I'm not much of a potter, a pretty poor husband and certainly no gardener, nor your hairy ape-man. But I <u>can</u> cope with stormy oceans of pain and unhappiness and other's distress, plus floods of joy and laughter and the incredible humour that people and life throw in our path day by day. It's never an effort.

Love <u>for</u> you, love <u>to</u> you, love <u>in</u> you, love <u>around</u> you, love Chris.

My solitary holiday visit to see Chris passed all too quickly and the journey home was a painful reminder of what I was returning to. My real world.

August 1982 Hampshire

Most Especially Dear Chris -

The longest, saddest drive I've ever had. Not helped by the motorway diverting confusingly so that I had to make a massive detour. Then torrential rain and what felt like a tortuously slow journey behind caravans and maundering drivers. But otherwise an uneventful ride - just me and my misery with my body and mind throbbing with the pleasures of our blissful week. So many joys, and sadnesses too. Approaching home was perhaps the worst bit but it was finally an enormous delight to see the children again and to feel their pleasure at seeing me - especially little Alice who just wanted to be held and cuddled, over and over. They seemed older and calmer - so perhaps it is me that's the disruptive influence. I don't know. Not only had Zarek coped, he'd painted the bathroom. Why couldn't I do that ? Felt almost redundant. Alice's goldfish Boo-Boo was I'm afraid, floating on the top of the fish tank unnoticed and very dead. A happy release I should imagine although the other two fish can't have enjoyed the taste of their putrefying friend in the water.

Thought of you sitting somewhere in your van yesterday feeling sad and grey and sort of knew that your loneliness would more likely have been for Jodi than for me and also that some of our bedtime conversations with you on your elbow drinking tea were really being shared with her in your mind rather than me beside you .... ah me. I think you have to write and ask her finally if she will ever come back to you. While you hold on to a sad forlorn sort of hope that she might, you make it impossible for any other relationship to take root. Perhaps that's how you want it - using your lack of confidence, your bad experience, your fears as an excuse for deferring the ultimate challenge. But the longer you go on doing this, the more habituated you will become to living with unfulfilled hopes and expectations. Of course it will bring problems and pain whatever the outcome, as well as joys and satisfactions. And should she reject you, at least you will know that she has the responsibility for the decision, rather than you having hung on to the ambivalence of the situation for fear of the outcome. Please do it Chris. I need you to.

So many pretty things in my suitcase when I unpacked it. Perfume and books and panties and postcards. So much brightness and love, so much of yourself you have shared with me, wanting things to be nice, wanting to get it right despite the void you say is inside you. You know how much I appreciate it, know I notice you noticing, so if I just say thank you, simply, for everything, I know you'll understand how much it has all meant to me.

So now Chris, I'm back here again, with you there. This time I have so many more little details of your mind and body etched in my memory to comfort me. I mentally embrace and enfold you - all that I have to share is yours. And most particularly, my gratitude.

Today, it must be Tuesday ? Get you to your cellar and then maybe go and pick up that transatlantic telephone line and get whistling. Jodi always said you only had to whistle and she'd come .... so I guess she's there. OK ?   Love and all over kisses from Lizziexx

It had felt like such an open, honest, sharing, loving relationship. Could I have managed without it and how much was I deluding myself ? I sensed that Chris was really preoccupied with Jodi which he was avoiding for fear of hurting me. He tried hard to play down this obsession but one evening during my stay, he talked about getting a new oven and buying a VW Polo, both things she'd wanted, within the following few months when he had hoped she would visit. I wondered whether it was my imagination but I'd noticed that whenever we'd spent time together, he seemed to try and insulate himself from feelings about me by talking about someone else. Once it had been Vanessa, his last wife, once another old flame Louise, and then Jodi. Each time I had felt hurt until I remembered the pattern almost as if he had been saying "you're getting too close; you've touched me but because of all the past pain I've experienced, I dare not show you for fear of future hurt." But all this contradicted the open, honest, sharing value of our relationship and sometimes, other things slipped out. "I can't imagine being without you," and "I depend on you more than you do me." I knew I was getting to him but felt that he didn't trust himself to cope. Didn't want to cope with me and my three children. And who can have blamed him for that ?

I got used to doing things on my own that summer with the children but it was hard. Days by the sea near where we lived, were fun for the children, but for me it was a constant round of loading the car with child and baby paraphernalia, buckets, spades, towels, cardigans, food, fruit, treats. Then feeding, weeing, rubbing dry, getting sand out from between toes , placating - it felt endlessly isolated and all against a subversive backdrop of worry about the future. How I envied the Mums and Dads who arrived with their kids and settled down for a day on the beach with their sandy sandwiches and their tea trays, their cricket and their brave little flags atop collapsing sand-castles. It was those rituals that gave one a sense of family, time, place, holiday.

I really missed an adult companion to share all this with but I certainly didn't miss Zarek. His idea of a 'family holiday' was to detach himself and read his newspaper or practice his violin wherever the holiday was taking place, while the children and I did whatever there was to do there. The business of whether one did or didn't have sex with someone (including one's husband) was almost peripheral to the notion of companionship. I didn't take a lover because of sexual frustration. The damage was done long before by Zarek's constant denigration of me as a person and my ability to fulfil my role as wife and mother. He had established himself as a sort of monolith, totally unapproachable and impervious to any sort of rationalisation. He'd been so busy fulfilling his fantasies about his intellect and self-importance that he'd missed completely the world which his body with his mind, could have enjoyed. As a wife I should perhaps have tried harder to accept all this. As a mother I definitely should but as a fellow human being I simply couldn't if it meant being treated as a 1984 'B' grade citizen. It was not like that all the time but the bad times made me mistrustful of the good and I withdrew from the relationship because the demands made of me were too heavy. It was tragic that it couldn't have been the other way round, accepting the bad times because of the good - but it defeated me.

Every day of that holiday was a struggle but Thursday 26th August was just a struggle too far.

To start with, like a bucket of icy cold water. Slosh. Brrrrrrr. Shiver shiver. A letter from my solicitor to say that the divorce was moving, that both Chris and Pete were named and that we would have to share the costs between us.

Rang Chris who was thoroughly decent about it, despite his poverty. Realised after I'd put the phone down how very worrying he must have found the prospect of yet another bill to meet.

Rang Pete who wasn't. He'd been hinting all along in a half serious, half joking fashion that it was 'my' divorce and that he shouldn't have to pay anything towards it. Fucks for free. Which made him much less of a gentleman than Chris.

12.30 Phoned solicitor for advice. The divorce paper we'd been sent had to be returned by each of us within eight days and Pete was going away so wouldn't be able to meet that deadline. No advice available as my solicitor was away too but his assistant, Mr. Black was going to phone me later.

12.45 Kids arrived home hungry. Got lunch.

2.00 Phone call from my sister who had just flown in from Montreal and was waiting at the station to be collected.

2.15 Collect her from station trying hard to look welcoming and relaxed. Fill her in on all the details and lunch.

2.45 Phone call from Hilda, just back from Peru or somewhere and most anxious for up-date. A welcome dose of moral support - we agreed to meet the following week so that I could take delivery of two ponchos she had brought back for me.

3.10 Mr. Black rang back and turned out to be a very chatty sort of bloke, full of reassurances. Described some of Zarek's attitudes as "absolute crap" and said that he couldn't make head or tail of a recent psychiatric opinion he'd done for him. Seemed very confident that it would all sort itself out - felt just a weak glimmer of hope for the future.

Other people's children arrived to play, Alice woke, rest of afternoon punctuated by whoops and screams and childish demands.

3.30 Damn. Forgot to check with Mr. Black that Pete's papers had been sent to my solicitor and not to his home address so rang back to the secretary to make sure. And they had, thank God. They'd also received my copy of the petition so it was all, at last, beginning to move. Felt relieved.

3.40 Rang Pete to let him know that papers wouldn't be plopping through his letterbox and he practically jumped for joy, especially when I told him costs would be shared between the three of us.

3.50 GP's receptionist phoned to ask if I could have my appointment to have my coil replaced a week earlier as it should be done during a 'red alert' when everything is nice and 'soft'. Certainly, anything to oblige - I'd get my thrills somehow, even if the more obvious methods were temporarily unavailable.

3.55 Phone call from Zarek. Was Alice alright this morning ? He'd had to take her with him to the dentist and wasn't sure if she was OK ? Eh ? Why not ? What had happened ? No explanation but he was apologetic for this morning's row and really wanted everything to be over as quickly and painlessly as possible. ZAREK I DON'T BELIEVE YOU.

4.00 Approx. Rang Chris. By which time it didn't feel like me talking but some hyped up maniac in a mad mad world. Felt saturated by the day's events but needed to explain the eight day requirements to get the divorce papers back to my solicitor. The document seemed so official and I felt worried and apologetic because it imbued an already horrible situation with even more gravity.

Supper time conversation with my sister who had suggested that instead of eating the cabbages in the garden which were riddled with caterpillars, that we should eat the caterpillars instead !

At 10.15 whilst doing the ironing, I suddenly felt as though a lift was going down inside me. Oh my God, this is it. THIS IS IT.

20. Autumn 1982

It was impossible to tell whether supporting Chris with his difficulties was a way of distracting me from my own, but it was certainly time-consuming. I could understand him wanting Jodi so much even though I couldn't help myself wishing that he didn't. He seemed to be using her as a talisman to protect him from his life's real potential so that even with all his caring, his honesty, his loving concern for other people, he could avoid a fatal flaw in his personality - the fact that he hadn't been able to achieve the fundamental satisfaction and stability of an enduring relationship. Maybe it was because he'd never had a father around to show him how a man/woman relationship could work, how to consolidate a long-term partnership. Not having had the opportunity to be part of a family unit in which a father and a mother worked together to bring up their children, it was all guesswork. We're none of us conscious, those of us that are lucky enough to have had the same two parents throughout our childhood, that this is part of our learning but I guess it must be. Chris's ten months of fathering could hardly have been enough.

The fact that he worried so desperately about money, that he was frustrated by lack of job satisfaction, that he constantly felt as though he'd missed the boat and was trying to catch up in a sieve, that he got frightened by the blackness of his own misery and depression, these things mattered less than his inability to stick with and by another person. They might even be said to be the things that made the fun-loving, 'life-and-soul-of-the-party', everybody's-friend-Chris-Daly who he was, always feel that he had to compensate for perceived inadequacies - like two sides of a coin. May be it was hell for him but he was stuck with it for the rest of his life and anyone who lived with him would need to understand that, otherwise repeated failure was inevitable.

Jodi was an ambitious young woman. She would have worked, studied, achieved what she had set out to. In all probability she would be highly successful and eventually highly paid in whatever she settled for. OK he said she was a softie but she must have found some way of coping with her vulnerabilities without him, once back in the States and she'd get better at it as the years went by. He would have become frustrated by her ambition and her achievements. It would have eventually eroded their relationship leaving him feeling even more bitter, more of a failure than ever. It seemed to me to be important to cherish the best that they had had together, but not to let the remorse and guilt that he felt at not appreciating her enough, destroy him. I knew she'd be alright and could even have been all the things he wished for himself. Certainly he could have felt proud of how he'd helped her and also proud that he was able to let her go, if only just. Felt proud that he had been a catalyst in her young life, bringing about change whilst remaining himself unchanged. Well, more or less. I saw him as a loving and lovable man but I also saw his life stretching on, miserable beyond belief but joyous beyond expectation and wondered if he could endure it that way. Unlike Jodi he lacked ambition. All he wanted out of life was to be creative and to be loved by everyone, especially women. Would that be enough ?

In response to these apparent insights, Chris was hugely appreciative (called me his 'old sense box') but puzzled at how I could understand and tolerate him still wanting Jodi more than me. For me however, this was a no-brainer. She'd gone. She wasn't coming back and the world that he had shared with her no longer existed except in his thoughts. It would take time for her image to fade but I was confident that eventually, it would and besides, my children were my number one priority. For Chris there were other distractions, such as the offer of a weekend visit to an old girlfriend in Richmond which she would pay for, which I chose to ignore. And there were other more immediate demands on my attention ......

A letter from my solicitor informed me that I was required to attend a Mediation Court.

'The object of this appointment is to identify conflicts and problems with a view to agreed solutions and so to enable the divorce to continue with reduced pain to the parties (and children) and end their marriage with as much dignity as possible.'

That's what it said but far from reducing the pain, it only served to increase it making the final break ever more real, bringing it closer. There were other small tasks too, like visiting Greg's headmistress who was startled when I told her what was happening, which left me panic-stricken and terrified. Zarek meanwhile was busy issuing orders as though I was some kind of scullery-maid who should really remain below stairs. Would I clean out the accumulation of flies from the double glazing. Would I 'take control' of Alice so that he could practice his violin. Would I use up the bananas, rotting in the larder when at one time he always used to gobble them up before I even got a look-in. Then I would hear him being jovial and avuncular on the phone with his secretary or ingratiatingly pleasant with one of his colleagues and I'd find myself wondering which Zarek I would be facing when it came to the final confrontation.

At times like that, I'd pour out my heart and soul on paper to Chris, rushing for my pen like a junkie scrambling for her syringe, as though a fix of words would restore some kind of balance in my skewed life. He never failed to respond to my cries for help and to be in tune with my feelings so that I felt a bit of him must be me to understand so well. There was nothing he could do but listen, but he was unfailingly generous with his time, his letters and phone conversations to the extent that at one point I suggested that instead of spending money on paper and stamps for a letter to me, he should go instead to the butchers and spend the equivalent on spare ribs to give himself a decent meal.

We plodded on that autumn, the season running its course in spite of the emotional quagmires. The freezer was stuffed with beans and courgettes and that year there was a glut of apples and pears, all of which, according to Zarek, had to be processed, windfalls and all, no matter how tiny and maggoty. He had also grown loads of onions and tomatoes, as well as a few green peppers. With the hens producing four eggs every day, we only needed a cow to be more or less self-sufficient. He had regularly grumbled at me for not taking enough interest in what he produced from the garden but in fact I loved the whole idea of home produce. What I didn't love was that he grew so much and then expected me to use every single scrap so that it became a real chore. The children wouldn't eat runner beans and yet every year he produced more in spite of my pleas not to. I felt as though he was intent on heightening the magnitude of my inability to dispose of it all.

Talking of maggots, another worm had turned. I hadn't seen Pete for months but had to arrange a meeting with him so that he could sign his bit of the divorce paper. Never one to miss the opportunity to improve the shining hour, he seemed to think he was entitled to payment in kind for his signature and when I refused, and it was obvious that I meant it, he grabbed the divorce acknowledgement of service, screwed it up and made as if to get out of the car. My world somersaulted. It was hard to believe what was happening - I felt as though I was being skinned alive. I got it back but driving home, huge howls of bitterness and desperation overtook me. There seemed to be no-one in the world I could trust. No-one.

And the children, who had no other reason to trust me than that I was their mother ? What would be the expression on their little faces when I said to them "Mummy and Daddy aren't going to live together any more"? I needed some concrete plans, to be able to flesh out the reality for them but it was hard to know where to start. One thing for certain was that even though it seemed like madness to leave the comfort and security of the home we were all familiar with, I couldn't stay. It was as though the place would have been forever contaminated by Zarek's deadly influence like nuclear fallout. And it wasn't just a vague miasma that I feared, it would be the regular contact he would demand with the children and the control which he would still have managed to exert even if he no longer shared our home. With my parents living on the east coast and Chris a bit further inland, I settled on East Anglia as a likely area to head for, but there I needed to find a job, a home and comparable schools for the children if I was to create a convincing alternative for the court to consider.

Whether I could have coped without the debatable kudos of being Dr. U's wife, the money, the general comfort of our existence, whether I could manage the children on my own, and how much I was dependent on his help I didn't really know. In conversation he had said "but you're incapable of bringing up the children although of course you could have unlimited access." Which made me all the more determined that I could manage on my own. If all we had to look forward to as a reward for staying together 'for the sake of the children' was a lifetime of frosts and thaws, of struggling to make decisions when we knew we couldn't agree, of tension, of inactivity and wearisome mess, then the outlook was bleak. On the very rare occasions when I allowed myself to mentally escape from all these feelings, I couldn't sleep for the excitement of the possibility of being – myself. However, feeling tough enough to confront the decision to leave with the children, meant that I was also tough enough to consider staying. But was it right that their childhood should have such a distorted flavour of family relationships ? Which would be worse, I wondered.

All of this was debated at length with our Australian psychiatrist friend James who was visiting this country to prepare for a sabbatical in Cambridge the following year. We had known each other since our early Day Hospital days when we were both in the honeymoon phase of new relationships, mine with Zarek and his with a clinical psychologist, Jennie. Inevitably our conversations were heavily laden with psychological theory and interpretation and over the years we had shared many convivial evenings, nights and early mornings. Talking, joking, conversations I'd hardly understood. He'd always had a mellowing effect on us but this time, there was a feeling that it was all coming to an end and he left us shaking his head despairingly, saying that he doubted if either of us would find what we were really looking for.

21. Summary letters

My penchant for letter-writing involved some dear friends including Rachel, whose children I had helped to look after many years earlier. I respected her wisdom and compassion unequivocally and it was therefore a comfort to lay out my thoughts and feelings on paper, to see how she would view my situation.

Very Dear Rachel

You can see from the size of this sheet of paper that I mean business ! Thank you very much for this morning's letter with all its love and concern, ideas, suggestions and offers of real practical help. It is SO reassuring to know your feelings and I do wish you were nearer so that I could work my way through it with you - ultimately of course, the decisions have to be mine but I value and respect so much your judgements and the attitudes which you as an individual and your family represent. I feel I must take any opportunity to ventilate as much as I can of all this business.

First of all heartfelt thanks for your offer of any such reference as may be required, either on paper or in person, by the court or welfare officer or judge. I really have no notion at this stage whether one has to approach it like this - my solicitor hinted that if Zarek was going to push the 'insanity' thing then it might be useful for me to get an impartial opinion from a shrink, but that's the only clue I've had so far about the need to call in 'witnesses'. The awful thing is that I really do feel he wants to put me on trial with him as chief witness for the prosecution. I don't want to have to stand up and answer all his allegations nor do I want to have to make a whole list of accusations against him, but I suppose with such a brief opportunity to settle something so momentous, I may have to. But that's all a long way off yet and assuming I get legal aid, the barrister will presumably advise as to the best way to approach such things.

But how perceptive of you to really get to the nub of things - ie. my <u>real</u> feelings about the children. It's really all very complicated and I'm not sure I can get it down in any sort of order so I'm sorry if it all comes spewing out like yesterday's meals !

The first thing that seems to demand attention in my mind is the all-pervasive influence of Zarek's attitude and his expectations for the future. Very early on when he discovered my 'misbehaviour', he presented me with a package deal - 'You clear off and leave everything, the house, the children, the lot and I'll give you unlimited access and will keep quiet about what you've been up to. Then you can be free to go away and start a new life without being encumbered. The children needn't suffer the trauma of having their lives upset and they will see you very often, spend holidays with you etc.' With the implied feeling that they would barely notice my absence. <u>That</u> hurt - the fact that he was trying to make me sort of evaporate – also the emotional blackmail. He subsequently suggested that if I went 'quietly' then he would preserve the anonymity of my extra-marital activities. If I chose to contest, then he would *be merciless. Anyway, with all this hanging over me, I've felt I had very little room for manoeuvre. He chose to name both my two lovers on the divorce petition to make it look worse for me and also I think because if he can be seen to be the wronged husband, his reputation, both personal and professional, will remain intact.*

My initial reaction to his original package was angry indignation but there was also a part of me which couldn't help agreeing that it might be easier without the children. I could <u>see</u> that Greg and Daisy could probably survive fairly happily staying here, but my reaction over Alice was a purely emotional one - I simply could not tolerate the thought of losing her. I suppose it's because she's so little, I still feel she needs me whereas the other two have more identifiable personalities in their own right. After much thought I decided I would have to approach this with Zarek. I'm so worried that he's going to use <u>anything</u> against me e.g. if I suggest not wanting custody of all the children, he'll say it's evidence of my indifference to them. Whereas in fact it's as much the realisation that I <u>cannot</u> say that either I or he has total rights over them - we have to compromise somehow. Anyway, he rejected totally and instantly the possibility that I might go with Alice only, so I was confronted with the decision that I would have to fight for custody of all three. And that is a sort of relief.

I went over this with my Marriage Guidance Counsellor, the turning point being when she asked me how I'd have felt if my own mother had left my father to cope with my sister and I. My instant gut reaction was one of anger and I can remember replying that fond though I was of my father, my mother was the keystone of our family. Then I realised that I've never had this sort of feeling with my own children/family. I definitely feel last in the pecking order - and she suggested that if I did have all the children, I might get in touch with feelings I hadn't been able to experience in relation to them before. Which felt good. But also I had a sneaky feeling that if I felt as though I was at the bottom of the pile, then maybe they wouldn't notice my absence so much and that perhaps Zarek was right.

I have to include a post-hoc aside here. One of the things my son Greg has subsequently told me was that when I left, it felt as though his childhood had ended. Um..........

You mention in your letter "occasions when we yearn for freedom from the demands and responsibilities that parenting involves" and I've scribbled YES under demands but NO under responsibilities, which leads to a complicated muddle in my mind about who is/has been responsible for setting up the family traditions, no, emotional patterns - can't think of the word. I've always <u>felt</u> that our children were particularly demanding and that Zarek insisted that I should pander to their every whim. Their needs had always been paramount - I wasn't expected to have any. But I wonder if I'm wrong. Maybe they'd be just as demanding anyway, maybe bright children are - yours were and as I've heard you say of other people's, they turned out alright. And it's all too easy in my present situation to say that because Zarek seemed to be playing a so much more dominant role in establishing the family culture, then it's his fault if the children aren't how I'd like them to be. And yet I know that <u>nobody's</u> children come out how they'd like them to be so *it's really unfair to offload the responsibility of this on to Zarek.*

So yes, I do yearn to escape from the demands. The responsibilities I don't know. In the sense that I've already mentioned I think perhaps it's easy for me to use Zarek as a scapegoat but on the other hand, I don't feel he's ever really allowed me the <u>real</u> responsibility of parenting. So often he's over-ruled my judgements or countermanded my decisions - one gets into the position of avoiding making any, so that in a way I long for the real responsibility of saying yes, this child is mine and I'm a fundamental influence in the formation of his attitudes and principles.

It's interesting that although my own rejection of Zarek is total, I don't feel it is imperative to remove the children from his influence. During the last few months he's been doing some very mad, nasty things to hurt me, but I still feel that he cares very much for them and would do everything he thought reasonable to bring them up as best he could. I know they wouldn't turn out as I would want them to, but they wouldn't be <u>bad</u> people. And yet I really do dislike him so much. I haven't got to the bottom of that one yet.

I spent a week away from them all during the summer with Chris - all very officially arranged through my solicitor, and although I wasn't conscious of missing them (too short a time to tell), I was very conscious of the absence of purpose in life without them. And I did worry a lot about Alice. So I suppose if I can find another purpose it won't hurt so much ? I don't know.

All of which is writing very much from the point of view of thinking of <u>not</u> having them - but I know that having them would mean rather more. Incredibly hard work, many emotional demands, upsets due to the trauma of the break-up, lower standards of living. But a lot of achievements to encourage and enjoy, friendships to foster and relaxed fun and laughter which we've so much missed out on - the house is quite different when Zarek isn't around and I can remember once in true psychiatrist's style he asked "why?" I wanted to do a particular family activity and when I replied "oh, just for fun" he said "who wants fun?" as though it was a cardinal sin to enjoy oneself.

Maybe all that I'm saying is that I think they need me for quite a while more than I need them, but that I accept that I have a responsibility to gratify this, their need, to the best of my ability within the given circumstances.

So how much do they need me ? Alice and I need each other at the moment. With her I can't somehow look further than that. I don't feel any special bond with her, it's just that she's younger and I feel that what I can give her is special to the newness of our relationship. And no nanny or crèche is going to provide an adequate substitute for it. Contrary to Zarek's plans. Also maybe I still feel that there's time to really be responsible for her.

Daisy ? Well, I've always felt particularly close to her - even when I'm cross with her, I know she knows I really do like her apart from the loving parent bit. I guess a lot of it stems from the early days when Zarek paid more attention to Greg. I've a specially soft spot for her and maybe indulge her a bit. Getting her into the GPDST school here was a great hurdle for me – an external manifestation of her intelligence, social acceptability etc. I now see that this was unnecessary - she's an eminently educable little girl who will mop up like a sponge everything that is put in front of her brain. I can't bear to think of her coming in from school and me not being there - but perhaps I must as even if she's with me, I might be at work or whatever. She's recently been fussing excessively over comparatively insignificant problems, bed-wetting too although she doesn't express overt anxieties about either school or home.

Greg ? For me he's the difficult one, so much cast in Zarek's image, both physically and emotionally, so that inevitably much of my anger at Zarek has been projected on to him, poor little chap. But recently we've been getting on better - he's been showing much more interest in doing things, going out etc. and sees me as someone who is usually keen to gratify this interest because I like doing things myself. But, he's very easily 'bought' with food bribes - a situation set up by Zarek in the early days, and generally has his eye on the main chance, but who can blame him for that ? Think he might be the most vociferously dissatisfied at our reduced circumstances, but also think he's emotionally pretty secure and could be a good support to Daisy who might react rather more strongly to the split; that doesn't make sense though does it - easily bought/emotionally secure ? Hm.

I do know that it would break Zarek's heart to lose these precious children but I also know that I'm not the incompetent, dependent moron he would like to have me believe I am. Just this morning he was shouting at me with terrifying loudness and ferocity about my incompetence and that I didn't care for the children properly. I managed to retaliate with the fact that I'd cared well enough for him to go to France for a week, just before Alice was born, but mostly I forget detail and suffer a sort of emotional blindness in the face of his fury. Even in writing this, I've been overwhelmed by a stunning insight. The reason we've stayed together hasn't been for the sake of the children although it could seem like it. We've been staying together because I needed to. And now perhaps I don't.

Well, that's about it Rachel. Except to say how much I value, appreciate and need all the loving support and concern you so kindly sent me. Heartfelt thanks dear friend. I do hope you are recovering from all your perfectly dreadful ailments and that the family is pampering you sufficiently ! My love to you all, Lizziexxxxx

October 1982 Hull

Dear Lizzie

Love and greetings. Many thanks for your long letter. I feel much closer to you on reading it and also felt so much <u>for</u> you. Inevitably you must go backwards and forwards and round and round all the same facts/feelings/fears/fantasies. You must feel so boxed in even though it's probably less of a trap than it seems from the inside. Firstly, you are really doing well - life is jolly complicated and the impulse to throw your hands in the air/bury your head in the sand and scream must be pretty strong. Perhaps it's an idea to give in to it from time to time otherwise things may snap - also, it's not a sign of weakness but a recognition of reality to rage and *scream sometimes. However, we can't do that all the time and the ability to make space and start to sort things - feelings/hopes etc. is one to be prized.*

Second. Thank you for taking me in to your confidence about things and what's going on. I am strengthened in my view of you as generous, warm and responsible.

Third. It's a bugger (life, the universe and all that) and I wish I was nearer and could pop over.

Fourth. Having stirred things up with such an outpouring, it occurs to me that lots more bits may come tumbling after. If you want to go on writing, please do but -

Fifthly. I don't want to comment on what you actually say about the children, not because I approve, disapprove but because the inertia of a conversation carried on like this means that replies from me may completely miss the boat if you've moved on. I did feel however, that your caring about them and recognition of your own needs (and Zarek's for that matter), came through so go on trying to understand yourself and what different bits of you respond positively and negatively to bits of them. The permission at this stage is to look at you and at them subsidiarily, in what bits of you they latch on to. To look at their need, for their own needs will come, but you must have confidence in the validity of your own needs - both for your own health and eventually for theirs. You're not static, any more than they are.

Lots and lots and lots of love and hugs Lizzie, through the post, from Rachel.

22. Still autumn 1982

We plodded on throughout that autumn. The legal requirement of a mediation appointment was delayed because Zarek's solicitor was unable to attend on the given date so we had to wait until another one became available. My own solicitor had arranged for me to apply for legal aid but that was cause for further delay. Nothing could proceed unless it could be paid for and in any case, my Do-It-Yourself Divorce book said that legal aid could take up to three months to be granted and that you couldn't apply until after a mediation appointment had established that there was a case to fight.

Worryingly, people had started to talk. I knew this from several sources. One was the wife of one of Zarek's hospital colleagues who lived in our village. Zarek had obviously been blabbing at work and when I met this woman she made sympathetic noises so her husband had clearly shared our news. "No, of course it wouldn't go any further because of the children", she'd reassured me, but although I believed the decency of her intention, I doubted the outcome. We all find it intensely difficult to respect confidentiality with that sort of information and my guess was that it would soon become gossip, gossip based on Zarek's interpretation of the facts. I felt he could say what he liked because people already had established opinions about both of us, but it was still intensely scarey, not just because we each saw the situation from opposing perspectives, but because following my indiscretion with Pete, I was terrified of wrecking his marriage. Also, I could see what Zarek apparently couldn't, that he was destroying his own reputation in the way he was going about it.

I knew this from his other colleagues wives as I was starting to get supportive phone calls from them, telling me that Zarek kept a 'Red Book' at the hospital detailing all my misdemeanours, both past and present. So apart from infidelity, every time I cooked something he didn't like, or left a light on or failed to stitch a missing button on to his shirt, it was recorded. This made me feel that nothing I could do was right so not doing anything was a way of not being wrong. His attempts to show this book to his colleagues were usually rebuffed and there was a sense of shock and disgust from them at how he was reacting. They may also have had their own experience of his patronising behaviour.

While the difficulties of our relationship remained private, I felt he still had a shred of credibility but once it seeped out, I felt he was destroying himself as much as he was attempting to destroy me. With one or two local friends, he'd referred to Chris as a Bohemian potter, quite unsuited to bringing up his three children regardless of the fact that there was never any plan that he should. One friend described the gossipy way he had presented our situation to her as appalling, as though it was nothing to do with him but all the fault of his wicked wife. I was cast as the thoughtless, selfish hussy rushing off into the arms of her lover (or several) whilst he was left to give his adoring children a decent upbringing.

A decent upbringing for them was what I wanted too, but by me, not him. I could see that it would be months before our knotted marriage was untangled and it felt much too soon to be disturbing the children's equilibrium with anxieties about the future. One advantage of both Greg and Daisy attending schools outside the village was that they had few local friends. Children are just as prone to gossip as adults but the limited number of village children they had contact with, reduced the likelihood of this happening. Even so, I can remember screaming at Zarek about my main fear. "It is of no consequence or concern to me personally what you say or to whom you talk about our affairs but IF THE CHILDREN HEAR ABOUT IT THROUGH SOMEONE ELSE'S CARELESS TONGUE, I SHALL NEVER FORGIVE YOU. EVER." When I'd mentioned about the wife of his colleague who has children the same ages as ours at the same schools, and therefore knows all the people we know, he had retorted "You stick to your crowd and I'll stick to mine." To which I couldn't help myself replying that I rather wondered who his 'crowd' were.

Enough ranting. That autumn was exceptionally wet making weekend diversions for the children, hard work. Swimming was a good standby even when I forgot their buoyancy aids. No doubt Zarek thought me even stupider than usual but Daisy and Alice, who used them most were better off without them. Alice in her droopy drawers, obviously liked the feeling of having her feet firmly planted on the bottom, even though the water nearly reached her chin, and Daisy actually tried to swim rather than just kicking around with her float all the time. It made me more conscientious too as I worried about them going under and therefore helped them more. The children all loved their swimming sessions although the water was like pea soup and you couldn't move for arms and legs and inflated arm bands and hairy bodies. I remember one man whose whole body was covered in stiff black hair - a bit like a pig with the skin still showing underneath. Some of the women were no better - not hairy but blobby. One woman had boobs that were totally disconnected from the fifteen years out of date, elasticated, boned, wired, cupped costume they were supposed to fit into. They started half way round her back and then sort of bubbled out of the front in their excitement to getaway. Only trouble was that instead of being high and bouncy, there was a concave bit before they started bubbling, only slightly above her waist.

Zarek sometimes accompanied us and Greg made good progress under his tuition. His method was to walk backwards with his arms out, pushing people out of the way while Greg swam towards him. The baths were often very crowded especially on Sunday mornings so it was the only way to make a space but it struck me as rather typical of Zarek's approach to life generally - to walk backwards, pushing unseen obstructions out of the way, regardless.

According to Zarek, Alice at just over two was ready to go to a crèche which would improve her sociability, speech, and toilet training. It might well have done, but the implication here was that her apparently slow progress in these areas

228

was due to my neglect. Failed again ! Neither I nor Zarek had ever wanted any of the children to be cared for by anyone but me until they were old enough at three, to go to Play School, but suddenly, he'd decided to remove Alice from my care and take her to a nursery that was conveniently attached to the hospital where he worked, every day. It was probably the sudden change in his attitude that intensified my reaction to his idea which to me felt punitive, but it resulted in a shattering argument one morning just before the older children left for school. According to Zarek, I wasn't just one bitch of a mother I was two, as I stood there with Alice in my arms to prevent him grabbing her. Poor Greg, frightened by this tirade, was pulling at my arm saying "You're not a bitch Mummy," but as Zarek stormed past the window outside, he pulled a face at Alice as if to say, "I'm sorry, I can't do anything about her." At which point I spat at the window….

Mercifully, children only know the world that is familiar so although Greg, Daisy and Alice were exposed to these awful scenes, that, for them was 'normal'. They had outings, parties and treats such as Daisy's birthday lunch box which contained special choccy pud and peanuts and crisps and meringues as opposed to the usual yoghurt/sandwich routine. She'd requested Spaghetti Bolognese and, wait for it ….. profiteroles for her birthday tea so I'd made a great pyramid of them in the afternoon and studded it with candles and a Happy Birthday flag at the top. Even so, having been completely continent, she'd started bed-wetting and I couldn't work out if it was because she was picking up sour vibes from me and Zarek or if she was putting so much into school work that she was simply too tired to wake up. For Zarek of course, "it's the start of her regression" and all my fault. The same might have applied to the cat who that day had widdled on Zarek's bed, two enormous puddles. More recriminations of course - I should have kept her out regardless of the pouring rain which she hated.

Zarek's view of his contribution to our family life was unequivocal.

*"If only you would get up early enough to attend to the needs of the family, our whole life would be different/better/under control. **I** am the only one who really **cares** for the children and I **always** get up to give them a drink or attend to their needs during the night. Even if they waken at 5.00 a.m I will talk to them, joke with them, read to them and give them breakfast." "But Zarek, what about our needs for sleep ?"*

"I like to have the television on at mealtimes. There is no reason why it should be switched off even though we are eating Sunday lunch. I have just as much right to have it on as you have to have it off. Therefore it will stay on," .... for Weekend World, a topical commentary on international politics with the children becoming bored and irritable because of having to keep quiet ?

I was consistently over-ridden and found it impossible to withstand the stress. No wonder I sometimes felt like an exploding pressure cooker. I'd breast fed all three children on demand day and night and with Alice that had gone on for over a year as she didn't want to stop. I'd tried to devote myself entirely to meeting their needs but it didn't seem to have been enough for him. I'd thought it perfectly reasonable for children to learn that their parents have needs too but my own were definitely at the bottom of the list. I felt as though he was depriving me of the most worthwhile aspect of motherhood which I was well able to cope with - a sense of responsibility for my children but the effect of all his harassment, made me want to opt out. Our family relationships had become distorted so that our children, although bright and loving, seemed to me to be unnecessarily demanding with the expectation, learned from their father, that the world would fall at their feet. There is no doubt in my mind that mixed race marriages are vulnerable, especially once children appear on the scene. We tend not to be aware of cultural differences until they are contrasted at close quarters with our own. Love will conquer all ? Sadly this was not my experience.

At half term in October, I'd made another fleeting visit to see Chris. It was an act of desperation, my only outing since early August, apart from a school meeting and baby-sitting for friends. As I'd feared, Zarek had immediately shoved Alice into the nursery, in spite of his being on holiday that week. I went away on the Tuesday and Alice had attended the nursery on Wednesday, Thursday and Friday - Zarek's idea of 'looking after' her. When I returned, I found Greg talking in his sleep a lot, and Daisy's bed-wetting had assumed flood-tide proportions if I didn't lift her by 10.30. Both children had said that they thought I wasn't coming back which I found utterly heart-rending. The future was obviously beginning to make itself felt and my absences were clearly disturbing them, so had to be curtailed. Nevertheless, that particular escape provided a useful opportunity to look around East Anglia where I was hoping to live and work. I visited the hospital which seemed interested in employing me and had the possibility of accommodation as well as crèche facilities, also several schools in Bury St. Edmunds.

Yet again, my visit to Chris was a kaleidoscope of colours, smells, tastes and sounds; things to touch and feel, a sensual feast, compensating for the weeks of emotional famine that I endured the rest of the time. He was always so easy to be with and this made it easy to do things for him, so easy to give and receive suggestions without them feeling like criticisms, so easy to laugh, so easy just to be together. With Christmas orders coming in, he was starting to feel better about his future and there was also the possibility of some supply teaching. He was so much happier when he wasn't having to worry about money all the time so that his recurrent feelings of failure and worthlessness were much less apparent. He had hardly mentioned Jodi during this visit and her shadow seemed to be fading whereas on previous occasions, she'd always been lurking, somewhere in the background. I felt that he valued our closeness but knew that until I was clear of all the Zarek horrors, it would be impossible to discover what the future held for us, if anything. One thing I'd noticed in the bar of the local theatre where we'd gone for a drink, was that it happened to contain an unusually high number of middle-aged predatory ladies - so unbecoming to screw around; I really didn't want to get like that.

The readjustment to my Hampshire life after spending time with Chris, even just a few days, was as usual, hard. I'd felt woefully numb throughout the journey home and was bothered to find all the children looking <u>so</u> tired, and Zarek too. Poor little Alice looked perplexed as though she was making the best of a bad job, but really just wanted to collapse into my lap and be the baby again. So was the letter that awaited me from my solicitor good news or bad, that on 16th. November our Decree Nisi was to be pronounced ? Odd that it was the anniversary of the first time that Zarek and I had made love.

23. November lifelines

November 1982

Dearest Chris, I've got to come out with it - I've missed you so much this week. Great aching wanting-to-be-with-you feelings which you must know all about. But there's nothing to be done but squash it all back inside, like a lump of proving dough that has grown too big for its tin. Or let a bit of it hang out for a while, while I write this letter....

I was thinking about the arrival of another letter, that one from the court with the date of the Decree Nisi - which was good news for me but for you must have seemed like just another bill. I'm <u>so</u> sorry about that - you're the last person I'd have wanted to inflict that on and you haven't grumbled or said anything about it which makes you a number one gentleman. Which you always were anyway in my estimation.

I think Zarek has been through my handbag again this morning as two personal letters were conspicuously near the top. The letters weren't that important but I do find it very hurtful that he seems to think he has the right to own my life. There was another session yesterday of him telling me what he thought was best for me. How I long to be away .... He had an hour's long distance phone call yesterday evening in Polish and coupled with one or two recent references, I suspect that the 'nanny' he intends to acquire is none other than his elderly Aunt from Poland. She's a sweet soul and would look after the home very well but speaks not a word of English.

Now, Greg has requested an apple pie (why is it all 'men' love apple pie ?) and I want to rake some leaves up before it starts to rain so I guess I'd better finish. Tonight there's a big bonfire and fireworks in the recreation ground which should be fun - and everybody in the village goes although it's a bit hard to recognise people, all muffled up in the dark. Could invent some lovely games !

So, dearest, much missed Chris, keep well, take care and enjoy yourself - things are looking up and if they aren't now, then they will soon ! Lots of love, Lizziexx.

PS. Lots of cursings and shittings from me yesterday. Having cleared the sitting room and living room, the sweep refused to do the boiler chimney because Zarek hadn't put the fire out. So only one chimney was swept and I'll have the whole horrible performance all over again. Bum.

November 1982 Hampshire

Hello Chris - me again. And even more desperate to talk to you - even tried phoning to see if you were back early but no such luck. Last night I consoled myself a bit by twanging away on my guitar but I must get a decent book of chords so that I know what I am doing. After that it was a few fugues, few fugues, few fugues on the piano but this evening, it's my pen and paper that I turn to yet again for comfort. Don't think this will be worth your replying to so forgive me if I burble on a bit. I do miss you so much ....

Last night I told the children I'd take them to the local Guy Fawkes celebration - a giant bonfire in the recreation ground with loads of fireworks. We were having the usual hunt the glove, hat, mitten, thick sock, boot performance in the hall when to my amazement Zarek said he was coming too. He's never bothered before and I suppose I ought to have felt pleased but if only he'd done it last year, and the year before and the year before that, it would have been different. As it was, I just felt irritated that he was barging in on our expedition. It could have been a super 'do'. The bonfire was magnificent - twenty feet across and blazing above the tops of the houses on the perimeter of the field. And the fireworks were smashing - some really exciting ones plus some horrors that sounded like banshees - all very well organised. As it was a village do, we knew practically every second person we bumped into but it wasn't too crowded. There were hot dogs and cold drinks but some mulled wine wouldn't have gone amiss and I longed, when the fireworks were over, and everyone gravitated back to the warmth of the bonfire, for some music and a bit of Chris Daly magic. For us it was a disgruntled evening which inevitably rubbed off on Greg and Daisy, when it shouldn't have been. Such a waste.

And today hasn't been any better. It's becoming increasingly difficult to maintain any semblance of basic politeness to each other. I only hope we can survive the next few months without actually coming to blows because I know in that instance that I'd come out worst, if at all. The effect on the children is to make them crotchety and demanding, Alice particularly today. So I was accused of neglecting her and being a useless mother. Fanny Hill he called me. He cannot see how he disturbs and confuses the situation for all of us. I feel so helpless against his accusations and resentful that he constantly diminishes my efforts and standards. What a struggle. And it's our wedding anniversary - ten years of satisfaction deteriorating into hell.

I suppose I'm missing you so much at the moment because your world is the one which feels real to me now. Normality has vanished from the bizarre situation here and the thought of another half a dozen weekends, then Christmas, then maybe some more is hideous. Yet again, I say I long to be away but mustn't succumb to the temptation to jump into my car and drive off, even though it's endlessly tempting.

Incidentally, I notice that Zarek has only taxed it for six months so at least he thinks that everything will be over by April thank God. Two large dents have appeared in the side of his Austin Princess but when I asked how they had got there I was told to mind my own business so maybe I'll never know. It looks as though someone reversed into him when he was stationary.

Nothing more to say now - sorry this is so dreary. All my love, yes, of that particular sort of love, all of it. Lizzie.

November 1982 Hampshire

Dear Hilda -

Forgive me for following up so immediately, our lovely telephone conversation with a letter but it's something I would have gone on to talk about had the children not been around.

You remember how I said that whenever I went to stay with Chris, at the end of the visit or after it, he always managed to work in some reference either to Jodi or some other old flame as a sort of insulation to protect him from having to express any feelings about me. Or maybe indirectly saying that he couldn't allow himself to get involved with me too heavily at the moment. Well this time it was slightly different - see what you make of it. What he said was "maybe it would be the best thing for you, living independently with the children but having lots of friends and nice times. There would still be the horror of lonely nights but it could be OK."

Now on the face of it, that sounds pretty cool, but really I think he was talking about himself. I've never expressed any horror of lonely nights but he gets really spooked on his own at night - often leaves a candle or light burning, has the cats in with him and takes Mogadon to help him sleep. In the past, he's even been glad to sleep with someone he didn't want to screw, just for the company. This also sounds pretty cool but when I thought about it, it made me wonder if perhaps what he was saying was, no, I can't cope with the anxieties of you plus three children but I want you to have the same sort of situation as me so that we can go on being this much good for each other. Whether this would ultimately prove sufficient for either of us is impossible to tell. I feel fairly confident that I will have the opportunity to establish other or another permanent relationship at some stage when Chris may revert to being an exceptionally close friend who's helped me over a very bad patch. At the moment I feel very much committed to him and this time he hardly mentioned Jodi or the hopes he once had for their future and I didn't feel he was thinking much about her either.

Now I know you'll be tempted to say of course he seems like a lifeline out of your present situation but the future could be different. And so it could. But we are such good close <u>friends</u> he and I, that I feel very strongly that things could be right. (And then I'm reminded of what joy the thought of a lifetime with Zarek once gave me - Christ !!)

We had such a happy busy time together - it all feels so much more real than anything that happens here. One evening, Chris had been anxious to demonstrate his prowess as a steak and kidney pud. maker. So we had this big fat feed and then made love in front of the fire in his enormous but cosy living room. It's a wonderful clutter of 'arty' furniture, super pictures, clockwork toys, candles, miscellaneous junk. Then jingle jangle jangle went the front door bell, door always open so in walk some friends who retreat rather hurriedly when they see we are sitting naked in the firelight with Chris strumming on his guitar. He'd thought he'd locked the door and I'd been so incredulous that anyone might just walk in that I sat paralysed ! Typical Chris, he rang them the next morning quite unabashed and said they should have come in and taken their clothes off too !

What with one thing and another, you may be wondering about the desirability of a Chris Daly as a companion but I can only tell you he's as good for me as he ever has been and although I worry about him/us, I am totally convinced by his integrity and find him as delightful company as ever. More if anything, since he obviously cares and is deeply concerned about me.

Lots of love to you Hilda, Lizzie xxxx

November 1982 Berkshire

Dear Lizzie

When I saw your letter lying on my typewriter when I got back from the dentist this morning (awful, three injections, I can only talk like a severe stroke patient and dribble gruel down my chin) I said to myself sternly that I would read it now but answer it later, but of course it's too hard to do that with your letters, when I read them they prompt so many thoughts and responses, that I'm answering it now and to hell with work ! (Anyway, someone who poses as a writer and can make a sentence that long, shouldn't have any aspirations about working as one !)

Liked the naked in front of the fire guitar scene. I bet his friends were riveted ! A friend of mine had a similar experience when she met up with a bloke in Salzburg. Having failed to get it up the night before, he was inspired by a goodly amount of marijuana (and, she confessed, her lechery) to make love on the carpet in front of a roaring fire (these men have seen too many movies). He had a woman flat mate and when my friend anxiously asked "what if she comes into the room ?" he'd said she wouldn't and of course she did. They were apparently in the middle of some heavy in and out stuff when the flat mate's door opened and then closed again, very softly. My friend was completely put off her stride (rhythm ?) but she said it enhanced his performance no end which was maybe what he wanted !

Anyway, on to Chris's 'horror nights' remark. I think your perception's right that he was talking about himself, and the dilemma he faces must be very sharp. <u>Everything</u> is in favour of you living together if it wasn't for the children. And companionable sleeping together is one of <u>the</u> joys of co-habitation, and that's the joy he'll be largely deprived of if you have the children. You still seem to need to reassure me that the relationship with Chris <u>is</u> special and not an escape. I know, I know, I really don't doubt it ! But I am distanced from it all enough to know that this joyful business wouldn't last if you were permanently together, which is why his 'lots of friends and nice times' remark is pertinent. That's the sad thing about most marriages - once routine sets in, couples stop doing all the fun things they enjoyed in the early days. So what I'm saying is, you have a very real chance of total happiness by living near, but not with Chris, and having patches of joyous togetherness rather than routine company with its inevitable tiredness, depression and bickering. All the more reason to try strenuously at the mediation meeting to get Zarek to agree to a joint custody arrangement, or partial custody or whatever. It's <u>so</u> necessary for both of you - emotionally and practically - to share the kids. They're all Zarek has to live for, whereas you have so much more. Actually, as you can see, I'm feeling sympathy for Zarek at the moment. He's such a lonely isolated person, he'll <u>never</u> meet another woman who'd tolerate him, and I suddenly have some empathy about how he must feel, knowing that *you and Chris have this wonderful friendship, seeing letters full of feelings going back and forth, and knowing that honestly speaking, you could manage emotionally without the children better than he could. Sorry to say this; well, you know it, but with the day to day horror of living with him, you can't possibly distance yourself enough to see his point of view, or want to.*

The saddest thing is that he's undoubtedly a loving father but undoubtedly also a lousy one. And children are too valuable and vulnerable to risk for the sake of an adult's satisfaction. But what if - as will happen - the court finds in your favour ? It would be so hard to then negotiate access for Zarek, because he'll be so full of rage, spite and revenge, he'll no longer think what's good for him or the children, but only what's bad for you. Oh God Liz, it is hell, isn't it ? I can only begin to know what you're going through, but my heart goes out to you.

Incidentally, I seem to have lost track of the children. They are such a rich part of your life and you seem to be able to keep things going for them, regardless of so much other awfulness. You tell me about things you do together but are they aware of what is really happening around them ?

Can you tell what bliss it is to be able to write what I feel again ? Now you can understand why my other letters may have seemed stilted - I knew they were not for your eyes only but that Zarek would be plundering your handbag or any other places where you attempted to hide them - what a nightmarish situation. Establishing a sort of 'poste restante' with your helpful neighbour where you can have things sent without fear of intrusion, is a brilliant idea.   Lots and lots of love, Hilda.

November 1982 Hampshire

So how's it going, for you there Chris, my Sweetheart ? You sounded a bit bogged down and frantic when we spoke on Sunday but maybe that was because of my interruption and the fact that you were just getting going, and were up to your elbows in clay. Things always feel much better when you have really got stuck in and interruptions can be annoying - its' a bit like leaping into a cold swimming pool - takes your breath away at first but it's great once you get swimming !

Shouldn't have much to complain about here really but still feel low all the same. I don't know why I should feel upset about Zarek wanting to take the children to Majorca next Easter. I certainly wouldn't want to go with him - but it does seem so much the grand gesture rather than relating to their actual needs. And again it's Alice I really worry about. Poor little scrap has been quite ill with a really bad cold this week. Which I've also had. On Monday night she couldn't settle and cried and cried saying that her ear hurt. Zarek rushed out to get some antibiotic at 10.00 pm and I couldn't console her and ended up speaking sharply to her because I was feeling lousy too. So then I felt fifty times worse for not being the endlessly patient and all-comforting mother. Then this morning we all overslept and when I sent Daisy to get dressed, having told her three times and with increasing urgency to hurry up, I found her upstairs playing so she wasn't ready when the school run car arrived. And I went on and on at her when the real reason I was cross was because I had wanted to protect her from the last minute rush - she _would_ have had time if she had done as she was told, _when_ she was told. But she couldn't understand that and perhaps I shouldn't have expected her to. This awful situation is confusing for us all - one really loses touch with realistic judgment and what is a reasonable expectation.

Last night I looked at Zarek sleeping in the chair and felt overwhelming pity for this man who had made himself so alone. I can see so clearly how it has come about but I know there is nothing I can do to change things - I just wish it wasn't or hadn't ever been a part of my life.

Things are coming together for the large party/grand bunfight I've arranged on Saturday for the children and they are very excited. I've come to the conclusion that a party for thirty or more requires little more preparation than one for a dozen. I've written everything down that needs remembering so it's just a question of assembling it all. The unpredictable bits are Zarek and Greg. I've tried to keep Zarek informed as closely as possible with the proposed plan of events but I don't know what I can expect in the way of active involvement. Greg is likely to get highly excited and disruptive but I think I'll take a football and if the boys want to, they can go outside and let off a bit of steam. Daisy is eager for Pass the Parcel and Musical Chairs/Arms/Statues - for her a party isn't complete without all the games that everyone else plays and even Greg was making some very positive suggestions in this direction so _maybe_ this time it'll be different and he'll really want to be involved. They've both spent hours decorating boxes for their 'presents' - let's *hope they get some ! Greg has requested Marmite sandwiches and bits of cheese and pineapple on cocktail sticks. And I've spent hours making chocolate crunchies and meringues and orange cup cakes and marzipan traffic lights - no bought cakes at all even though kids often seem to prefer them. The piece de resistance is to be The Cake. I plan a green caterpillar with liquorice bootlace legs - what d'you think ?!*

And now I'll join the hens in the garden to rake yet more leaves and Zarek has just rung asking/commanding me to put the rabbit out !

Keep well, work hard and here's a great swoosh of loving thoughts to wrap around you like Ready-Brek ! Lots of love, Lizziexx

November 1982 Hampshire

Hi Chris. I suppose it's because I don't really have anyone to talk to that I have this irresistible compulsion to sit down and write at the end of each day, no matter how weary I feel. Which makes me wonder if I'd really be so good at going it alone ?

Anyway, write I must. And I __am__ weary and it __has__ been a frantically busy day and I do wish that instead of writing, I could just snuggle into bed beside you, having talked about it all already, having shared the fun, the worry, the everyday this's and that's which are what I expect from a normal existence. I do miss it so. I think of it gradually getting chillier in your comfy house and wonder if the man has been to look at the heater, hear the chop-chopping noise as you give the cats their breakfast or the jingle jangle of the front door bell, see the garden ever bushier out of the back door, smell the bathroom, feel the screech of the ironing board. It's all so vivid.

Knowing how busy you are at the moment with the unexpected arrival of the supply teaching, a financial God-send, that you told me about on the phone, I was intellectually at least, glad that you didn't have time to write. But emotionally, well, that's another matter and today I've been struggling with the knowledge that you have been keeping me going on an emotional lifeline on which I am now totally dependent. In January 1981, my awareness of my problems was formulated in terms of "if only somebody could get me out of this". Then it went into abeyance until six months later, Pete popped up. He filled the vacuum that had been created by my increasing detachment from Zarek, helped me to take the first step away from all the horrors here. But it couldn't have lasted, nor was it right that it should and although I didn't consciously look around for someone else to grab hold of my lifeline, it was <u>convenient</u> that it should come floating in your direction because you're a sucker for lame ducks and people in need of help.

Today I've realised that I couldn't have done this on my own, even knowing that it had to be done. Although I feel incredibly grateful for all that you have done for me, I also feel guilty for dragging you into it. People keep saying to me "How can you stand having to go on living there ?" and I hadn't realised before today that I couldn't if it weren't for you because instead of private weeping and pouring out my soul on paper, I'd probably be cosily locked up in some looney bin, having gone completely berserk. So, I feel ashamed at using you so and frightened for the future. About which we talk not at all because we both know that for a variety of reasons, at the moment there is no point. Chris, if you feel I've elbowed my way into your feelings to a place where you don't want me to be, give me a boot up the arsehole pretty smartish would you ? It might hurt but at least it would be over quickly !

On Saturday, forty little children will be pounding their way around our village hall - a sort of birthday/Christmas swansong party I guess. Sad, but they won't know it. We're paying an entertainer £14 to keep them happy so he'd better be good ! At the moment, the caterpillar cake is four pudding basin shaped lumps of bright green sponge cake but I'm about to work a transformation ! Then there'll be bridge rolls, peanuts, crisps, sausages, pineapple and cheese, jellies in paper dishes, doughnuts and lots of little cakes, all things the children have requested and they love.

Daisy said today that she hadn't got a present for me but that she'd give me her Gonky. This is her most treasured possession - her dark brown cot-blanket that has trailed around with her for the last five years. I feel doubly blessed.

My feet feel tired and my legs like hot balloons from having been on them all day. Wish we could go to bed, wish you'd look at me, touch me, kiss me, sleep with me.

How the wind howls outside.

Night night.   Love Lizxx

Standing back - Early 1983

24. *Hiatus*

And so the days and nights ticked by, marked more by the passage of letters with their thoughts and feelings, than events. Time felt indolent and heavy, especially without the distraction of family and friends making visits. I'd guessed they felt it best to leave us alone until our troubles were sorted but earlier visits had helped to insulate Zarek and me from each other. Our emotional bankruptcy seemed more conspicuous in the absence of these distractions and made me wonder how I'd managed to like him for even some of the time, for so long. Even so, there had been times when I'd felt sorry for him. After one bout of sniping, he'd said "I don't want any arguments in these last few weeks." Fat chance, I'd thought until I realised that even though we couldn't even *speak* to each other without arguing, he was trying very hard in his own way to create a positive memory of our family existence for the children. That was heartbreaking in the face of what seemed to me to be his dotty perceptions of reality, and also the fact that we couldn't do it for real. I'd found myself wondering whether, when it was all over, I might have an unquenchable yearning for our former life together. I can now say with absolute confidence that in spite of everything that subsequently happened, the thought has never again entered my head.

Absence of knowledge about the future created an awful hiatus in life inducing both anxiety and lethargy. I found it almost unbearable when Zarek talked about the changes he wanted to make to the house, holidays he would take with the children, purchases he would make - a goat among other things for goodness sake ?! How was he able to view the future with such certainty when for me it was a blank canvas ? In my mind, the only substance it had was a life without him and the thought of cranking up the machine to establish this, setting up a home, looking after the children, dealing alone with all the decisions and responsibilities associated with holding a family together, was terrifying. But, silly Lizzie - weren't you doing it already ?

My antidote to the panicky feelings this induced was to reach for my pen and send yet another letter to Chris. Our letters were like a continuing conversation as though we didn't want each other to miss out on great chunks of our lives, rushing by. Everything ended up on paper - all the worries and excitements and thoughts and experiences which relieved the choking bottle-neck of anxiety with which I was living. It helped Chris too. Losing Jodi had made him feel empty, black, worthless and the fact that I'd lent him my shoulder to cry on and never complained about him going on about her had helped. So he said.

The children's party came and went. Forty of them milling and fizzing with excitement. It all passed in a flash with help from other mums so that screams of joy or pain, laughter and tears seemed to get mopped into a melange, an essence of children's party. The little boys tended to chase around getting more and more excited and rough, like in a school playground, whilst the girls gathered in clusters, chatting and giggling. They were much more competitive than the boys, anxious to play games 'properly' and especially to win the prizes. Expecting everyone to join in was a vain hope. Some were too young to understand, some too shy but some just wanted to charge around letting off steam. Eventually they had all departed, my lot with their 'present boxes' adequately filled with the usual collection of cheap toys of five minutes interest value, and each of the little guests with their party bag of left-over caterpillar cake, novelties and an inflated balloon. It had seemed to go well enough and Greg and Daisy were wonderfully well satisfied - definitely worth all the effort, but phew, what a lot of effort there was !

A bit later, Zarek had suggested that we should have another children's party at Christmas. Having just got over one and with the unbearable thought of having to attempt to co-operate with him, I refused. "But why not Mummy ?" asked Greg and Daisy at bathtime that evening. When I said it was because we didn't work together very well, they were very matter-of-fact. "We don't like you quarrelling. You should separate." Greg had it all worked out. "I know. We could live in a big tall building and I could live at the bottom with Daddy and you and Daisy and Alice could live at the top." To which Daisy agreed - all very simple. Smiles. No hassle. Wish it could have been that easy.

It was about now that we had had our mediation appointment high jump which felt like a rehearsal for the real court room drama. This was due to take place after Christmas when decisions were to be made about the fate of the children, about all of us. I'd done my homework, having retrieved all my papers and letters which had chronicled events, from the 'safe house', home of my good friend Mrs. Jennifer, where I'd lodged them away from

Zarek's prying eyes. I'd wanted to read everything through to make sure I had all the facts at my fingertips. What a harrowing five years it had been and thank god I had forgotten a lot of the rage it had all aroused. To have lived with it at the forefront of my mind would have been totally crippling. The trouble with my 'safe house' arrangement was that having got my chronicle back, I didn't know what to do with it. That particular afternoon, I was visiting a friend in hospital and knew that Zarek would be home before me. Would he go straight to my bed and feel between the mattress and the base where I'd hidden papers in the past ? Should I take the bulging carrier bag with me to the hospital like an impoverished 'Bag Lady' ? But what if I crashed the car or it was stolen ? Hide it in the garage or the utility room ? No, too vulnerable. I finally settled uneasily on the children's toy cupboard but then worried constantly until I finally arrived home and was able to return the carrier to its safe lodgings.

The actual appointment was disastrous and distressing. Zarek had sat there looking supercilious, being the know-all consultant and smoking a pipe which looked really silly. I just sat and cried, enabling him to observe that as a man, he didn't have the same opportunity to manipulate the situation and gain sympathy. The only positive outcome was that it must have been obvious to the Welfare Officer who conducted the interview, that there was no way we were going to reach any agreement about an amicable divorce. In any case, there was no rush as my legal aid application wasn't processed until after Christmas.

The finality of what was happening began to impose itself as I watched with horrible fascination as the clock ticked round to 10.30 on Tuesday 16th November when our Decree Nisi was actually pronounced. Felt numb and withdrawn all day, as though I was living in a glass carboy with all my loving friends and family looking in sadly and compassionately from outside, but helpless. I suspect that Zarek felt the same as he went to bed very early although the fact that the TV aerial had blown down in overnight gales might well have had something to do with it. No television.

For me, momentary glimmers of joy pierced the gloom, like when at bathtime, Greg had described Alice with wet spikey hair as 'Pock Runk'.

Then there was the sleepy little voice from Daisy as I potted her one evening, "Mummy the sweet Mummy, even though you're very old."

A different voice from Zarek who had been nagging me for never emptying the ashtrays (of course not true). "Arguing yet again," said Greg. "No, I'm teaching your Mum good manners," was the response to which Greg replied "But you haven't got any yourself !" Out of the mouths of babes etc !

And a letter came from a local GP and his wife, John and Camilla, who had been long-standing friends of ours. In the 'good old days' when Zarek and I still considered ourselves to be husband and wife, we often had dinner with them - always very civilised and cultured evenings. I knew that Zarek had met John at the hospital and had given him the usual line about me. Their letter was ostensibly to give us their new address because they had moved, but it was sent to me, not Zarek and expressed much love and concern that we shouldn't lose touch. These moments were like tiny toeholds on this terrible overhanging rock face that I was clinging to.

Another aborted attempt at getting the boiler chimney swept, made me feel murderous. The boiler had always been Zarek's responsibility so it seemed reasonable to ask him to put the fire out in anticipation of a further sooty visit. "Oh, I haven't time now", he'd said that morning. "I'll be back at one so I'll do it then." At the appointed time, the phone rang. "I'm tied up now and can't get away. Here's what to do. It's very simple." In which case why couldn't he have done it before ! Simple it may have been but with children to collect from school, Greg at home because of his asthma, and shopping to get something for them all to eat, we were late back so they were all cross and hungry. And just as I'm on my knees persuading the last of the still hot embers into the ash pan, in walks the sweep. I had quite a thing about the gentle unseen precipitation of soot which is always a consequence of the sweep's visit, no matter what method he uses or how careful he is. I'd cleared the sitting room and the kitchen, yet again, and once more, he couldn't do it because the chimney was still too hot. What with this and three bad-tempered children, I was close to total disintegration. Fortunately for me, this sweep, a clean-looking burly man with yellow hair, kindly said he'd come back the next day which meant tolerating the chill, the various inconveniences and the anticipated clean-up afterwards a mere twenty-four hours. Why did it make me so angry? I wish I knew.

Although Chris's letters vacillated between abject misery and depression, there was also fun and an endless stream of engaging anecdotes .....

"If only you could have seen it here at teatime yesterday. Firstly a friend from down the road, Christine, called with her two nice youngsters for them to glaze two pots they had made and I'd fired. We saw to that and then she went on and on, down in the cellar which was my pottery, about her love life and all the while, four of us shuffling around with me trying to work and saying yes/no, but not really listening - I've heard it all so many times before. The kids were being good but fiddling with things and me edgy that they'd knock pots over ..... then Anne Macey called to borrow a desk lamp to keep her school tortoise warm. Then Wendy from next door, who appeared to have been at the whisky, came in calling down the hall "Ooooh! Isn't it COLD ! - So COLD !! ....." and leaving the front door wide open. And "Where shall we all have tea then, here or next door ? .....As long as it's not COLD!" I gave Anne a pleading look and she managed to shepherd everybody down to the front door and into Wendy's. This at 5.00 pm. Yes, I had to smile."

November 1982 Hampshire

Dearest Hunk

(OK so maybe you're not exactly Mr. Universe but for me, it's soul that counts and boy, have you got soul !)

So, as I said, Dearest Hunk -

(Goodness - this little scribble before bedtime - you don't think it's a masturbation substitute do you ?!)

Humph. Dearest Hunk -

So easy now that my mood has changed to write a STRONG and CONFIDENT letter but yesterday evening I was weeping gently into my whisky and not knowing which way to turn. On account of the loneliness you see. It does get you down a bit doesn't it. I hadn't realised how low I'd sunk but now that I think I've been to the bottom (except that I've said that so many times before), I hadn't realised how deep down it was. But the penny has finally dropped. IT'S ZAREK WHO IS NUTS ! And what have you been telling me for the last year ? IT'S ZAREK WHO IS NUTS !! Now I really know, so I have to share it with you, you see. Feel good.

People ask me why/how I've put up with Zarek and the situation here for so long but in the early days, it wasn't 'putting up with' - I wanted to do everything and be everything for him. No Buddy - you haven't seen the half of my caring, once I really put my mind to it. Then gradually after the children arrived our differences became more pronounced until they finally amounted to a degree of incompatibility which we both found intolerable, which is why we have to part. I couldn't go on living like that. I don't stand up to him now because it's like voluntarily walking in front of a firing squad every time. It's impossible to duck the bullets so I prefer not to step out there. I do tell him what I think but it makes absolutely no impression so I've stopped believing in it as an effective means of manipulation. It couldn't be the same with someone else.

Now I shall lumber off to bed. Too many late nights - sleep deficit I think. Night night sweet soul. And much love from Lizziexx.

25. Parents and children

After sitting in hospital with a big tummy waiting to have her baby popped out by Caesarian, my duet partner Bronwen produced a son weighing in at 11lbs. 3 ozs. As the Portsmouth midwife put it "a dockyard job". All was well but I didn't like to think of how she and her babe might have fared if it had happened fifty years earlier. She and Big Baby, visited for lunch not long afterwards which delighted Alice as she adored babies. She would rush up to anything in a pushchair with excited cries of "baby, baby" and one afternoon when we were out shopping, she'd settled herself in the vacant side of someone else's double buggy in order to chat to the other occupant who, until her arrival was sleepily sucking a dummy and then proceeded to scream blue murder !

Bronwen's experience with Big Baby made me overwhelmingly grateful for the safe and normal arrival of my own three children, regardless of the mad world in which they had spent their early years. Looking back, I'm amazed at how well they coped. Yes, they'd wet their beds and had temper tantrums but these were all things that happened to a lot of children as part and parcel of childhood so who was to say whether they were reactions to our tricky circumstances ie stress related, or phases that they simply needed to grow through.

Greg was a cheery boy, very large, very tall, slightly tubby and always grinning. His size was deceptive, creating an expectation that he ought to have been behaving better, like an older child. It was no fun for any of us when he was overtaken by an asthma attack resulting in trips to the hospital to be nebulised and he always had a Ventolin inhaler in his pocket. Darling Daisy was our skinny Lizzie - very fay with lovely big brown eyes, light brown hair and the sweetest expression - a pleasing child with not an ounce of malice in her, characteristics she has maintained to this day.

I felt sad for little Alice. Although she was two when our family life really began to disintegrate, she was conceived and born in an atmosphere of hostility, devoid of parental love, not for her but for each other. Her brother and sister were close together in age and became good supportive friends as their lives progressed. For her, being several years younger, she was always on the fringe of this friendship and carried the dissatisfaction at being the odd one out with her, into adulthood. In spite of this, she was a pretty, sunny child sharing her brother's streaky blonde hair and with a mischievous sense of humour.

I could be challenged on why I had indulged myself with a third pregnancy when the relationship with my husband could best be described as 'uncomfortable'. Naivety is my first answer, that I simply thought that having another child might cement our family life together rather than fracturing it further. I'm embarrassed at the ingenuousness of this explanation and so would prefer to move on. Once Alice had been conceived, had quickened, had drawn first breath, her existence and the love that it generated, was there in both heart and soul, equal but different from my love for Greg and Daisy. The question of whether she should ever have been given life became irrelevant.

Different permutations of these three precious children had to be managed in different ways. Greg was much given to little boy's pooshitbum talk and rather bombastic behaviour which meant that the girls' needs could be overshadowed. In his absence, they were much easier to manage as he tended to dominate the scene. It was Daisy who tended to get squeezed out as Alice was at a disruptive age, always wanting to join in but not having the skills to manage very well. This often ended with everyone screaming at each other. When Alice was snoozing and Greg was playing with a friend, Daisy and I were actually able to have conversations and do things together like drawing and painting and making Christmas cards. She cut out lovely strings of trees and high-heeled robins and stuck them to card in pairs. It didn't matter that they went on a bit crookledy and looked as though they were hoppity skipping in a three legged race. Sadly Zarek was never very kind to her, comparing her unfavourably with the other two. His justification was that if he'd been more involved with her upbringing (instead of me), she'd have been 'alright' by which he meant not wetting her bed.

Friend Stella was much better organized than me. She too had three children and when they did things together she always had three sets of everything - felt tips, scissors, sellotape, glue and glitter which meant that each child had their own collection, so no fighting, well, less fighting. It always fascinated me that in her former life, pre-children, she had been a scientist so her descriptions of any illnesses, for example a tummy upset, were couched in empirical terms, size, weight, volume, frequency etc. Whereas my descriptions of symptoms, as someone with a more psychological and artistic bent would be in terms of feelings, "Greg hasn't been himself recently, has completely gone of his food and is very clingy...."

Stella and Pete also worked efficiently as a team when their children had their birthday parties. They didn't do anything particularly high-powered as parties went, but shared the responsibility for the children who responded to their guidance by doing what was expected of them, behaving reasonably and enjoying themselves. This made me appreciate just what I was missing with Zarek. And when the parents, all known to me, arrived at the end of a party to collect their offspring, I was conscious of my own isolation and the lack of any real family activity within my own home.

Other families were generous with their concern and support. Rachel and William, whose children I had cared for so many years earlier, had invited me out for lunch in Guildford. It had turned into one of those rare and cherished days to be stored in one's memory and taken out and dusted down, whenever the going was tough. The sun shone and the hotel they took me to beside a very swollen river Thames, was perfect. I could have sworn that the portion of steak and kidney pud that I was given was as much as my own mother would have made for four ! Also, the staff were so considerate of Alice's needs that she eventually fell asleep in her high chair, leaving us to talk in peace without the distraction of a demanding toddler.

Some people one has the good fortune to meet can become more than both friends and family. The former one only knows part of and the latter one knows too well. I'd known Rachel and William and their children since I was seventeen and although in the intervening years I had seen them infrequently, there was a tremendous love and understanding which overcame the barriers of time instantly. There was a calm deliberation in the way they listened carefully and then reformulated aspects of my circumstances or opened up new ideas. William took enormous trouble to reinforce all the positive things I could try to do to build up my confidence. He pointed out the shortfall between my own opinion of myself and that of my friends with the suggestion that I should pay more attention to them. He even suggested that I shouldn't worry about feeling hollow inside and that having an affair was an emotional and symbolical way of filling the gap and carrying on when I felt as though I'd reached the end of my tether. It was such a special day, I felt a different person when I arrived home. One thing for certain, if I was to believe my friends, I had a very proper obligation to fight for the children and minimize Zarek's influence.

With another Christmas on the horizon, I had hoped to take the children to stay with my parents for a few days, especially as they had been asking if they were going to see Grandma and Grandad. As usual this had to be negotiated with Zarek from whom I received a prolonged tirade about my parents being "duplicitous dishonest liars" and Chris, who we would also be visiting, as an "undesirable influence." As a result of this I'd decided to get tough over Christmas via my solicitor. My legal aid appointment had been and gone and my attempts at looking honest but poor were obviously successful as the outcome had been a decision to meet my legal costs for the custody battle. This gave me confidence to tackle his anticipated negative reaction head-on. As expected, the communique I received from his solicitor announced that I was to take the children for two days rather than the requested five, because of my mother's 'extremely bad chest' and the 'cramped conditions in which they lived' which made my Mum and Dad in their warm and cosy home sound like something out of a Dicken's underworld.

26. Bombshell

At the start of December Chris had announced that one of his many attempts to find a part-time teaching job had at last been successful. This was just as well as he'd been going through a particularly bleak and regretful phase, worrying about not having money, worrying about having lost Jodi, worrying that I might be hoping to take her place, worrying about the state of the world at large and wracked by self-doubt. I passed on some of Rachel and William's wisdom, about believing positive things that other people had said about him and to reassure him about Jodi. I didn't feel that anybody could take her place in the emotional sense, nor did I want to try, but as far as being 'the woman' in his life, yes, that might work but until I was through with all the rubbish I was having to deal with, there was no point in even considering it. I knew I could be good for him but I didn't feel in any way, second best, just different. My suggestion was that he should spend his first pay cheque and half term holiday after Christmas, on a flying visit to the States to sort things out once and for all with Jodi, a suggestion that came to nothing.

Trying to help Chris sort himself out led me to wondering why *I* was still in such a mess, why was I still living with such a despotic man ? I listed my reasons:

1. I was still there because my children went to good schools and taking them away abruptly would not only disturb them but would make Zarek liable for a

266

term's fees. In the first place, I wasn't that nasty and in the second, a court might make me liable for the equivalent of half that money.

2. I was still there because until some kind of settlement was reached, I couldn't afford to move anywhere else.
3. I was still there because if I moved out, I could lose my claim to half our jointly-owned house.
4. I was still there because I could better tolerate the stress of staying than my parents could tolerate that of having me and the children decamping to their home in Essex, even though they were prepared to.
5. I was still there because it was easier to handle all the negotiations at close quarters rather than being geographically distant from my solicitor.
6. I was still there because moving away wouldn't resolve anything any faster – it still had to be worked through.
7. I was still there because I couldn't face the upheaval of moving hastily away to somewhere temporary and then another upheaval when I found a permanent home for me and the children.
8. I was still there because it was only a relatively short time until I could leave. Having put up with Zarek's idiosyncracies for so many years, it wasn't a door-slamming-I'm-off type of situation. That wasn't how I did things.

Odd though when I remembered how certain I had been that Zarek was the person I wanted to spend my life with, who made me what I wanted (at that time) to be. The trouble is that we only find out who we are and what we want through our relationships, using others as our sounding board, and this may be as much from becoming aware of the incompatibilities as the positive aspects. This led me to see that I probably shared the responsibility for perpetrating *his* idea of himself and perhaps *I* had changed beyond anything he had expected, so that I was no longer acceptable to him, hence our intolerable disagreements.

Whatever the rationalisations for our situation, with Christmas approaching, I had become aware that unless I got Zarek a present and some for the children to give him, he was likely to have nothing at all waiting for him under the Christmas tree. This was sad, but I could only see it as his own fault and I rather wondered if he would notice even if the children might. These thoughts were much more charitable than he deserved. Out of the blue there came a bombshell.

This is what he sent round to my family, close friends and around twenty other people (not ones he had EVER contacted in the past), with Christmas greetings:

Friday 10th December 1982 Hampshire

Dear Mum and Dad

You may be surprised to hear from me, as I habitually do not indulge much in epistolary activities.

However, as you perhaps know from Lizzie's pre-emptive correspondence, we are now divorced ! The decree should be made absolute in a few weeks' time. The divorce was undefended on the grounds of her adultery with two co-respondents involved - one of whom was the husband of her best friend ! I believe that Liz is now engaged in a frantic re-writing of our marital history, much the same way the Soviets do cosmetic surgery to their great Encyclopaedia Sovietica after any of their political idols fall from grace. I suspect that she intends to settle with one of her boyfriends, and I wish her the best of luck. Unfortunately she intends to uproot the children, exposing them to the uncertainties of her new life.

I intend to obtain the custody of the children, as I think in short, as well as in the long-term, their life and progress could be more stable and secure if they remain with me. I realise that the dice are heavily loaded against me, as traditionally any woman is considered to be a "natural" good enough mother. I am sure not everybody entirely agrees with this.

I hope that this news does not surprise or upset you too much.

The children are doing and coping very well in the circumstances and I am trying to cope as well as I can. The life will be much easier for all of us after Lizzie's departure. May I take this opportunity to wish you a very happy Christmas. Yours, Zarek.

This letter appeared to have whizzed to the four corners of the earth in double quick time and elicited a variety of responses. Isolated from detailed information about events of the preceding decade, this might have seemed a fairly reasonable if clumsy explanation of a failed relationship. Most of the recipients however had already formed their own opinion of this relationship and a flurry of shocked and supportive responses came in my direction.

"……. it was obvious that your relationship was already so mutually destructive as to lead inevitably to a parting. So, it was no great surprise to me that you had decided to separate…….I hope we shall always be friends and wish that I could be closer to comfort you."

"…….I haven't the right to take sides although I've seen how dreadfully he has treated you."

"……. I perceive you as the stronger of the two of you - despite all Zarek's qualifications and I know you'll survive. The most important thing of course, is to try and keep some kind of perspective regarding the future of the children. They still need <u>both</u> of you……"

"……. have received a horrible letter from Zarek, which made us both feel very <u>angry</u>……."

"…….though he had to talk about how painful this news must be to me, somewhere, however distant, there seems some acknowledgement of pain, even if it has to be attributed to others."

"…….we received a letter from Zarek explaining his side, but why he wrote to us beats me. We only met him once or twice so what does it matter what we think, and we're *unlikely to meet him again. We're on Lizzie's side no matter what ."*

This last letter was a bit of a barrel-scraping exercise as it was sent to my parents by a rather ancient uncle and aunt who we saw about once every twenty years. My solicitor's reaction was the same as everyone else's. He said he wished he got such interesting communiques in *his* Christmas mail. He'd written to Zarek's solicitor saying "This Must Stop" but actually thought it could do his case more harm than good. One of Zarek's colleagues sent me a card which said inside "Who's got the Christmas card list then ?!" so I immediately returned a postcard to him saying, "Yes, and didn't he do well !"

There was only one person that I knew of who responded to Zarek rather than me and he was someone with whom we had had no contact for several years. He certainly wasn't someone with whom I had had 'pre-emptive correspondence' and as a bright guy, he would have known that Zarek's letter was only a fraction of the story. Since the break-up of his own marriage several years earlier he had specialised in well-known and very glamourous actresses, real head-turners but without too much between the ears - what men might describe as a 'good lay' but definitely not intellectually challenging. It made me feel like phoning him and saying in a sleazy voice, "Hello Darling, d'you want me to give you a nice time ? It's half price on Wednesdays."

One friend telephoned in a panic because Zarek's letter made her think we had already parted and she was worried she had 'lost' me. She'd said that although 'the letter' was a shock, she wasn't surprised at the news and could have guessed because last time she visited us, the house looked dirtier and I looked paler !

The children had broken up from school and once more I'd tried to fix up a progression of visitors, outings and diversions to cover the holiday period, all of which were to be punctuated by a continuing production of Christmas decorations, Alice permitting. This was tricky as she screamed blue murder if she couldn't join in but in the process, produced an appalling mess with glue and glitter everywhere. This made the other two disgruntled as she messed up their efforts. The impact of Zarek's letter made me fearful and created an undertow of anxiety to that Christmas. Cards didn't help either with their seasonal greetings and good wishes. In the past we had always sent and received a lot and had enjoyed the news that they brought with them. This year those addressed to us both felt no better than impersonal circulars, greeting a relationship that no longer existed.

In addition I was getting a barrage of criticism from Zarek because Alice at 2 ½ had shown no inclination to use the potty in spite of my best efforts. Friend Bronwen had suggested a musical potty that 'tinkled' every time she did. Years ago I'd have laughed it to scorn but I was becoming desperate and scoured Hampshire for one without success. Zarek's theory was that if she had gone to the creche, she would no longer be in nappies but as far as I could see, she'd shown absolutely no interest in being dry. To be honest, I was pretty fed up with the nappy routine too and had decided to make a determined effort by potting her every twenty minutes. Not a single drop of urine went into the potty and although I knew I needed to be encouraging, I also felt it was me that needed a bit of positive reinforcement to sustain my efforts. Instead I had Zarek standing over me with his ever ready criticism and too-clever-by-half suggestions. All of which made me feel murderous. Again. Added to this, Greg had been really difficult and demanding so that I just wanted to get away from him which resulted in him crying and crying one evening because he knew that in trying to gain my attention, he'd pushed me beyond my limits and I'd rejected him. Impossible situation. Poor little boy, loving me because I was the only mother he had, while I felt I made such a bad job of it.

Chris' contribution to my Christmas was a pretty (sexy) pair of knickers and a tape of Vaughan Williams and Hely Hutchinson, lovely evocative music that reminded me of mediaeval winters with occasional crisp sunshine but mostly heavy grey skies and chill silence only occasionally broken by the bark of a distant dog; drifting smoke too from cottages across the valley and gawky black trees outlined against the snow. I particularly associated this with an earlier winter in 1963, when the countryside was frozen over for a couple of months and I was doing a student placement in a remote part of Gloucestershire. I was pretty unhappy as my first great romance had come to an end so I used to go for long walks across the snow-laden fields and really wallow in my misery. Then I'd return home to the stifling warmth of the Nurses Home where we were billeted, longing to find a letter from my love, which of course was never there.

In his circular letter, Zarek had informed the world at large that I was intent on rushing off to remarry or cohabit. When I challenged him on this he'd said "but all the evidence suggests the contrary." Apart from the fact that there <u>was</u> no evidence, even if there were , I didn't see how anyone could have described the progress as 'rushing'. It made me feel like cutting my tongue out to present to him and then saying or rather, writing, "Here - IT SPOKE THESE WORDS - THERE IS NO EVIDENCE !"

A Welfare Officer had been to visit us just before Christmas and although I knew these people were masters in the art of charming inscrutability and there were the usual unpleasantnesses, contradictions and deadlocks between Zarek and myself during the session, it wasn't all bad. The children were very much in evidence and gave an excellent demonstration of a lot of the things I saw as symptomatic of our differences. As usual they were very forthcoming and sociable but they gobbled up all the biscuits I'd put out to accompany tea, with me saying no and Zarek saying yes and every time they came into the room, it was me that they related to and not him. So while he was busy outlining his schemes for the family punctuated by "Lizzie will you take charge of Alice", or "Lizzie attend to her she's screaming", or "Lizzie she is smelly, change her pants" - which I'd just done, it was patently obvious that I was the one who actually got on with the job while he issued commands and theorised. We were given appointments to be seen separately after Christmas, to go into things in more detail and I started to feel just a tiny bit more optimistic about the outcome, that it might just work in my favour.

While I was buying Christmas flowers for a couple of deserving friends, putting marzipan and decorations on the Christmas cake, doing last minute shopping and anticipating filling stockings for the children, Chris was making his own preparations in his very cold house in Suffolk.

Christmas Eve 1982. In bed 8.30 am Suffolk

Hello Lizzie -

What a <u>grooosum</u> day outside ! Yesterday there was ice <u>inside</u> the window pane, just above my head and today, the garden, little housing estate and far meadows look caked in cold, wet clammy gunge. <u>This</u> I'm afraid is the typical traditional English Christmas weather - you can't really depict it on a Christmas card, can you !

Kitchen downstairs is warming up with gas heater and oven, and tuna and egg flan I've made (sneaked back to bed afterwards with pot of tea) to take to Jo's, plus four loaves (two solid with garlic and olives) hopefully reviving after an unfortunate start yesterday evening. Threw the dough together but was out all evening and when I got in at about 1.00 am, they'd all collapsed, probably due to intense cold in the house. Had hoped they'd perk up in the oven but have just had a gander and they seem to have settled down even more sadly. Oh dear. What a waste of half a pound of black olives ! My fault for stopping out late - whisky, mince pies with one lot of friends, then on to another arty crowd where I seemed to fall, not between two stools, but between the gross pot bellies of their 40/50 year old aging hippy friends and the filthy denim and displeasing haircuts of their

275

children plus punky hangers-on. Me ? Well, nondescript I guess in black trousers and white Guernsey. (Joy! - have just taken flan out of oven and it looks just like an illustration from a cook book ! Bread though ? Desperate !!) After that popped in to see neighbour Joan who'd had Di and Jo in for a drink. Just as well they'd already left - I'm not sure how I'd have coped being in a room with three women I'd made love to. Doesn't that sound degenerate !

Yes, it's been a cold week. Seem to have spent every day fiddling, wrapping odd presents, sending off last cards, cooking, cleaning, wandering to the shops. On Wednesday we went carol singing and collected over £57. It went well but maybe I'll tell you about it when we're snuggled in front of the fire with a fistful of whisky each and soft music playing in heaps of cushions and pillows and duvets and we're already half undressed in the candlelight and my fingers have already discovered you ready and your light touch has reared me to an alarming hardness that dips prematurely and impatiently into all that rich readiness. Let's see. Let's see how long we can defer that delightfully precious agony shall we - please don't give in and let me have you early, will you ! Ooooooh-er !

Oh dear. Back to earth. The loaves look awful - absolutely solid. I'll have to make another lot. Later today, as I've so often done in the past, I'll cycle out to a little church near here with mediaeval wall paintings in the plaster and sit quietly and read through the Christmas story and think of all my dear friends everywhere. After that it's back for supper and then I think I'll go to the Watchnight Service .....

P.S. 11.30 am. - Petrol tank filled. Gas bottle renewed. Cling film and more olives for more bread purchased. Will cook <u>us</u> a tuna flan for New Year's Eve. Just seen a <u>very</u> old boy in town with bright yellow leg-warmers on ! Joy. Down with the tea. Up with the spirits and leg-warmers. <u>Up</u> with Christmas ! <u>Down</u> with the blues ! Up with 1983 ! <u>Down, down, down</u> (slowly)with your knickers ! And up up <u>up</u> - yum - with you know what ! Happy Christmas Lizzie - Happy Fantasies - and Joyful Realisations of the same <u>SOON</u>. Love, lots of it, Chris XXXXX

With Christmas over, I was able to escape with the children for three solicitor-sanctioned nights away, two with my parents and one with Chris. This was New Year's Eve, which I can remember and I can't remember. A blur of super sensuous sensations of warmth and softness and hardness and smooth skin; hair, wine, music, lips, loins, being in him, on him, under him, around him. A consolation of having experienced hell on earth was that it gave me a heightened perception of heaven and those early hours of the new year were definitely it. I'd been there, I'd been there.

Chris and I took the children to the coast that day, a final treat before returning home. And for me it was a total joy to be out sharing the wintery sunshine with someone to talk and laugh with, to push the buggy, carry a bag, pick up a fallen child, warm my hands, fool around with Greg, dig the sand with Daisy, all things that I'd never done with Zarek because it hadn't occurred to him. Having shared small day time personal intimacies, it was sad that we couldn't have stayed together to share the closer ones of night time. Travelling back home that evening was in a word, soggy. It was like having a wet blanket thrown over my head and then tied tightly round my neck. And of course, when we got home, four letters addressed to me had all been opened.

27. Time-serving

Having defrocked, undressed, disrobed the Christmas tree it was time to think how to fill time. Time is such a precious commodity, it seemed unreasonable to urge it on or let it slip through my fingers, but there was so little joy in my life at this stage that it was hard not to associate it with a prison sentence. The alternative was to find distractions, things that would absorb my interest so that it passed quickly but as my main distraction was largely denied me, ie visits to see Chris, it was inevitable that anything else simply didn't work.

I'd been advised by my solicitor that the courts attached quite a lot of significance to the Welfare Officer's report and that I'd be able to see it before the case was heard. He also said this might take several months so clearly nothing was going to happen in a hurry. Nor did it. I was sorry to see the Christmas tree go, so was Alice when she called into the sitting room to say hello to it, as she had been doing each morning throughout Christmas. There it was , forlornly dropping its needles on the carpet with narry a bauble in sight. And it was hard for me too, knowing that there wouldn't be another such tree, right up to the ceiling and covered in lights and tinsel and decorations, glittering and pretty. It had all been pretence of course, but it had been part of our Christmas tradition and would be missed. One year the cat had got right into the middle of it and had bitten the flex resulting in a sort of feline electro-convulsant treatment. Mercifully she had survived so maybe it was more like a massive one-off dose of aversion therapy.

Now, imagine a vast hall/gymnasium, about the size of, say, six badminton courts. At one end a lowish platform, its sole occupant being a trim, yellow-haired lady in a shocking pink body-suit. Then imagine - 200 women (and one man) - big women, small women, fat-uns and skinny-uns but mostly with big bums wearing every conceivable combination of sportswear - from swimming costumes, leotards, tights, leg-warmers, tunics, tennis skirts, shorts, trousers - even everyday clothes - with shoes and without and on the whole, fairly tatty. This was Popmobility, a weekly diversion which I and three local friends decided we needed to lift us out of the post-Christmas/ new year doldrums.

Activate all these women plus man into a fairly well synchronised sea of waving legs, then arms, then bottoms, bobbing in the air. Add the sound of giggles, groans, a distinctly audible hissing (when we had to kneel on all fours and cock one leg up behind us like a peeing dog), puffing and grunting - and there you have it. Considering half of the group could barely hear and only occasionally see what they were actually supposed to be doing, the fact that we were at times, vaguely co-ordinated was little short of miraculous. And my goodness, it was strenuous - my body hadn't felt such fatigue for a long time - not even after a night of love-making when the mental/emotional stimulation and relaxation round the whole thing off. This was hard physical work - but not much else. Four of us had planned to go together but the most glamourous one didn't turn up and the other two were conventionally garbed so our particular contingent blended into the scenery with complete anonymity. There were a few glossy, lycra-clad bodies but mostly in shades of lilac and brilliant purple which made one VERY fat lady who was wearing it, doubly conspicuous. There was a viewing gallery at one side of the hall, which adjoined the bar so it was inevitably crowded with men, eager for an eyeful but quite honestly, with so many to watch, it must have been difficult to decide whose bum, tits, legs related to whom - although maybe that didn't matter.

The exercises were mostly variations and extensions of ones I had already learned, the difference being that with music, one had to keep going for much longer and much faster than I was used to. And it was hard to see and hear and concentrate, especially when lying on one's back amidst a sea of waving legs. The one man present with his girlfriend, managed to look fairly composed for most of the time - which I thought must demonstrate a singular mutual devotion. And afterwards in the changing room where I and most others didn't bother to shower but pulled fresh clothes on to sweaty bodies, there was a flurry of towelling and powdering and deodorising from the giddy youngsters, obviously off for an evening with their blokes.

Another scintillating round of Popmobility the following week left me not just tired, but STIFF. But it was better, much more enjoyable as we had elbowed our way to the front row and could therefore hear both the music and the instructions. "This one's for yer pectorals" yelled the instructress (this particular evening resplendent in turquoise body suit with pale pink leg-warmers and matching belt).

And then by way of explanation to the expectant multi-shaped women arrayed before her, "Yer pectorals is what keeps yer boobies up." And my God, a woman behind me really needed it. Her boobies looked as though they were beyond retrieval. We next had to lie on the floor on our tummies ("if you've got something to lie on, put it under yer didgery-doo" yelled the instructress), stretch our hands and legs out straight and then lift both off the floor simultaneously. Lots of times. The well-endowed lady behind me had boobies which never even left the floor, probably in relief that they no longer had to undertake any gravity defying activity. So they just spread out a bit and made themselves more comfortable. The session finished at 8.15 but by 8.00 it was me that was finished.

I enjoyed the exercise, enjoyed the fact that I could keep going, was supple enough to make a pass-able attempt at everything - but didn't dare jump with my legs apart for fear of my leaky bladder. But I did find that it only absorbed my body and it's an odd feeling to have one's mind completely isolated in such a huge roomful of busy people. At home I lay in the bath for an hour afterwards and felt both tired and rather flat. But it was a change and good to be out with pleasant friends, not talking about divorce and relationships and problems but normal everyday things. Time-serving ? Yes, but distracting and even entertaining.

Learnt from Bronwen, married to one of his colleagues that Zarek did indeed have a thick red folder full of 'evidence' at the hospital - which he attempted to show her husband. This of course included copies of all our letters he had been snaffling, including illustrated ones with Chris' drawings of detumescent pricks etc ! I guessed that anyone who showed even a passing interest/sympathy would have had it pressed upon them but hopefully most, like her husband, were too decent to want to know, but I daresay the Welfare Officer examined it quite closely. Thinking of all the things Chris and I had said to each other, over the last few months which may have been included, I hoped that he had sensed an alternative reality in it all, rather than accepting Zarek's interpretation. In fact I hoped he <u>had</u> read it most carefully, appreciated the warmth, humour, concern, indignation, desperation of it all rather than seeing it as a manifestation of my nastiness - which was all Zarek could see.

He needed distracting too and had taken a part in the hospital pantomime, as the Grand Mugwump in Dick Whittington. It meant he was out most evenings rehearsing and then for one week, out every night for performances with two on the Saturday. I dutifully took the children, imagining that there would be odd looks and cold shoulders but they hadn't materialised and the outing had been enhanced by a chance encounter with old friends and their children. I hadn't seen the wife since the arrival of their third child and there she was, an attentive five-year old ! Apparently Zarek had garbled our 'news' sotto voce as they arrived but they admitted they had heard it a month earlier. I'd found myself prefacing every meeting with people I hadn't see for a while with "have you received a letter?" but it seemed there was no longer any need. The jungle drums had obviously been beating.

The pantomime was …….. a marathon, three and three quarter hours of amateur plodding that lacked both wit and sparkle. I appreciate professionalism but I also admire amateur enterprise and they had tried very hard to make it a good show but apart from a troupe of rats, nubile young girls wiggling their bottoms around in very abandoned fashion, it was mind-numbingly boring. At least Alice enjoyed it. She shouted and screamed whenever there were loud bangs, applauded and hissed with gay abandon and bounced enthusiastically whenever there was music. Daisy concentrated and paid great attention while Greg vacillated between excitement and boredom. I spent quite a lot of time trailing around the various hospital lavatories with Alice, the one she favoured most being part of the Board Room Suite. Even so, I had to change seats early on in the show when with her on my lap, I felt a familiar warm flush spreading down between my legs - *her* accident, not mine !

In spite of my plans for the future, I found the thought of coping with all three children on my own daunting and yet I couldn't see why since that was what I was doing most of the time anyway. In fact it was worse than that because there was a fourth 'child' who was completely beyond any kind of management. He frequently nagged me about not giving Daisy piano lessons. He couldn't see that the children were tired when they came home from school and by the time I'd given them supper, cleared up mess, and persuaded Alice to go to bed, there was only an hour of their evening left, a precious hour of playing time, and by then, I was tired too.

It was even harder with little Alice who went to a toddlers play group some mornings. This exhausted her, so I sometimes let her sleep in the afternoon but the consequence of this was that she would waken very early the next day. It was a no-win situation. I could usually anticipate when she would need a snooze and would work really hard by playing with her, talking to her, taking her for a walk before getting her to settle for an hour. Then, as likely as not, Zarek would come home and say she shouldn't be sleeping and would get her up. Result, one very bad-tempered, screaming child and one stressed and bad-tempered mother. On one occasion, my patience snapped and I walloped her, hard, then had to spend the next half hour defusing my guilt and cuddling her back into liking me again.

A typical day at this time went something like this:

7.00ish - Rise and shine, unpack dishwasher, pack lunchboxes, give everyone breakfast, clear away, chivvy children, then OUT. Go with Greg to pick up lift to school. Alice comes too which is when we walked around the block to post the letter I'd usually written to Chris the previous evening.

9.15 - Quick dash into Petersfield for shopping - 18 mile round trip. DAMN. Went to Post Office for envelopes and stamps but forgot to send urgent parcel for God-daughter. Dash home, toss Alice into bed for a snooze and dash out again with parcel. Shame on me for leaving her but the local PO is only two minutes' drive away - that's when I don't have to remove my car from the garage, unlock the garden gates, open them, drive out and shut them all up again to stop the freely ranging Henny Pennys from escaping.

10.30 - Back at home, washing the kitchen floor, changing the goldfish water (Catty and Superfish still thriving despite frequent attempts by the cat to supplement her diet), wash the bathroom walls which are FILTHY - mould, cobwebs, toothpaste splats and worse. Load washing machine with Greg's bedding and bits. Redistribute dry clothes from airing cupboard.

Munch a couple of bits of Jarlsberg cheese (poor man's Emmenthal) and then collapse with paper and fag for half an hour before rousing Alice. Gave her lunch of Noodle Doodles and choc spread sandwiches which she gobbled up in double quick time (for fear I might eat it ?) then watched TV programme with her and played with her 'loony' ie balloon. Hung washing out, then us, out for a walk.

Met lovely old man in the churchyard, thankful that he'd enjoyed his long life. Enjoyed being among all those resting souls with the snowdrops peeping through and hearing someone being positive about their old age. Dawdled home, paid garage bill where Alice's 'loony' burst and fell into an oily puddle.

Started to prepare tea when Alice discovered Daisy's old doll's pram so kitted her out with bedding etc. so that she could trundle her dollies around.

4.00 - Off to collect Daisy who has Friday afternoons off school and had been playing at a friend's house.

4.10 - Meal preparation in earnest. Greg home and suddenly there's pandemonium because his birthday present from

Grandma, a Space Invaders game, has arrived and everyone wants to see/play with it and I'm desperately trying to clear up mountains of hats, coats, football gear, dirty overalls, gym shoes/shorts/shirts/shoe bags/mud on carpet/notes from school, lunch boxes to empty and satchels to make ready for the next round.

Television on. Alice has to be potted. Zarek is in and rushing through tea in order to be out again before five with Greg to see another tutor in preparation for his school entrance exam.

Then a bit of a lull during which Alice adds the contents of the brick box to the existing mess of dolls, toys, clothes etc. everywhere. Finish tea, watch local news - glassy eyed.

6.00 - Zarek and Greg back. More chaos, more demands. Mummy will you tie this bit of string to my Action Man life raft? Mummy can I have a piano lesson now, a sweety, a choc spread sandwich, waaaaah from Alice. Furious bellows from Greg whose game has been interfered with. Zarek goes out to his orchestra rehearsal and I stagger upstairs with Alice who is now screaming because she can't take the pram up with her. A lady wrestler with exposed nipples on Southern TV. Alice to bed at last. Resist the temptation to lie down with her and drag myself back to the living room where, in addition to bricks, dollies and Action Man life rafts, Daisy and Greg have created a 'house' by upending all the chairs and covering them with cushions and a doll's blanket. Greg loses interest and decides to play his new video game ....

Finally got them all to bed after Greg had thoroughly explored a mysterious little hole in his sheet which of course, soon became the size of a football.

Such was the ebb and flow of a day in the life of Mrs. Ordinary of Hampshire. Incontrovertibly, one day followed the next. Could it be different I wondered ? Another waking nightmare, in addition to all the sleeping ones that disturbed me .....

Chris meanwhile was still struggling with Jodi's absence, which he constantly referred to in his letters. She hadn't contacted any of their local friends during Christmas and to me it was obvious she was weaning herself from her whole English experience, including Chris. I longed to bring his obsessive pain to an end but could see that he was in a Catch 22 situation. Living alone again made him conscious of what he was missing, but another relationship would remind him that it wasn't Jodi so he'd be dissatisfied either way. And in any case, while he was experiencing so much remorse and misery, no other relationship was going to have the opportunity to develop anyway, and this didn't mean with me, but in general terms.

I'd often asked myself, in the light of events over the previous year, whether my reaction to Chris' desperate plea for an opinion just before Jodi went back to the States, was entirely honest, or whether perhaps subconsciously there was a grain of self-interest hidden in my negative response to the possibility that they should marry. In which case, in view of his subsequent suffering, I should certainly have felt more than a twinge of guilt. But I didn't. I felt that she had to go and that Chris could never have married under such pressured circumstances. I think it was one of the few times I'd dared to give a straight opinion on something so important but I felt it was right for them both. Had I foreseen the consequences, the devastating effect on Chris, it might have been sufficient for me to keep my mouth shut even if it didn't change my mind. It's much harder to imagine what might have been right for him and I was left with a trite generalisation - what's right at one time isn't necessarily right for all time - for any of us. Which is maybe what life's all about and why we need to resort to magic, mysticism, religion or grand causes to make up the shortfall between what we plan for ourselves and what we actually achieve. Chris' woeful failure to achieve what he'd seemed to have set most store by, an enduring relationship to make all other things possible, was what might have made him precious to other people. He cheered, comforted and reassured them that despite not meeting their goals, life could still have spontaneous pleasure and excitement. And so, like me, and all his friends, neighbours, callers, mistresses - we came back for more and more - we were insatiable. And perhaps therefore we by our demands, deprived him of the opportunity to truly develop himself so that he was left feeling peripheral despite all the love he inspired.

His reaction to this was predictable:

January 1983 Suffolk

Wotcha Lizzie-Babe ! Tea and Christmas cake break ! Just back from test-flying two kite prototypes - OWL and PLANE down in the meadow for a few brief moments. OK but wouldn't fly without tails to stabilise as wind was so strong - too strong really - they are only made of paper after all !

I don't mind <u>what</u> you say about Jodi - it's the truth anyway. But I can't bear that this great, most gorgeous chunk of my life with a very special person slipped through my stupid insensitive fingers and I hardly noticed. Her pain scarcely registered with me at the time. But there's lots more to it than Jodi. I'm so conscious of waste - neglected potential, blunted mind through lack of use, laziness, frustration - so <u>many</u> things to do. I could spend a whole week, two weeks developing these kites. Garden <u>such</u> a sorry mess. Upstairs 'studio' come to nothing. Weariness. Bombs. Thatcher chaos - the jungle just beneath the veneer of civilisation - a society that might fall apart at any moment. Why <u>bother</u> with it ? And you may <u>think</u> I do a lot for other people - I do no more than any reasonable person would. So can you imagine anyone, let alone Jodi with all her keenness to get on, wanting to be hitched to such pessimism, cynicism and negative thinking ? And now <u>you're</u> saying you'd take me on ?!!

Beware Lizzie - "The Piscean man uses a gentle self-effacing manner to get support, sympathy and concern from a strong woman. Once he has seduced his victim, he will rob her of her ideas, strength ...... whilst maintaining the façade of innocence and helplessness. Pisceans are swampy. They enjoy pulling their victims into their chaotic, confused lives in order to pull themselves out of the mire thro' the evolved minds of others." - Not bad eh ?! And by the way, YOU in this particular book are down as Scorpio, the sex-obsessed demoralizer !!

Pity you're not here. We could go to bed and read it, laugh and then lie on top of it and make love ! Keep truckin' Baby !
XC

28. Mr. Dunlop

A strange sort of quiet had started to creep stealthily through the house, as though it contained someone suffering from a terminal illness who didn't have long to go. Everything was tinged with sadness and poignancy - writing labels for Greg's birthday presents saying "with love from Mummy and Daddy", talking about preparations for the school he was hoping to go to and his future, realising that although we'd never had family togetherness, soon there wouldn't even be a home to unite us. The Welfare Officer, Mr. Dunlop, who had already visited us, wanted to make another visit to seem me, a separate one to see Zarek the same day, and also to see Greg. He'd played down the significance of this encounter - "the others are too young, and I shan't be asking him who he wants to go with." But I wondered what he'd recommend. Suddenly I was confronted by the heartbreaking and profoundly hurtful reality that I could be losing my jolly, happy uncomplicated son, who needed both me and Zarek. "He knows of course that you are splitting up ?" the Welfare Officer had asked.

"Actually no, because I was hoping when the children had to be told that we'd have some definite arrangements to tell them about, so that it didn't all seem so uncertain."

"Well, there are only two possibilities aren't there - either he goes with father or he goes with mother."

This meant to me that by the following week when the next visit was scheduled, Greg had to know that this devastating change was to take place in his life. I decided to try and think of it like boarding school and for all I knew, Greg might prefer to be with Zarek rather than me. But losing a child ? How can any mother live with that, whether it's through death or divorce. In the worst living nightmare of all, I trembled with fear and revisited all the permutations which I'd already gone over and over in my mind. If the girls were 'too young' to be asked' could I assume that they would automatically stay with me ? Would that be a sort of solution ? Alice on her good days was such a rewarding and positive little girl. And Daisy, without her aggressive brother to compete with was a very sweet and amenable child. We'd have time to draw and paint and, yes, I could even teach her to play the piano. That evening when I went in to see her after she'd fallen asleep, she was lying there, thumb in her mouth as usual, with a round circle of lipstick she'd drawn on each cheek like a little Dutch doll......

I started to think vengeful thoughts, thought of the chickens bubbling away in a stewpot, thought of all the extraneous junk that could go to the saleroom (those two horrible kitsch pictures for a start), thought of moving, setting up a REAL home somewhere different, thought of compiling weekly menus with the children without Zarek's interference, of things they liked and were prepared to eat. Thought of no more dirty shoes on the carpets (because of no more hens), less furniture bashing, more concern for possessions, less television watching, more sweetness and kindness to each other. A different kind of life altogether. I suppose my increasing awareness that there *could* be an alternative life was useful in that I could see how it might shape up but it also drew attention to the contrasts between that and my current existence. And what was happening there and then was reality whereas the future was at that time, a figment of my imagination. For example, the day before the Welfare Officer's visit was due wasn't that bad. Swimming as usual, rows as usual, Greg off to one of his tutors that afternoon as usual; Zarek turning up with some meat he wanted to cook which of course the children said was delicious, giving him the opportunity, as usual, to gloat over all the meals of mine that they had rejected. Alice was briefly in paddy mode and turned to Zarek rather than me and I could see him interpreting it as usual, as evidence that she preferred him to me whereas I saw it as evidence that she had learnt how to play us off against each other.

The evening prior to Mr. Dunlop's visit I went to Greg to say goodnight and told him. Told him that his Mummy and Daddy were going to live apart. Tried to be very matter of fact. It's not going to happen for a long time. He'd spend time with us both. Yes of course he could keep his Lego with him. Yes he can still work hard for the entrance exam. No, I don't want to separate either but we have to. Don't worry. It'll be alright. We have to make the best of it etc. etc. He seemed to take it all very sensibly as I had hoped, and then asked for Zarek to go and say goodnight, as usual.

Went downstairs and told Zarek. Who hit the roof. Fortunately not me. He denied all knowledge of his appointment with Mr. Dunlop the next day, said that Greg was in enough of a state about his forthcoming exam and he hadn't wanted him to know about our split until it was over.

Why hadn't I discussed it with him etc. etc. Although I could agree that the timing wasn't brilliant as far as Greg was concerned, I was sure about my own appointment to see the Welfare Officer the next day and also that he had definitely told me he'd arranged to see Zarek at the hospital first and that he'd said Greg should be told about his future, before he saw him.

"Then he must have spoken to my ghost. I know nothing about the appointment blah blah." He went upstairs to see Greg and then stormed out having first demanded Mr. Dunlop's telephone number from me. As it was 9.00 pm I said he'd never get him and in any case, all my papers with phone numbers were elsewhere because of his nosiness. "Where ?" he demanded but of course I wasn't going to let on. "I shall ring him at home" he said, and somehow, he did.

There was no point in trying to explain anything, even if I could have got a word in edgeways. He didn't wait to hear what I had said to Greg and would never have tolerated the idea that it was precisely because of this kind of reaction, that it was impossible to discuss anything with him. I hoped that the Welfare Officer could see this as a classic example of Zarek's capacity for making muddles and messes out of any situation, how he stirred things up. The only person who was most in a state about Greg's exam seemed to be Zarek. That night Greg wasn't sobbing himself to sleep, he was more concerned about his Lego than anything else although later he did have undefined nightmares that frightened him. Zarek couldn't accept what was to happen because he had dictated everything from his pillar of self-righteousness and couldn't stand not having control of the situation. Ideally, of course it should have been discussed and presented gently and convincingly to the children by us both as a united decision. But if that had been possible, we wouldn't have been separating and I had acted in good faith on the recommendation of Mr. Dunlop. I had assumed Zarek knew of his appointment, assumed that he knew Greg was to be seen too (in fact this had been requested by Zarek) and that as he hadn't said anything to him about the visit, then I should. And having told Greg (and also told him that of course he should talk to Daddy but not to anyone else as it wasn't going to happen for a long time yet), I then went straight to Zarek, wanting to do the decent thing. Should have known he'd explode. When/how could I get away from this dreadful man ?

The next morning at 9.45 I had a phone call from Mr. Dunlop. He couldn't understand what had happened and sounded a shade put out by Zarek's reaction. Said he wasn't going to be put off and was coming to see me anyway. That morning, Zarek had asked me when it would be convenient to make another appointment to which I had replied that it was a matter for me and Mr. Dunlop to sort out, not him. It appeared that the Welfare Officer had rung Zarek at the hospital to make his appointment and had spoken to his secretary so as far as Zarek was concerned, it was her fault, not his for not checking on forthcoming diary entries. Typical. In spite of the fact that Zarek blamed his secretary, he was the common denominator in all the confusion that surrounded this episode although on reflection, maybe Mr. Dunlop should not have made an appointment for such a personal matter with the secretary.........?

He turned out to be very perceptive. I didn't have to tell him much for him to understand Zarek's attitude - that I wasn't good enough to bring up the children, that the first affair was a necessary escape route, that my relationship with Chris was different, that I needed to establish myself independently, that the children were young enough not to have strong community ties here but could just as easily get established elsewhere, if they were with me. He said that in his experience, people who transferred from one relationship into another permanent one straight away, as I might have done with Pete, invariably came to grief. And seemed to regard the situation with Chris, as sensible caution. He seemed unconcerned at my inability to present concrete alternative proposals for the future - clearly understood the difficulty of the situation and I would imagine, was aware that I wouldn't suffer financial hardship as do some couples whose joint income is low. Filled him in on the details of Zarek's recent activities but could tell that he understood how shattering it was for <u>him</u> with a second failed marriage and so much at stake, so much to lose. Told him how scatty Zarek was about co-ordinating and organising things and how I didn't feel he'd ever cope, or be able to provide continuity to their childhood.

He was obliged to be non-committal but he seemed to be implying that he could see no reason why I shouldn't have the children, the only difficulty being the distance I intended to move away. He said there was no point in asking the children because at their ages, you could get them to say anything. Which you could. So in all, my feelings were of cautious optimism.

I told Mr. Dunlop about the mix-up over his visit - and a good many other things too. Apparently Zarek had insisted (on a fair's fair basis) that when he had the re-scheduled appointment, Greg should be there again too so he took him out of school early. The oddness and inconsistencies of Zarek's behaviour became more obvious as time passed and I felt confident that unless there was a very strange judge at the hearing, I would definitely have the girls and probably Greg as well. The situation didn't have to be finite - if Greg decided when he was older that he'd prefer to be with his father, then it could be arranged.

However, after Zarek had seen Mr. Dunlop at work he came home equally serene so maybe he felt he'd been able to counteract much of what I felt had been achieved during his visit to me. Moving the case on, my solicitor had advised me that he thought a tough lady barrister who could stand up to Zarek's hectoring might be an appropriate representative for me in court and the next stage was for her to prepare my affidavit.

Knowing that all the expenses were covered by Legal Aid, I had hoped that everything might be settled by the end of February but a solicitor friend I spoke to said that it could take up to two months from the time affidavits and reports were submitted to the court - which could make it March at the earliest. Her suggestion was that I should get an injunction to remove Zarek on the grounds of past violence and present menace !

29. Guilt

"Almighty God, Father of our Lord Jesus Christ, Maker of all things, Judge of all men; We acknowledge and bewail our manifold sins and wickedness which we from time to time most grievously have committed by thought word and deed, Against thy Divine Majesty, Provoking most justly thy wrath and indignation against us." *Book of Common Prayer, The Communion.*

Was it a sense of guilt, followed by fear of retribution in the form of wrath and indignation raining down on me like thunderbolts from heaven, that brought these words of the General Confession to mind ? I doubt it. A more likely reason was that I had attended the induction of a new vicar at our local church which had been conducted using the old-fashioned King James Bible language, which I loved. Loved the sheer poetry of it and also the inevitable reminder of the hours my sister and I had spent in church as children, hearing it endlessly intoned for matins and evensong and communion services. It did nothing to bring 'faith' into my life but it did give me an appreciation of the celebratory aspects of religious belief, which I have never lost. I loved the beauty of those words and was in awe of the diligence and dedication which inspired people to give of their creative best in building beautiful cathedrals, creating amazing works of art, writing inspirational music and words for a posterity which they could only guess at.

Much as I enjoyed the church 'do', it left me feeling low. I avoided the bunfight afterwards despite the lure of lots of unsexy clergy and Mrs. Conway's legendary vol-au-vents. My existence at that point in time felt so static and isolated. There was nothing I could contribute in a crowd of people talking about their families and holidays and the future. I didn't feel I fitted and didn't want to pretend. This hurt, and highlighted my isolation. Not that I was physically isolated but that I inhabited a different world. I also felt pretty choked off when Stella told me about someone we both knew in the village who had been a 'customer' of Zarek's but was 'much better' since she gave her husband his marching orders - and he went. Could it really have been that easy ? My solicitor must have completed umpteen divorces since I first saw him, and there I was, still plodding on and feeling as though I was wading through treacle.

I had confronted a different kind of beauty and moment of exhilaration when I drove into Portsmouth to collect the girls from school earlier in the day. I came sweeping round a broad bend in the motorway to face the Portsmouth skyline - a broad horizon with the sun catching one part of the estuary like a horizontal neon tube supporting a curious mixture of rectangular office blocks and huge crane rigs all in steely grey silhouette. Stunning.

From then on, things had deteriorated rapidly. I thought before collecting the girls, that I just had time to dash to Southsea Post Office to post a letter and Alice and I set off in fine form. Her neck was festooned with cotton reel necklaces and she'd insisted on taking her Father Christmas balloon with her and a plastic 'fly swatter' sort of bat. She

300

knew she had to hang on tight to the balloon (wouldn't have a string put on it) but the more we hurried, the more it kept on escaping so that in the end, half the people in Southsea seemed to have spent part of their afternoon helping us to retrieve it - and of course the prevailing wind was blowing away from Daisy's school.

When we finally arrived, a bit late, Daisy was waiting outside in tears and there was a message for me to go in and see her teacher. They'd been doing Romulus and Remus and Daisy had pestered me to allow her to take a pottery oil lamp to school which my sister had brought back from a holiday in Israel. I had refused until I found something suitable to pack it in - a cardboard box filled with polystyrene bits so she took it with her, with many threats as to what would happen to her if it got broken. Well, her teacher handed me the pieces with many apologies - I suppose it was silly of me to have taken the chance and I felt sorry for poor little Daisy who must have had such an unhappy day. Funny really because I'd often wondered if it was something which was mass-produced in some little back-room in Jerusalem, for the tourists. (Like the icon that my architect boyfriend once bought in Greece which lost half its paint on the wrapping paper.) Having seen the pieces of the lamp which were very brittle and flakey, I felt a bit more convinced that it was authentically old.

Then Alice biffed one of the other little girls (who has a famously fussy mother) on the cheekbone with her bat which must have hurt although I don't think she needed to stagger quite so dramatically after she had got out of the car and went up the garden path with her hand over her eye.

Finally, Zarek demanded to know, immediately I put the plate in front of him, how I'd cooked the frankfurters he'd purchased for supper. I'd dropped them into hot water but he said they should have been steamed. Ah me.

No, finally when I got back from the Church induction service at 8.45, Greg and Daisy were still larking around upstairs while Zarek sat in front of the TV in the living room. I asked "Why aren't Greg and Daisy in bed ?" and he immediately left the room and went upstairs - which was one good thing.

And maybe only a few more months of doubt and anxiety and ups and downs - already one month of my 1983 wall chart was nearly completed - maybe only two more to go ?

 The following evening after some over excited bathroom games which inevitably led to me getting cross, Greg collapsed in tears. I lay down in bed with him and gave him a big hug and a cuddle. "I had this worrying thought Mummy," he sobbed " that you might go away and leave us and I love you all the time, even when I'm naughty and when I'm good....." and again, the horrible enormity of it all pierced me like an icy dart. So I came downstairs and made a big apple pie (one of his favourite puds) and a few final mince pies with the pastry leftovers.

30. Children and schools

Knowing that I would need to present some concrete plans to the court for the children's future, I rang the Independent Schools Information Service (ISIS)to see what was available in East Anglia. As Zarek had been prepared to pay for their education in Hampshire and presumably would find something comparable more acceptable if they were to be moved, I looked for similar opportunities - a question of continuing their education in the manner to which they had become accustomed. ISIS had an accreditation system so only the schools that could meet the accreditation criteria appeared on their list which was posted to me a few days later. This had a wonderfully clarifying effect and I zoomed around the house all morning doing a lot of cleaning, for once, totally undistracted by daydreams. Here was a bit of reality I could grasp at long last. I spent the afternoon cooking and playing with Alice and apart from the three lots of shit I had to clear up, two from Alice, one very squitty lot from the cat which I discovered when I put my hand in it, oh, and the split lip I got when Alice stood up suddenly and knocked my teeth, it was definitely A GOOD DAY.

The school situation was interesting. There seemed to be nothing suitable in Bury St. Edmunds at all - mostly because they all charged huge fees per term which was out of the question and were either boarding schools with a few day places, or posh prep. schools. This suggested that the people of Bury were either an exceptionally wealthy bunch or that the state schools were pretty good, good enough for the fairly middle class people I got the impression lived there. And good enough for my children.

I discovered that there was an independent boys school in Ipswich with a prep. school attached, very similar to the school in Portsmouth which Zarek was desperately coaching Greg to get into. So if the court thought Zarek could and should continue to pay for their education, then it would have to be Ipswich even though it wasn't my destination of choice. The idea started to take root. Felt that if I was coping on my own, it wouldn't be a bad thing to be in a place which could provide all the amenities I was likely to need. Also it was that much more accessible to Essex and my parents, and to roads south for the long trips to Hampshire which would presumably have to be part of the routine. So, if it was state schools it was Bury St. Edmunds, and if it was private, it was Ipswich and that was that. Almost.

Greg had been attending a small local private school since he was four. He was a big bouncy mature child who had frankly outgrown the limited play school opportunities which would have had to suffice until he was five, so we were pleased to have found this alternative. He'd settled in very happily. Its kindly caring atmosphere clearly suited him and it provided an unpressured but comprehensive education up to the age of sixteen, for children who didn't get syphoned off to other schools. A phone call from his headmistress had surprised me. She had been asked to provide a reference by the new school in Portsmouth for which Zarek had been coaching Greg and was startled because she had known nothing about the anticipated possibility. I was startled too because I hadn't realised they would contact her before a decision was made and knew that it should have been discussed with her. Oh dear. What she was really expressing was her dismay that our 'sensitive, artistic' child's educational future should comprise jumping through the various hoops required by the straight-laced, academic, no-nonsense school in Portsmouth, excellent though it was. What she actually said was that for Greg, she couldn't have picked anywhere worse.

I dutifully relayed this information to Zarek although it might have been more in my interest to get her to sign a written statement to that effect and save it as a coup de grace for the custody hearing. I knew it wouldn't influence Zarek's plans but Mr. Dunlop needed to know.

Chris meanwhile was having his own school dramas. He'd started his permanent part-time job after Christmas and was settling in well, probably because the things that he taught like pottery, art and craftwork included making mobiles and making and flying kites, all much more fun than boring old sums and writing. He'd gone into a classroom where he was to teach a new group and had written his name on the blackboard. Mr. Daly. Then he'd noticed one small boy sitting at a desk in the front go bright red and look very uncomfortable.

I'd known that Chris had had a child and was providing a small sum to his mother for maintenance but that he wasn't any part of his life, nor had ever been. Chris' relationship with the mother Rosie hadn't quite been a one night stand but it had certainly been temporary and he maintained that she hadn't told him she was pregnant until it was too late to do anything about it. For this child to surface, a chirpy seven year old, sitting in front of him in class must have been devastating. Devastating for the little boy too as he clearly knew the name of his father, a father he had never seen and had only heard about from his mother.

Chris' immediate reaction was to want to make up for those years of lost fathering but I was worried that whatever he was biting off with little Charlie, might eventually turn out to be unpalatable or hurtful. Worried that he might say to another child in confidence "That's my father" and it would then fly round the school like wildfire with who knew what consequences. Mercifully it didn't. Chris set about establishing a routine of contacts and they got to know and like each other, sharing suppers, walks in the nearby meadow, building go-carts, kites, castles, all the sorts of things that appealed to both Charlie and Chris who could clearly see that Rosie had made a good job of being a single parent. He was proud of the fact that Charlie was a fine-looking, intelligent child who had told his Mum he thought Chris was "excellent". And he said that deep down, he felt as though a piece of a jigsaw that had been floating around for seven years, adding to his unrest and dissatisfaction with his life until that point, had finally dropped into place.

I had been worried about the impact on Chris of meeting a child who had only ever been the merest twinkle in his eye and a standing order on his bank statement. Worried about the impact on Charlie too, as some people when they eventually meet a missing parent are disappointed or have a sense of resentment that this person has opted out (for whatever reason) of the obligation to share in their upbringing. Further thought made me realise that my anxiety about this news was more likely to be me feeling jealous, a shameful jealousy really, that they were both finding a part of themselves that they had never had the opportunity to fulfil before, and that sharing these feelings might dilute whatever was left for me. I'd have liked Chris to think that my concern for him was selfless, but it wasn't. I knew that it was mean, greedy, insatiable Lizzie, always insecure about my parents' love, always feeling sure that they must love my sweet, docile, generous, well-behaved older sister more than me. Which they probably did - she must have been a much easier child to manage. But why should I be jealous of this burgeoning love that Chris was feeling for his son when they had every right to find joy in each other ? Mea culpa, mea culpa.

Reflection enabled me to see that the jigsaw piece that had dropped into place was to do with Chris being able to give Charlie something that had been conspicuously missing from his own life ie his feelings for the father who had died in the first year of his existence. It must have been very precious for him to experience at last, something of which he could have had no knowledge until then, the love between father and child.

Chris had talked about not daring yet to look right into Charlie's eyes to see if he could see anything of himself there which drew my attention to his own inscrutability. I'd looked into his eyes often enough but could never read what I saw apart from when we said goodbye. He was someone who noticed every minutest detail, nuance of light and shade, shift in a fold of clothing, twitch of a tiny muscle. But he never gave anything away. What he saw was a great deal more than anyone imagined but I think this was partly the artist in him, translating everything into line and form on paper. Seeing *so* much seemed to make him wary of what he gave away with his eyes. From the very occasional remarks he'd made I knew that even when we were both totally absorbed in the most intimate of love making, there was an additional part of him that was observing and deriving sensual pleasure from what he saw as well as the reactions of our bodies to each other. Saying goodbye was one of the times when he was emotionally vulnerable and couldn't quite keep up the guard.

A final confession: I'd felt humbled that Rosie had managed so well alone with her little boy when I'd <u>had</u> a husband, a father for my children but we'd made such a mess of things.

Limbo - February 1983

31. Thin ice

By mid –February, I was beginning to feel like a stuck gramophone record. Nothing much seemed to be happening to move our case on and Chris' job and a sudden influx of orders for pots meant that he had less time to write to me although he said he missed what he called the 'gentlemanly joys'. Me too - found I was even casting discreetly lustful eyes over the dozen or so clergy at the induction service I'd been to - but nothing to get excited about ! Not that there was much with Zarek, even before the decline - maybe once every two or three weeks. And a paucity of letters from Chris didn't stop me writing. My daily 'fix', outpourings of words, almost seemed like an addiction that had to be satisfied before the day felt complete.

By this time, Zarek and I had settled on a compromise for Alice who was attending the crèche for two mornings each week. It made me feel even more lost seeing her depart, crotchety and sucking her 'nonny', delighted to be off with Daddy in the car but nevertheless missing her usual morning snooze. Within a few weeks she was coping much better - no tears, no wet pants but a very tired and impatient little girl to bring home, so much in need of cuddles that she could hardly bear it when I put her into the bath or prised her from my lap to put her into her cot to sleep. She'd made friends with Chalky the nursery guinea pig and a little boy called Tom so it seemed to be doing her no harm. Even so, she had been reacting very strongly to our differences, screaming blue murder and pushing me out of her room yelling "Go way Mummy" when she didn't want to wear the clothes I'd picked for her. Of course she should have been able to choose for herself but the need to get three children ready and out of the house sometimes made prolonged negotiation impossible. She would then rush to Daddy to whom it was all evidence that he was the preferred parent. Probably at that moment he was, but he couldn't see that it was <u>because</u> he was giving in to her, couldn't see the value of attempting to *support* my judgements which seemed perfectly reasonable, so that she would learn to respect them too and see a united parental front. Originally I'd hoped that Zarek and I would have been able to achieve an amicable way of sharing the children's future but I could see that the constant hassle and interference I would have to put up with if the children were with me would make that impossible. I wanted to get as far away from him as I could.

Chris could see this too and any account of Zarek's unreasonableness generated a scalding diatribe in response "…….*to think that he's a psychiatrist is really beyond belief. He's a fool, a blind arrogant fool. An obstinate dangerous fool because he's fucking up a tender young life that's been given to him in trust and not as an extension for his bloated ego etc. etc.*"

Once he wrote about sending me strong powerful vibes to catch me gently under the chin and hold my head above the waves but this simply reduced me to a morning of blobby weeping so that I could hardly see what I was doing as I mopped the kitchen floor. Alice had caught a cold which Zarek said was my fault for keeping her out for too long and hadn't I learnt anything in ten years, blah blah blah and I wept all the more at that trusting analogy of someone holding my chin up in the water. I'd lost sight of that kind of honest confidence in somebody else, being able to relinquish all the emotional and physical tensions necessary to keep myself afloat in this hideously stormy sea - needing so much to be able to let go even for a few moments and *allow* myself to be held.

According to my Oxford English Dictionary, limbo was "*a region supposed in some beliefs (ie Christian) to exist on the border with Hell as the abode of the just who died before Christ's coming and of unbaptized infants.*"

More relevant was "*An unfavourable place or condition, likened to limbo; esp. a condition of neglect or oblivion to which people or things are consigned when regarded as superseded, useless or absurd; an intermediate or indeterminate condition; a state of inaction or inattention pending some future event.*" Quite.

Greg was struggling and came home from school one day complaining of not feeling well - a bit of a headache, indeterminate aches and pains, feeling sick, no appetite etc. The next morning he was weepy and didn't want to get up although there didn't appear to be anything wrong with him. Eventually and reluctantly he did get to school with a note to his teacher to call me if she felt the need. I knew that he was concerned about the entrance exam he was to sit the following week, and news of future uncertainty in his young life can't have helped - both good reasons to be worried but Zarek very cryptically said he'd like to speak to me some time (like a servant being summoned for a dressing down).

Later he said did I know Greg was depressed and then asked, and I gasped with incredulity considering all that had gone before, "you know that he knows about our separation ?" - Remembering all the business with Mr. Dunlop, I couldn't understand this so I asked him what he thought we should do and he said, "You know the whole problem would be solved if you moved out as quickly as possible." At which point I stomped out and rang my solicitor. Livid.

One evening I called my friend Hilda, complaining of boredom and she said "But Lizzie, there are so many interesting books to read and programmes to watch - you *can't* be bored," failing to comprehend that my inertia fed on itself generating a total disinterest in things which under other circumstances would prove interesting, stimulating or challenging. Besides, the drama I was actually participating in was real and absorbed all my attention. I had nothing left for fiction or fantasy.

There were however distractions. The children had asked to revisit Bird World and to everyone's surprise, Zarek came too. I was never particularly interested in birds, but it was a stimulating place, well kept, even in mid-Winter and with a lot of trouble taken to create suitable environments for the birds and display them to advantage. I must confess though that the Andean Condor who was looking miserable last time we were there, was still looking miserable – possibly its natural expression ? Zarek sloped around showing only passing interest in the birds and with no concern at all for

Alice who needed watching all the time - kept on dropping her mittens into the enclosures or sticking her fingers perilously close to the parrots' beaks or climbing over fences and chasing the peacocks. Then when the children wanted to go into the Aquarium, Zarek just hived off and sat in the car. Couldn't imagine how he thought he could look after them on his own.

Another time I went with Bronwen to Jaeger in Southampton where I watched while she bought a very expensive dress. Another woman was choosing one from the rail, "I don't know about this, green really isn't my colour." Nor was it, although it would have been difficult to think of one that might be. Middle-aged lady with nondescript permed grey hair, nondescript face with nondescript make-up on it. And <u>what</u> a nondescript dress - so maybe it suited her perfectly - a green, stripey, blobby pattern on white, shirtwaister style with long gathered sleeves - wouldn't even have done M&S credit (in my opinion). But then, while she was trying it on, there followed an incredibly involved discussion with the assistant, "well, it would have to be shortened here, and taken in there, and perhaps the sleeves gathered on elastic rather than cuffs etc. etc." And it cost even more than Bronwen's dress !

Zarek arrived home that evening carrying two very smart toolboxes, belonging to Bill, a former patient of his. We called him Breadknife Bill and he professed to being an odd job man, wanting to help the 'doctor' by mending our oven. Being half blind and with very shaky hands, there were limits to what he could do but some years ago he had managed to stick a knife in his wife, for which he had done time. Mending the oven took him three hours, several cups of coffee and umpteen roll-ups. His wobbly hands meant that he kept on dropping the minutest nuts and screws on the floor and half way through, he showed me a horrifically long scar on his leg where he said an attempt had been made to remove some veins to replace some in his heart. "Didn't work" he said, so they used plastic ones. He adored children and loved cuddling and playing with Alice. What a contrast between her sweet innocence and his sad, raw and shabby life.

I might have happily settled for boredom , limbo and a few low key events had I known of the next terrifying episode that was about to confront me.

It had all started at a coffee morning which I didn't attend, when Rosemary Rintoul, who was not best known for her discretion, decided to make a public statement. "Did they know" she'd said, "that Zarek had sent a letter round at Christmas time describing Lizzie's activities, and wasn't it awful." I'd heard this from Stella who had been there and who was at that point in time, completely unsuspecting that one of my activities had involved her husband. As far as I knew, the letter had not gone to anyone in the village but I couldn't be sure. It made me feel as though I was standing in front of a firing squad, comprising all the village wives I knew, including Stella and at the words, 'Pete Clarke', they would all fire. The Rintoul woman, whose husband worked with Zarek had probably heard all about the contents of his 'little red book' of evidence about me. Apparently she had said that it was unfair that it should all be seen from my side so she was putting a word in for Zarek.

The interesting thing about gossip is that if it is about you, you are unlikely to know of it but as far as I knew, no-one had been seeing our situation from anyone's 'side' , least of all mine because I'd kept so quiet and out of people's way. I'd have been very surprised if that had been enough to get me the local sympathy vote. But it was terrifying and made me upset, angry, frightened. Having narrowly avoided any scarey revelations when the divorce papers were first circulated, was my cover now to be blown ?

It made me wonder too, what any of us *really* knew about each other . I could imagine the sort of gossip this woman might have been attempting to revise. "Nice woman, decent mother, but he's a real oddball. Isn't it awful what she has to put up with - it's not surprising it's all gone pear-shaped."

What indeed do we know not only about each other, but about ourselves since our behaviour is determined and rationalised by the value bases that have been shaped over time through the acquisition of knowledge and experience. This means that we become self-justifying systems, believing that we have good reason for doing, saying, being what we are. That is how we are. We also seek networks that reinforce this self-justification so I belonged to a network of 'nice' women and 'decent' mothers. Were they all matched with decent blokes and good fathers ? I doubted it. I also doubted that many of us could maintain this with any constancy given the inherent 'excitement' which is a significant part of our emotional physiology, manifest as it is in various behaviours - joy, misery, sexuality and above all, anger. But would any of those nice women and decent mothers want their neighbours to know about this darker side of their relationships, or those of other wives at coffee mornings ? No. We all pretend, perhaps to ourselves as well as each other.

As far as I could see, all that had been going around were Zarek's beastly stories. It made me want to send a copy of the very detailed summary I'd prepared for the Welfare Officer to Rosemary Rintoul with a note saying "Please read this. If you must gossip, you might as well have your facts right." Although on the basis of what I have just been thinking, who knows what the 'right' facts are ? I didn't send her any such thing because anyone who'd been doing what she had, was going to make a mess of things, whichever way they handled it. A fire which isn't fuelled soon dies down. And if it didn't, if the worst came to the worst, then I would try lying first and hope that was good enough; it might at least create a confusing smoke screen. And failing that, when it came out, somehow, somehow, I would have to bear the consequences. I didn't know how.

Apart from the ongoing nastiness of being there, it was my conscience that was killing me. Couldn't bear to think what it might have done to Stella, Pete's wife, if she had found out......

Oh dear. The ice was beginning to feel very thin indeed.

32. Employment

A letter had arrived, inviting me for an interview for the Occupational Therapy job I'd found out about in Bury St. Edmunds. I'd made it very clear in my telephone enquiry that I had no idea if and when I might be available to start work, should they choose to employ me, but it was a start and made me feel as though the future did exist even if it was a long way away. It also created the opportunity for one of my rare visits east to see Chris. I told Zarek that I would have to be away for a couple of days to further my plans and for once he raised no objections and said that if necessary, he'd take time off work to look after the children. Any other time he'd have said, "But I cannot be off work on Monday (Tuesday, Wednesday etc.), it is my busiest day, I have patients to see and it is all arranged," but this time he couldn't wait to get rid of me. I guessed he was wanting to accrue credit in demonstrating his parenting skills.

The weather around that time was awful - very snowy which of course the children loved. Endless parades out and into the house, warm and dry going out and then half an hour later, mountains of soggy mittens, wet boots and icy red fingers and toes (60 of them) coming back in again. And what about the hens, picking their way even more delicately than usual. I wondered if they had an feeling in the ends of their claws ? It continued to be bitingly cold and once the enticing snow had disappeared, any attempt to get the children outside for some fresh air was sabotaged by Zarek saying that he wanted to do reading with them, or that their lives would be incomplete if they missed Robin Hood on the television. "A wonderful film," he had said. "I saw it when I was a boy" (c. 1935 - Errol Flynn ? !) but of course it was a different version. At least it was a distraction enabling me to have some time in the garden sorting out the grape vine in the greenhouse. Started with bark stripping - pulling off all the loose bits to stop parasites from lodging underneath – a lovely job like picking dead skin off one's feet ! Then dusting all the knobbles created by sprouting leaves from previous year's growth with flowers of sulphur, before tying the whole vine up neatly and sweeping all the earth scratted up by the hens back into place.

Letter writing continued.

February 1983 Hampshire

Dearest Hilda

I did so enjoy our meeting today and my need to scribble to you now is a clear indication that we ought to have been able to spend a great deal more time together - but even our relatively brief lunchtime natter gave me enormous pleasure as I hope it did you. Things that I have to tell you now are partly continuations and partly associations which got left behind because of the need to pour out as much as possible within a limited time span. And also there are fresh ideas resulting from the stimulation of our meeting. Zarek's description of my writings as literary diarrhoea is not perhaps so far off the mark !

D'you know I truly feel sorry for him even though you said I shouldn't. It really churned me up this evening to see him playing with and cuddling Alice, telling her how much he loved her. And now he goes up to his room each night at about 8.30 and lies in the dark with the black and white tele on. Really low. I feel as though I'm experiencing his pain, even if he refuses to consider mine. And I feel so much more guilty about going off to see Chris when Zarek isn't being nasty. I guess I'm in for some unbelievably awful feelings when it comes to the actual separation. Can you imagine if he loses the case, the horror of helping him to pack his things and go ? A hideously painful freedom - best not to dwell on it.

But, this evening after Chris and I had talked briefly on the phone I actually caught Zarek with his hand in the till, so to speak ie hurriedly putting my handbag back where he'd found it after looking for letters. He said he was looking for matches but as they were in a jumbo sized box in the same cupboard, right in front of his nose, it was hard to believe. I hate all this pathetic posturing, lying and playing games. I really wouldn't mind telling him things if he asked, but he is obviously attempting to use everything to discredit me. He can't blame me for not telling him anything ….. so maybe I can't blame him for being nosey …..

Chris's relationship with his son is interesting isn't it. One of his problems (I think) is that he's the sort of person who needs to go on believing in Father Christmas or magic. I think that one of the reasons he rejected a permanent relationship with his son's mother was that he couldn't bear the thought that the child was the product of a fairly casual encounter, rather than something uniquely special, consciously created. For him, conception is something that you enter into with great deliberation. And yet for me, the reality of conception wasn't like that at all.

The same with his relationship with his American girlfriend Jodi. It wasn't actually spectacular. Good enough maybe and yet, as I understand it from the way he described it, fairly mundane. In his mind he has subsequently converted it into something beyond all other relationships and is consumed with remorse that he didn't have the sense to realise it at the time. Which has the effect of diminishing or belittling all other relationships, thereby acting as an insulation from further involvement and hurt.

He describes his son Charlie very positively and yet I know that deep down, he's disappointed at not experiencing some sort of unique vibe because the child is his flesh and blood. Which leads me to wonder if he's fundamentally disappointed in his own <u>inability</u> to experience such feelings both in relation to Charlie and interpersonally. He can be a great lover, but can he truly love ?

*My experience of parental bonding, is that it is largely generated initially by the total dependence of the infant on those caring for it and the total commitment of the parents to the child. I may have been conscious of 'ownership' in those early days - 'this is **my** child' but I don't remember ever having strong feelings about the flesh and blood bit. I certainly didn't expect to reproduce clones of myself. Subsequently tiny babies become very much their own person with varying and finally diminishing needs for caring* *adults who don't by that time need to be <u>actual</u> father and mother but simply a totally devoted person. I think Chris is disappointed not to have uniquely paternal feelings for this boy, but how can he when he's missed out completely on the first seven years of his life ? Not to mention the fact that his own experience of being fathered was practically non– existent as his father died when he was tiny and his mother never had another partner. He had no role model to learn from, no grounding in being fathered or in fathering. Apart from this, there is the fact that a father is by definition, not simply a progenitor but also a person in relation to a mother. Chris can be a wonderfully positive person for this boy to identify with at a time when he needs him, but not a father.*

At first I felt jealous of this relationship, especially as Chris seemed as usual, to have such an idealised expectation of it. But now I think he views it more realistically and yet again may have to cope with a degree of disappointment. Our own relationship can be seen, in this light, as an exceptional friendship because we share so many tastes, interests and sensitivities as well as being open and available to each other. We are also realistic about its potential and try not to build too many castles in the air and yet, by this very realism, I fear he may yet again undervalue what we have, and be therefore unable to commit himself. Can the leopard change his spots ? I doubt it.

Anyway, enough of this. I send you much love and hope that we shall be able to meet again soon. From Lizziex

Meanwhile, I had made arrangements to stay with Chris for a couple of nights when I went for my job interview, something we were both looking forward to.

February 1983 Suffolk

Hi Liz!

It doesn't matter about your arriving before I get back from my London visit on Sunday. You know where to find the key and I'll leave the heating and immersion on so that we can have lots of hot water and slippery soapings eh ? Yum. Read a film revue the other day in which a girl bathes and washes her pants while wearing them - gave me a nice buzz that idea ! And I'll get some food in for supper on Sunday eve - we really must try and eat something first ! - Not to mention booze a little ..... shall we sleep downstairs in front of the fire or upstairs bedroom ? Perhaps there on Monday after watching tele - just to prolong the ecstasy ?! Could try and make the damp patch 18" wide ! Or three or four in different places. Must have you on pillows this time - bottom and hips well up, nice solid deep mountings .... oooooooh .... how quickly I get side-tracked. It's that picture you sent me Liz, of the lady looking just like you after an hour of love-making ..... soft satisfied smile ..... tousled hair over moist face ..... hips thrust up, camiknickers falling away to reveal that secret, most private of places, the hint of swollen tenderness, of it having been plundered and worked and used until it flooded down the creases in your thighs and round your bottom making your underwear stiff with juices, everything a lovely wreckage of throbbing heat and spread stickiness, open and gorged upon like over-ripe fruit, its

324

secret yielded, spread, shared, both seducing and seduced. Must stop this, I'm nearly busting my zip ! Talk about your lost youth - I wish it was ten years ago when I could screw and come and come and come until my scrotum felt turned inside out like a pocket and it was just jerkings and thumps but with nothing left to spurt out. Now I'm far too quickly satisfied - wheezy to boot, with fags and no jogging since I started teaching. Perhaps that's why I talk and think and write about it so much ! Anticipation being almost as important as the act itself.

Cracked hands in contrast. Pain, discomfort, cold. Always think of Evans, one of Scott's final N. Pole party (who fell and banged his head and died before the final tragic camp) - he was repairing a sledge when the chisel slipped and very badly gouged his thumb which refused to begin to heal in all that fearsome cold. Think of it, pulling the sledge, sealskin boots stiff with ice, likewise, ice stiff sleeping bags. Trying to cook. And rig a tent. And keep cheerful. "The Worst Journey in the World" was what Apsley Cherry-Garrard called his book about it. Can never forget. Read it. You'll never feel really cold in England again.

OK Finis. Except to say that I think you were probably right in your analysis of the Rintoul lady's comments. Hope this finds you where it leaves me - hot, dribbly and gently throbbing ! See you soon XC

February 1983 Hampshire

Dearest Chris - how typically thoughtful of you to telephone this evening, rejoicing at the news that the job was offered to me. In spite of this, I had the usual feeling of wading back into treacle as I returned home - up to my neck in it. So it was like having a lifeline thrown to me from the unsticky beyond, hearing you talk about the everyday this's and that's which continue to happen when I'm not there. Told Stella and Pete about the job when I got back because the children were round there playing. This was great because I didn't have to bottle it all up and they said "Yes, that's the _real_ world", where people are direct and honest in their negotiations and you don't need to be always wondering what their ulterior motives are. Greg and Daisy too were curious, wondering how I'd travel three hours to work every day (ie imagining I'd be going from here) and Zarek also wanted to know about it but even though he was being reasonable (and had cooked a tasty roast chicken), I didn't dare go into details for fear of what he might do - it's so sad that we cannot trust each other enough to talk sensibly about arrangements.

Found myself giving very serious thought on the way home to the possibility of attempting to re-open negotiations now when I feel my position is so much stronger. Dare I suggest that he should reconsider letting me take the girls while he has Greg ? Which would be for his sake but not for Greg's. Then when I collected Greg from his friend's house, he was _so_ pleased to see me, so loving, said he'd missed me - but he'd miss Zarek too if he wasn't there. Oh the dilemma.

And I can't tell you what a struggle I had upstairs in your bedroom this morning before leaving, with the BIG weep. Didn't want to appear all tear-sodden and sorry for myself because what can you do? More cuddles, more comfort,

326

more don't worry it'll be alright in the end ? - But there <u>are</u> imponderables especially in relation to my feelings for you - but perhaps not the other way round. And holding on to that kite while we were out in the meadow just before I left, I wanted to stretch out my arm and feel myself lifted off the face of the earth to disappear into space, like one of Chagall's paintings ….. can't help feeling like 'your woman' when I am with you - that's the trouble. And yet I know that as far as you are concerned, I shall be just another baby that goes out with the bathwater.

Great big soggy blobble of tears bouncing up and down inside me all the way home. Mostly in my chest but then down to my tummy and up to my head, coming out in dribs and drabs, like squeezing out something the size of a rabbit pellet when you're constipated. Thought of being just another of Chris Daly's mistresses littering the countryside and at that, I nearly had diarrhoea if you see what I mean. That's what frightens me.

If I just about managed to put a brave face on things this morning before leaving, I know I'm not doing it now but please understand that I don't <u>want</u> you to send reassurances or to run the risk of being insincere. I <u>know</u> that your impartiality is as much for my own sake as yours and I appreciate it as such. Things <u>will</u> sort themselves out in time - don't be hurt by anything that I've said - it isn't meant that way as you well know.

So all I can do now is say yet again, thank you. For coming back on Sunday night, for all that happened in between that and taking me to Bury on Monday, for the long boring wait at the hospital while I was being interviewed , for lovely breakfasts, lunches, suppers, for leaving me to sleep after I'd woken you at quarter to three, for helping me to waken in the nicest way possible. (Didn't tell you how much I enjoyed that special warmth and closeness !) For the trip to see the school where I learnt that the state system could have quite a lot going for it and for kites which are so much more than bits of strong, cane, paper and plastic bobbing around in the wind and sunshine.

Lots of love Chris from 'your woman' in Hampshire ! Lizziex

33. Dreams and depression

It was inevitable that the effects of the prolonged stresses and strains I was experiencing should contaminate my subconscious. It reacted with a string of terrifying nightmares that bubbled to the surface and terrorised me when I was at my most vulnerable, asleep in my bed. They were so convincing that it felt as though I was awake, living a different reality.

One night I found myself walking up the road from Stella and Pete's house, trying to get home. It was very dark and one part of the road was quite eerie with poor lighting and the pavement rutted with thick dark hedges and trees on either side of the road. I desperately wanted to get home but didn't seem to be able to make much progress and couldn't breathe enough to be able to walk very fast. I could hear heavy breathing, flesh creepingly heavy breathing coming up behind me, and a vague shadowy presence dressed in long drab raincoat, with a hideous face and spikey green luminous hair, catching up on me. It vanished almost before it could be defined leaving me still struggling to get home. Then there was another one a bit further back but again catching up on me and then more and more dotted around behind me but all getting ever closer while I struggled to get home to safety. In the end I must have woken up because I can remember consciously trying to push the image out of my mind by thinking about Chris and lying in bed beside him.

Another night I felt as though someone was coming into the bedroom, a bristly, rustly feeling in the air which made me prickle all over. I thought it must be Zarek with the breadknife. Imagined grappling with him, knowing how much stronger he was than me. Somehow managed to escape and dashed to the bathroom, the only room in the house with a lock on the door. Jumped out of the window to the grass and bushes below then on to a different dreamland where I was finding myself in close confrontation with the man from the paper shop over the road. A pathetic fellow, a widower, always a bit unkempt, unshaven, smelling of alcohol - lonely I suppose, always chatty when we went into his shop where he gave Alice sweets. But there he was, pressing himself up against me by our garden wall in broad daylight saying "Come on, it's alright really," and me struggling and fighting to get away …….. ugh. Only a dream …….

Day dreams are of course a different matter. Dreaming of chat and fun and total ease of communication. Dreaming of the passion of our love-making, even though a little of me is holding back from total abandonment because of the impossibility of total commitment. Chris has a lot of me, but not all because that is how it has to be. I can still dream though of being gently unwrapped and put to bed. Of long looks and tender explorations with lips and tongue and finger tips. And then a closer union, the intensity of Chris' body in mine and so to that different sort of dreamland…….

I wondered about Zarek's dreams especially when I caught him looking at me one evening with such penetrating distaste that it sent shivers up my spine. It was like the hypnotic gaze of a snake at its victim and all I could do was stare back. What was he dreaming of then ?

There were days when I longed from early morning to be alone with my pad and pen, needing so much the escape and brief freedom that it afforded me. Instead I would moon around, dreaming, staring into space, weeping intermittently, wondering what to do next but never getting on with it. Windows need washing ? Well, maybe I'll get round to it tomorrow, and so on. The house/ the whole situation reeked of emotional stagnation and decay which became almost intolerable. My brief escapes seemed to make it worse and having the job, although good in itself, made everything harder to tolerate, harder to endure the passage of time. It was easy to jump into my car and escape to Chris' house in Suffolk, to take pretty clothes and try and look nice. Easy to be happy and responsive when I was away but that was the dream world. The real one was one of hatred and misery and despair. Zarek's terminating comment in one of our regular major rows was that I wasn't even good enough to smell his smells. Which might have been funny were it not so intensely offending. Which he meant it to be.

One of my local friends had said "I can't imagine how you manage; you still seem to be smiling and joking about things" but I found the public mask an easy one to wear. At home it was slutty depressed me, in tatty jeans, day in day out, shapeless washed out sweater, hair scraped back into a rubber band, house and garden neglected too. Tried, really tried to clean up properly after each weekend but with messy children and messy uncaring insulting husband, there was little incentive to make the place nice.

Thank God the children didn't notice. Daisy had stopped bedwetting and Alice's behaviour had improved a lot, possibly because she was more able to communicate her needs and understand those of others. She no longer wet her pants and sometimes chose to sleep in the bed beside mine although during the night would decamp to join her father. Thought of dismantling the cot and passing it on to Bronwen's Big Baby who was rapidly outgrowing his carry cot. The fact that Zarek and I seemed to be suffering more suggested that maybe we were absorbing more of the anxiety but it didn't seem to be doing us any good at all.

During this period in early March, the strain and uncertainty about what I could or should do in pursuing my quest for freedom from this crushing relationship, almost overwhelmed me. I looked at the main issue of what to do about the children from every whichway and continued to be agonisingly perplexed. With the likelihood of Greg getting a school place in Portsmouth, I knew that the alternative in Ipswich had to be pursued so that I had something comparable to offer when it came to the court case, so there was no time to waste. BUT might Zarek perhaps agree to him staying with him and the girls coming with me, if it would save him the time, energy and money required to fight it out in court ? My solicitor was non-committal but agreed to consult 'the other side unofficially and unprejudicially.' Having discussed this option one afternoon, it made me feel as though the bottom had dropped out of my world. It was teatime with the children about to come in from school and then Zarek home from work. It was unthinkable that any of them should see me in a disintegrated state so I'd tried to keep out of the way and hope that they wouldn't notice I was tear-sodden.

It didn't take me long to realise that there was no way that Zarek would be capable of compromise. It simply wasn't in his nature and my next turn of thought was that perhaps he'd been right all along and that I should leave him and the children in their familiar world, clear off to my newly acquired job and hospital flat and visit as often as I could. My only emotional possession in that event would have been the initiative to come in and out of their lives as often as possible. In victory, I'd imagined that Zarek would be supremely generous but then I'd wondered how I could have given him that satisfaction and that it would have been better to do away with myself completely leaving a sealed letter of explanation for the children when they were old enough to understand. I didn't of course. Thinking about the muddles he got into, the complications with child-minders, all the things I was forever mending, toys, clothes domestic equipment, the constantly surging tide of mess in the house that he never did anything about , the isolation of his kind of existence, not to mention the insidious influence of all his quirky ideas which I could see would increase as he got older, and my reaction was a huge OH NO. Torment.

Chris too was struggling but for different reasons. Although his days were filled with creativity, both making pots and with the children he taught, as well as in his social life, there was hollowness in the centre and his commitment to me was forever ambivalent. My days were full of the pain of an unhappy marriage and the consequences of its dissolution for our children, but with a solid core of love for Chris. He richly communicated support and sympathy as well as letter-sex but never love, whilst he obsessed about Jodi. There was endless discussion between us about where a future with her might have led, but no consideration of any future for us. He often talked about suicide, a bottle of whisky and a ton of pills on some remote hillside, seeing it as a 'tidy' way of escaping from his sense of failure, wasted years and opportunities.

"......a successful acknowledgement to the world that at least if I failed at living tidily, and failed at digesting life and communicating what I am and see and feel and think, I was at least able to close the door firmly and leave no mess and litter (like the scattered feeling of others I've left torn and shattered down the years). So often I feel I can't beat Churchill's Black Dog - so go join him – eternal sleep ? Rest ? Relief ? Ah, there's the rub as Hamlet knew. Would it be that ? Or some kind of perpetual hell ? What's the reality ? Joy or desperation ? Starting and ending always seem to be the worst and when I'm there it outweighs all the happy times which have always been stolen, as with married Louise or threaded with pain, like with Jodi. She needed all of me and I was just unable to give myself completely."

I had challenged this, challenged the idea that what was neat and tidy for him, would be the same for those he left behind. As far as I could see, the majority of his many friends would have been unaware of the depths of his desperation and therefore unable to understand why he had resorted to such an extreme final act. He was seeing it as a 'proper' and appropriate resolution to his problems. To everyone else it would be interpreted through their own perceptions, firstly of tremendous loss and then of sadness that he couldn't have somehow hung on to his vibrant life, giving the rest of us some justification for hanging on to our own miserable existences. Chris was seeing it as a successful death after a failed life whereas many people would have interpreted it the other way round, a terrible waste of a life full of creativity, stimulation, fun, colour and love. As others saw it, it would have been a successful life, savagely terminated. At a cynical level , to me it was a pretty gutless sacrifice. If he really wanted to make a WORTHWHILE sacrifice, he could have rushed to help me with my three kids. Which would have been as near to purgatory as he was ever likely to get !

I had written to friend Hilda without apology, describing these various miseries but knowing full well that she thought my really morbid letters the most interesting. And there was other news to share. Greg had been accepted by the Portsmouth Grammar School.

Both he and Zarek were beside themselves with delight and I have never seen such a look of ecstasy on that little boy's face as when I gave him the news. (Well, one other time perhaps, when I told him I was expecting Alice.) For me, joy at his success was tempered by the realisation of all the implications. The possibility I'd already discussed with my solicitor, to take the girls and leave Greg, now seemed to make sense. It was rational but the whole idea left me absolutely choked and reinforced my resolve to attempt to get Greg a place at the equivalent school in Ipswich. Then I discovered that Zarek had passed on the news to Mr. Dunlop, the Court Welfare Officer, presumably on the assumption that it strengthened the case for the children to remain with him. Mr. Dunlop's response was cautious, saying that even though he appreciated Greg's success, he couldn't ignore the headmistress' reaction when she'd heard we'd applied to the Grammar School, that it was the worst possible option for our creative son.

Zarek had ignored this and talked all the time about his 'Grammar School Boy' and how he should behave and what he would learn, echoed by Greg "I'm a GS Boy". In a village of barely 1,000 families with at least half of the fathers employed by a mammoth computer company or officers in the Navy, it was inevitable that educational ambition was a hot topic and everyone knew who had applied to the good schools and who had been successful. This didn't deter Zarek from suggesting a party for all those who had succeeded, regardless of the feelings of those who hadn't. I can't pretend that I too wasn't very proud of my son but in the circumstances, it all seemed like a horrible mess. Could I really confront Greg with the possibility that he wasn't going to that school after all ?

34. Marking time

March 1983 Hampshire

Hi You –

Shouldn't be writing now - too much to do, but here I am again - like Moira Shearer in her red shoes which wouldn't let her stop dancing. Remember my mother refusing to take me to see the film because I'd been naughty but perhaps it was a lucky escape for both of us. When I eventually saw it years later, it turned out to be only slightly less than boring and interminable. I'd never have sat through it as an eight year old !

Everybody out this morning by 8.45 so stripped our living room chairs to wash the covers. It's a hate job because the cushions inside are just great loose bags of foam pieces which shed profusely and cling to absolutely everything. The seats themselves look a bit like uncooked brown bread rolls when they are clean and plumped up but getting them apart reminds me of a picture which was in our Children's Encyclopaedia - Laocoon and his sons, wrestling with the Hydra ! I can remember once when Australian friend James was staying with us and I'd had to wash one because it had been wee'd on. I'd got to the stage of attempting to reassemble it when seeing me struggling because they are such a tight fit, he'd said "Can I help you ?" The least practical of men - a cup of tea yes, a boiled egg no, and he was offering to HELP - something Zarek had never done.

He's still reading your letters by the way. I think he imagines I have a secret plan to rush off and live with you and that I shall say one thing in court and then do the opposite. Which is _stupid_. Whatever I do, I'm not going to lie about it - too much is at stake for that and the court has to have accurate information to make any sort of reasonable decision. I'm sure he's looking for clues of further deception - it must be so frustrating not finding any, not to mention wading through all the paper pillow talk !

Odd the things we think of. I realised today that I'd never heard the word 'fart' until I was about fifteen and I definitely didn't say it or refer to its existence for at least another couple of years. It was certainly never uttered at home. Farts were things to be sat on very firmly, or to wince at with embarrassment if my mother (who seemed more prone) inadvertently let one escape. My greatest mortification at school would have been to have farted in the school hall during assembly and I can remember sitting there desperately concentrating with my little bottom pinched together as tight as it would go, praying that it wouldn't slip out. The next worst mortification was being in assembly without a handkerchief and, with one's head bowed in 'prayer' feeling a wet trickle coursing down the inside of one's nose. Surreptitiously I'd lift my head up to try and slow the flow, then furtively lick my upper lip and possibly resort eventually to a stifled sniff and finally, shame of shames, the sleeve. How we suffered in the pursuit of being ladylike !

Zarek says I am humourless but you make me laugh SO much - I mean _really_ laugh. I've spent years pretending to be amused at his intellectual jokes - he can make a clever play on words and has wit, but a real gutsy guffaw ? Never. Or hardly ever. Also envy your sense of style with scene setting - you always get it so right, the look, the feel, the smell of things and the sounds too. I'm not very good at it but my architect boyfriend had that skill. Kidded myself with Zarek that his totally foreign, different generation ideas could surely be adapted, but the compromises were always uneasy ones. He used to take a Polish newspaper called Dziennik Polski which had a fashion column in it. In the early days, he used to tell me how beautiful I'd look in the different styles but walking around Hampstead looking like a Russian babushka was not my idea of fashion when everyone else was wearing miniskirts and Courege boots and had a Vidal Sassoon haircut.

Thinking about the desperation you experienced last week, that everything was so futile, I'm wondering if it isn't something most people go through at some stage in their lives ? At the start of a committed relationship, there's the stimulation and excitement of planning for the future - the great unwritten book. Then there's the delight and anxiety of caring for babies and little children - totally dependent. But once they begin to spread their wings, wives begin to get bored and husbands find that the immediate necessity of providing for the family lacks its urgency, even though the costs and demands can escalate in range and complexity. As children's emotional dependency diminishes, their practical needs become those of adults but their ability to meet them doesn't necessarily keep pace. All of which makes the likelihood of tensions across the whole family seem inevitable with everyone having to make adjustments.

I'd guess that some people experience feelings of self-doubt at this time - has it all been worth the hassle ? And I'm sure that some come up with the answer, no. You have avoided the relationship/child-rearing responsibilities but are still taxed by the idea that the experiences you have had have not been ultimately satisfying. It might be argued that you still have the opportunity to seek other successes, as do any of us in different ways. When you told me about your friends who seemed to be taking each other for granted, I wondered how on earth one can avoid it, how it's possible to sustain momentum in a relationship. If you try too hard to be independent of each other, you can lose sight of why you are together. Hopefully one can learn to work with a partner so that the domestic side of things functions as efficiently, effectively and pleasantly as possible. One can also pursue interests both together and separately so that the 'taking for granted' bit becomes positively useful in some areas, creating opportunities for development in others. We each have to work it out for ourselves, but is it fair to expect someone you get to know so well over a long period of time to be permanently exciting or stimulating company ? And if they aren't then what can take its place ? The comfort and security of knowing exactly where you are with someone or alternatively, the excitement and risks associated with an affair ? There must be other options.

You're always saying how sane and well-balanced I seem, but if this is the case, why couldn't I have found a sane and well-balanced husband instead of being in the mess I'm in now ? Eh ?

Stupid of me yesterday. Went out without a coat - <u>knew</u> I'd be cold but didn't think it would matter. So guess who's got a nose that is running like a tap and a head that feels as though it's stuffed with cotton wool - no prizes ! Thought I'd go to bed early because of feeling rough but then remembered that the chair covers needed finishing off and that I'd got the ingredients for a cake recipe I'd been going to try for ages, so here I am as usual, approaching 11.00 pm - cake in oven, chair covers sorted, scribbling. Wonder if my pen is taking over my brain ?!

Zarek is being very quiet and withdrawn at the moment and we're managing to be quite nice to each other. Maybe at last he is confronting reality - I wonder what the outcome will be ? All loving Chris, your Lizzie.

Beyond belief - Late March 1983

35. Reality unanticipated

The reality Zarek was confronting was very far from what I'd anticipated - how misguided one's assumptions can be. Thinking that one knows what is going on in someone else's mind and making decisions on that basis is a very risky strategy. Indeed, on this basis, should my trust of Chris have been so unequivocal ?

15th. March became a very odd day indeed. It began in the evening when I overheard a bit of Zarek's telephone conversation, "..........going in for investigation........." it went and although I didn't hear much, it was clear that he meant hospital rather than anywhere else. "Are you ill ?" I asked him when he'd put the phone down, which he totally denied. He then said that he'd been told to go to Queen Alexandra Hospital either that evening or first thing the next day, which didn't sound to me like planned elective surgery. He said he'd be going in on Tuesday and coming out on Thursday. And so off he went the next day, delivering Alice to the crèche en route. I didn't know what to do or feel. Admittedly he'd been looking quite unwell and his skin was an unhealthy sallow shade. One of his work colleagues telephoned that evening, anxious to know what was happening as Zarek had said nothing. We commiserated on our mutual ignorance and I spent the rest of the next day, poring over Zarek's medical books and trying to put two and two together. In the end I decided he must have gone in for a liver biopsy, which as it happened was quite wrong. I had a confusing search that evening when I phoned the hospital as

I had no idea which ward he was in and if you ask for someone called Dr. So-and-so at a hospital they understandably think you mean a member of staff. Eventually I was told he was under an Ear, Nose and Throat specialist who had "just wanted to have a look down his throat." Rang his colleague again and discovered that Zarek had been in touch with him. I was right about the biopsy but not its location. Lumps in ……. the throat. All sorts of serious possibilities.

And so many thoughts that day. I was curious more than anything, a little bit worried too but not in the way a loving wife would feel for her husband under such circumstances. Having spent the previous twelve months detaching myself emotionally from Zarek, it was hardly surprising that I had few sympathetic vibes for him, just a sort of normal compassion as for anyone suffering or in pain. My mind had been busily running over all the possibilities, both good and bad. If it was nothing serious (and I couldn't stop myself thinking it could be a physical manifestation of all the stress and anxiety he'd been through), then the worst it could have done was to delay things a bit. That was bad enough. If, to go to the other extreme, it was something terminal, well at least it would be finite. Yes I wished him out of my life, but not dead, not like that. I guessed that under those circumstances, I would stick around with the children to try and bring some happiness or at least reconciliation, into such final awfulness. On the other hand, it might be an illness which was curable but with the possibility of recurrence and prolonged poor health. What might I have done then - leave him to suffer, knowing he couldn't cope with the children, so alone at such a time, and for how long ? Terrible thoughts, among many.

The outcome to the biopsy took time and in any case, the nurse I spoke to at the hospital was extremely cagey, which may have been normal confidentiality caution but I was his wife after all. I guessed she'd been told to be. I attempted to phone the consultant but whenever I did I got the same evasive reaction, either 'not available', or 'in theatre' and he never returned my calls.

My feeling during this period was one of entrapment rather than sympathy, that Zarek in a particularly macabre way was still calling the shots. As each day passed I became more and more convinced that his illness was a sort of solution to his problems. Not that they didn't exist, they definitely did, but that in some mysterious way, his body had taken over what his mind could no longer control. That it had created a way out, of sorts …………

That evening I took the children to visit him in hospital and for the first time for many months was able to look into his eyes, such sad, old eyes with nothing left there. I couldn't help feeling pity and sorrow for this ongoing suffering. A sort of 'so be it' feeling too - no fight left there, only resignation.

The next day was a mad dash, with Alice joining me some time during the night and then very awake from 5.15 onwards. There was nothing for it but to give her breakfast, which was what she was used to after all. I then put us both back to bed despite her protests. What she did between

5.30 and 6.30 I'd no idea but I slept which was good enough to see me through the day. I was just getting up some time after that when Greg appeared fully dressed, bearing a tray with two slices of bread, thickly spread with butter and marmalade, a glass of milk and the newspaper. So proud of himself, bringing Mummy breakfast. Got the children off to school and then went down to the hospital again with Alice to see Zarek. He was stern and non-committal, looking as though he'd had a recent rendezvous with a vampire, one small puncture hole in his neck, some obvious swelling presumably after various manipulations and difficulty in speaking and swallowing. He refused to be drawn on his condition and was tired, so our visit was brief.

Back home and just before lunch there was a phone call from Greg's school to say that he had been in the sick room most of the morning and could I collect him. I just couldn't face that as well and with only the vaguest of symptoms, not in evidence that morning, suggested he had his lunch before I rang again to see how he was, by which time he had recovered, thank goodness. As soon as Daisy was home, I had to take them to the baths where Alice had a swimming lesson and after a rather scrambled meal, bundled them all back into the car and to the hospital again. Driving was wet and nasty but Zarek was pleased to see them, and they him. When I asked the ward sister about the tests and when he was likely to be home I was again stonewalled, which must have been overheard by one of his colleagues who arrived to visit as we were leaving. This particular young man had always struck me as pompous and patronising at the best of times, but the humiliation of him overhearing me being refused very basic information about my husband's condition, sent a bubble of rage bouncing around inside my chest.

Lovely though it was, not to have Zarek's intimidating presence in the house, I was feeling lonely, hopeless and stuck by uncertainty, unable to plan anything and forced to live my life, minute by minute without any sense of a future. It reminded me of an old film by Bunuel called the Exterminating Angel. A group of Spanish people start off having an elegant and sophisticated dinner party. After a while they find they are unable to leave the room in which it is being held. First of all they appear to make plausible excuses to stay in the room but it becomes apparent that there is an unknown force actually preventing them from leaving. Over a period of time they are reduced to savage behaviour in their attempts to survive, and some of them even die in the process. Eventually they work out what they have to do to break the spell and escape, and the whole town goes to the Cathedral to give thanks for their deliverance. As the priest is about to leave the chancel having given a final benediction, he turns to say another prayer ……. and the whole situation, this time with everyone having to remain in the church, is repeated. That's me. Stuck. Every time I think that I can move on, something else happens to prevent it……….

For a couple of days, we all enjoyed the freedom which Zarek's absence afforded us, even though I was conscious that my reaction to his illness could well have appeared callous and unfeeling. I didn't want to be like that but because Zarek wasn't sharing his problems, it prevented me from showing any compassion. He simply wouldn't talk about it and so we had to continue going our sad and independent ways. Coming to terms with that was a struggle. I decided that I had to make things happen rather than drifting on without purpose so invited Stella, Pete and the three children to lunch the final day that Zarek was in hospital.

I got the place tidy and then whisked my lot out for a mystery trip to run off some of their excess energy. On a back road to Chichester there was a distant castle that we had often wondered about so we set off to find it. It turned out to be a brick and flint tower, roughly mid 19th century, ruined, horribly vandalised and filled with every conceivable variety of junk and much broken glass. Fortunately the children didn't bother to read and question the two foot high red daubs round the inside, "Sharon sucks cocks" etc. and we didn't stay long to explore - too hazardous in my opinion with so much tangled barbed wire, stinging nettles , used condoms and other rubbish around. No primroses, but some newborn lambs in one field nearby and lots of muddy puddles which the children enjoyed, plus the various county types in their Barbours and country tweeds walking Labradors and retrievers along the same path. Lunch was relaxed and easy but Pete didn't come as he had a lot of 'work' to do at home. Couldn't help wondering what sort of work he had to do on a Sunday and if he was frying other fish, but wasn't going to rouse Stella's suspicions.........

36. Diagnosis

March 1983 Hampshire

D'you know Chris, I simply hadn't bargained for this. Hadn't bargained for the total shock of today's news. I suppose it's a question of taking in new perspectives which I daresay will sort themselves out in time but I do feel completely shattered.

Here's Zarek looking ill and obviously experiencing discomfort in relation to his neck/throat - but behaving as though <u>nothing</u> has happened. This morning he mentioned making arrangements for Easter and the summer, the first time he's <u>ever</u> taken the initiative about this and I now know damn well that he's got CANCER and that he's going to take a month off work for radio-therapy and try to pretend it's holiday and that he feels alright. When it'll make him feel tired and sick and ill and if he has to have chemo, his hair will probably fall out. Isn't that terrible.

He's got cancer, I keep saying to myself. Zarek has got cancer. And it feels odd, like when I first started to use the word 'divorce'. But it soon gets incorporated into the vocabulary. Even if I confront Zarek with the knowledge that I know what the score is, I <u>know</u> he won't allow me to show any kindness. He'll say it's insincere - that I only want his money etc. etc. when like Joan, his colleagues wife, who had the decency to phone me today and tell me his diagnosis when no-one else would, my main concern is for the *children. When it was just a question of divorce ('just' - ha ! how perspectives change), I felt that if I could get things straight for me, then it would also work for the children but suddenly all the priorities are changed and I feel that things have to be seen to be right by them. They would never understand or forgive me for taking them away from Zarek at such a time. Indeed, could I forgive myself ? I doubt it.*

And I feel so upset that he won't allow me to show any compassion even though he's had none for me. And that yet again, he's got everyone dancing to his tune, not allowing me to share the responsibility for how this should be handled - especially in relation to the children. Of course it's early days yet and maybe we should try to be optimistic about the outcome - I guess his colleagues are just as shocked and confused about how they should react. But my initial feeling is anger with them. They've all heard him going on in the last few months, seen his 'red book' about me etc., expressed secret distaste at the way he's gone about things and yet there they are, sitting back on their bloody Hippocratic oaths saying that they mustn't tell me anything if he doesn't wish it. I feel angry that their Hippocratic oath doesn't seem to stop them telling their wives - but not me. They are my children too, and I have a right to be involved in these decisions. The situation is neither finite nor absolute but it has to be flexible according to these new circumstances which have changed everything totally.

Faced with the actuality, I know that I couldn't leave if Zarek were dying. The least I could do for the children would be to perpetuate the idea that Mummy and Daddy had a decent relationship rather than tearing the whole thing apart at such a time. And although I don't know the prognosis, a barrage of X-rays around the thyroid and pituitary glands <u>can't</u> be good news.

Asked Zarek about the Easter holiday today, visiting my parents and he gave a most emphatic and aggressive "NO". Which of course I don't have to accept - except that the whole situation has taken on another dimension. My impulse is to fly over to see you this weekend before he gets immersed in his treatment and really can't cope with the children. Could you possibly cope with me at such short notice ? Providing you weren't out <u>all</u> the time I'd be very good and quiet and not get in the way. But perhaps that's awful of me rushing off when he is so ill. I don't know. I don't know anything really. I don't want it to be like this, I really don't but if he has to die his way out of it, please God let it be quick.

Suddenly the reality of the cessation of life actually hits me and it's so much more momentous than ever I realised - all that I've ever said before has been verbal juggling. I am sorry.

Please keep this inky thread running - it's my lifeline. Love Lizzie.

….. can you imagine if it was you, or me, having to say "I've got cancer", anticipating the months of increasing pain, the useless treatments and the ultimate fearful dread ?

Zarek seems unmoved. I can't believe it.

Hi. Don't know if I'm going to be able to stay awake long enough to finish this but I'll try. Felt in need of a sedative so cracked open the last can of barley wine but it may get the better of me before I finish scribbling.

Awful day really (apart from talking to you on the phone). Rang Mrs. Jennifer who came round late morning - the early part having been spent mostly in tears. Zarek pretended to go to work but I know damn well he didn't and probably had his first radiotherapy session this afternoon, without apparent ill-effect. Yet again, tried to get hold of the ENT consultant who did the investigation but he was again thoroughly unavailable and hasn't yet responded to any of the messages I've left for him. Tomorrow I see my solicitor who may have some ideas and also my GP who may be able to discover how serious the condition is. That's what I need to know - if anyone can tell……..

Mrs. Jennifer was shattered today by my news and immediately thought of all the unthinkable implications - she is a dear stalwart soul - I don't know what I'd do without her. Stella is super too - very down to earth and practical, and always ready to help if it's needed. Zarek seemed relieved this evening - maybe the treatment, or the news wasn't as bad as he expected. Funny really that he's just as nasty to me but somehow I can tolerate it better without rising to the bait. Just wish he'd shut up that's all.

Pray that I can get away for a flying and all too brief visit on Friday - I feel that I shall go mad if I don't. And hope I haven't messed up any of your weekend plans. Might be better if you have a secret assignation, to hang on to as I fear my libido is at a low ebb and is likely to need more than a little nurturing ....

OK - so I'm now barley-wine boozed ! Hope to see you. Must. Lots of love, Lizziex

March 1983 Hampshire

I suppose I really ought to try harder to control this writing. I'd thought I wouldn't tonight but here I am again, spinning my lifeline out of ink like some quirky spider. And dragging you into my web too. Can't see it getting any better. Which is all the more reason for feeling so grateful to you for tolerating it so nobly. OK, OK so I've helped you ? No, not really - haven't made any real differences to your miseries have I. But we just plod on.

But there <u>are</u> moments of elation. Didn't tell you that I yelled my way across London Bridge and then into Sudbury on Friday night. Nice thing about being alone encased in a car. I yelled at the top of my voice - can't even remember <u>what</u> I yelled but the happy feeling coming down that last bit of road from Halstead is always there, past the garage, into Ballingdon Street, under the bridge - and whoopee, here I am ! Reminds me of a song by Dory Previn who was doing *the same thing, driving along and screaming - "I was doing it alone, I was doing it alone, I was doing it alone in a twenty mile zone, I was doing it alone, I was doing it alone I was screaming." So it's not just me !*

But then, the downside. Numb with misery. That's the expression for my feelings, coming back here. Not a good journey with rain all the way, quite a few hold-ups due to road works and a massive detour off the M11 in Chelmsford which meant that I had to trail into London via Brentwood and Gants Hill. Didn't get home until 6.00 pm. Pandemonium with the children delighted to see me - Zarek is right - they are so special and precious and unique. He'd obviously coped without too much strain and all was fairly orderly in the house. Should I feel guilty about my brief desertion ? I guess a few eyebrows would be raised if people knew, but they know so little about this whole terrible tornado that has swept us into its vortex over the last few years. How could they ever understand ? Wonder what the treatment will do to him tomorrow ?

Two boiled eggs, two slices of toast, two doughnuts, half a Mars bar and a glass of whisky later. Feel as though I'm encased in cement (although managed to do my exercises!) Can't turn my head or open my eyes to see the future although I daresay I'll manage the odd squit and fart to keep the systems operational ! Velvety blood red flowers from your garden on our kitchen window sill to cheer me. Bottle of your homemade wine in the larder likewise. Heartfelt thanks Chris for doing what you could - it means so much to me - I wish I could be more for you..

356

Many kisses Chris and memories of warmth and holding and closeness and loving. From Lizzie.

By the beginning of April, Zarek was feeling better. Not better better, but more like his usual bossy, grumpy self. He'd been going on at me one evening for not getting up to look after Alice, which to an outsider, in the circumstances, would have seemed entirely understandable. "D'you think I've set it up ?" he demanded. "Have I ? <u>Have</u> I ?" But there was no point in reminding him how he had bossed and bullied his way through Greg's babyhood all those years ago so that I never felt I had any freedom of choice in anything, only ultimately the freedom to opt out. Which is why Alice had established a waking time of five o'clock and not seven. He had determined it, not Alice, or me.

Various treatments were lined up for Zarek who could no longer preserve his cloak of secrecy. The cancer was in his tonsil which according to his medical books was a site that was unlikely to metastasise and therefore wouldn't spread. His surgeon was optimistic that he had caught things in time and with my increasing sense of frustration, inertia and despair, I made a decision to go ahead with the custody case. I was fed up with feeling pathetic, miserable and oppressed by my wretched situation and the feeling that my life was slipping away. My solicitor had assured me that I could stop the process at any stage but even so, I hadn't bargained for the terrible guilt I experienced as he wrote all the bits about Zarek's illness into my affidavit. It seemed like an awful thing to do, but again I felt as though I had little choice. I had to get away from this man, this house, this situation somehow.

My love affair with Chris, although emotionally nourishing, couldn't provide for practical support like childcare, or a shoulder to cry on when frequently misery overwhelmed me, or objective analysis when I had lost the capacity to think clearly for myself. Immediate friends, Stella, Mrs. Jennifer and Hilda were my mainstays and wonderfully supportive. Hilda was often abroad but her letters prompted useful thinking that helped to carry me through the most turbulent times. This was what she wrote from Paris when she first heard about Zarek's illness.

"I can imagine what you are going through and am so, so sorry at the disruption of all your dreams. By the time you get this you will, no doubt have started to formulate some alternative plans and I'll probably hear about these when I get back home. So Zarek does have cancer. The big question, of course, is 'how long has he got' and the next is what on earth do you do. I've thought about you and the situation a lot so will tell you my feelings about various alternatives, although I know that emotionally you may well find them all unacceptable, particularly the first one. Which is - well, Zarek has 'won' hasn't he ? It's the supreme irony ! (And you must try not to let guilt become too great a factor.) By dying, he avoids the humiliation of losing the court case and he regains the sympathy of 'friends' who were obviously siding with you. And the intolerably bleak future which I foresaw for him as a "tomorrow, and tomorrow, and tomorrow creeps in this pretty pace from day to day to the last syllable of recorded time" becomes a rush to the finish. A horrible, painful finish, but at least a timely one. Yes, it's victory alright. I keep thinking how, about a year ago, I remember saying that I was worried that Zarek would take

his life if he didn't get the children. But what I'm thinking now, is perhaps you could bring yourself to make the victory complete by communicating (by letter I would guess) your sadness at what has happened and a reflection of the real happiness you experienced together. Is it possible, or is it me romanticising and sentimentalising the 'final reel' or last chapter ? I wouldn't expect much sincerity, but it wouldn't be dishonest, and maybe it would help his last days, or is it years ? That's the complicating factor. Then, you could ask, still in the letter, what he wanted you to do. The thought of you nursing him to the end is obviously detestable to both of you, yet what on earth is going to happen ?

It does seem that you must stay put where you are, and I wonder if you are coming round to that idea. I know you felt very adamant about leaving your home before this new turn of events, but with Zarek no longer around, your latent friendships would surely blossom and you <u>are</u> involved with village life and of course, there's the security for the children of their schools. And when Chris is free, to come and see you, he surely would. And maybe you could visit there …….. I don't know. This is probably irritating to read because inevitably you'll have been thinking about it endlessly too and you'll have more up-to-date information, so I'll stop. Love Hilda.

37. Easter

With Easter imminent, Chris was preoccupied with a walking holiday he'd planned in Northumberland, new lightweight boots he was thinking of buying, the cost of the coach fare, Easter cards he had to remember to send, cat food to buy for the cat sitter and then his plans for the following term's teaching. He made no secret, even in the face of the distressing situation that I was dealing with, of his need for self-containment. This he saw as cautious honesty, especially as Jodi was still there in his thoughts, a distraction from any other commitments. Our relationship definitely wasn't one-sided but for him, basking in my devotion, that was enough, even though he could see that it must hurt and frustrate me. The last thing he said he wanted me to feel was that I was being used, to bandage wounds or paper over cracks. Zarek he saw as arrogant and intransigent, especially when he asked, "Who will look after the children if I'm gone ?" as though once the divorce was completed, I ceased to exist. As far as Chris could see, proceeding with the divorce was a no-brainer, in spite of Zarek's illness.

During the Easter holiday, Greg's friend Michael had arrived for a sleep-over. It had poured with rain all morning but the children were fortunately happy enough playing and watching television. Michael had informed us that his Daddy was 'nearly' a millionaire, and demonstrated a slight preoccupation with his health, may be because he'd been told that Greg's Daddy was a 'doctor'. By the afternoon the rain had stopped so we headed for the Southsea roller skate

park and had a <u>lovely</u> time. Apart from it being slightly
boring going round and round and across and back again,
into the wind, followed by it, I think I could get very hooked
on roller skating. I launched myself at the barrier and edged
my way round very gingerly at first but soon found that such
skills as I had acquired in the distant days when my sister
and I used to go ice skating at Richmond Ice Rink on
Saturday mornings, stood me in good stead and by the end I
was sailing round with a fair degree of confidence.

At least I'd broken the ice, although the one time I fell over,
much to the children's delight, made me appreciate that it
really was advisable to stay upright if at all possible.
Children tumble easily and with little ill effect but I could see
that it wouldn't be at all difficult to break an arm or wrist
with an awkward fall. Daisy had been before and although
her little spindly legs looked hardly strong enough to cope
with the heavy boots, she managed quite well. Greg never
really got the hang of rolling on the wheels and spent all his
time either on his bottom or taking little pigeon steps, but
Michael, well, I've never seen anyone fall over so much ! He
refused to help himself by staying within arm's reach of the
barrier, but launched straight into the middle with great
abandon. And every time he fell, he doubled up in agony,
clasping some part of his anatomy like a fouled footballer. I
soon stopped commiserating with him.

By ten o'clock that evening I'd decided that he was an out
and out hypochondriac. They'd been asking all day for a
midnight feast so I had assembled three platefuls of goodies
and took them up at 9.30. Neither Daisy nor Michael had
gone to sleep so I reckoned that the sooner they got it over

with, the better. Poor old Greg, who was dead beat, was wrested from the arms of Morpheus to gobble his up and then dropped straight back off again or perhaps I should say, returned with relief. Ten minutes later began a half hour struggle to convince Michael that he was not mortally ill ("pains in my head and in my tummy") and that I had no intention of taking him home to his Mummy at that time of night (he was nine, a bit older than Greg). He was thrashing around getting hotter and hotter (no temperature), hyper-ventilating and absolutely refusing to listen to anything I had to say to him. In the end I was a little more than firm (he'd already woken Alice) which finally resulted in peace and quiet. Felt so thankful that whatever the deficiencies in their upbringing, at least my children seemed to be singularly unpreoccupied with their state of health. I don't think I'm unreasonably hard or unsympathetic and if I hadn't observed his behaviour throughout the day, I might have been more worried - an amazingly histrionic performance.

However, it was good to have the distraction.

Zarek had seen fit to divulge that in order to make absolutely certain there were no remaining malignant cells, when he had finished the radio therapy, after six weeks, he was to have another operation to remove the lymph glands in his neck. This I took to mean that he would try to put off final divorce activity for as long as possible in the hope of demonstrating recovery. As for the possibility of him being awarded custody of three children, when everybody knew there had to be at least a five year remission period after cancer, well, pigs might fly. My desperation to escape

362

increased a millionfold. Nothing that he had done until then had made me feel the hatred that I was experiencing, just when his very life was endangered. I wished that I could be objective and feel some sympathy for Zarek but all that was inside me at that point was pure rage. I wept in anger, not sorrow. Wept as I loaded the washing machine, wept as I made morning coffee, wept as I sat on the loo. I didn't know what to do or how to bear the prolonged pain. Bear it. To have to carry on doing things with the children, maybe starting Greg at his new school, living in a home that felt more like a tomb. It was more than I could stand. My mother had telephoned a bit earlier, voicing her feelings. At that time I still had enough left to be able to say no, when someone's life is really threatened, you can't wish them dead, but in my present desperation, I did and that was a truly terrible feeling to live with.

Zarek had promised a conversation. "We don't need intermediaries" he had said. But the conversation became his usual peroration on me being incapable of looking after the children, how incompatible they were with the 'Bohemian' life I had planned to lead, that "mark my words" Chris would be like a fourth child, that he "knew" me, knew what I was "really like and how useless and incompetent" I was. I knew he'd never miss me and the awful thing was that in my desperation, I felt as though I was turning into a self-fulfilling prophecy, as useless, incompetent and lazy as he described. There was only one point at which I felt I'd penetrated his cast-iron defences. "So you think I set it up ?" he'd said. "Set up having to attend to the children every night for the last eight years ?" - which wasn't true of course. "No" I'd replied. "What you set up was the feeling that you were the only person who was competent to deal with them." And that got to him, I'm sure it did.

Two Easter cards had arrived from long-standing and dear friends, one for each of us. Zarek must have written and told them of his illness because knowing that the divorce was in hand, they expressed concern for the "further sadness and stress" in our lives. They asked how I was coping in such an emotional maze, hoped the children were happy and that something kind would happen to cheer me. Sadly, I found that if shown pity it almost made it worse because it required one to acknowledge one's need for it. This was intensified after a visit to the hairdressers where I had to be an unwilling onlooker while a mother and daughter, seated in adjacent chairs, spent all their hair-cutting, shampooing and setting time regaling the hairdresser with stories of the good life in Brazil where they lived. The mother kept on producing gold chains from her handbag, "I think Sharon/Kim/Jenny will like this, don't you ?" she'd said to her daughter. "Only £200 and it's worth £260 for the gold in scrap value." Parties, sunshine etc. how wonderful her husband was, who walked in with brandies from the pub over the road, half way through, the value of each charm on her gold bracelet, how awful the Rio hairdressers were "cold water for shampooing - I ask you" how the men wept in the streets when they lost a football match. And so on. It was a relief to get home where there was an enormous bunch of flowers waiting for me. "To our Lizzie" it said on the card. "With love and support from Mother, Father and Sister Margaret." I sobbed.

Zarek finally agreed to let me take the children away to visit my parents during the Easter holiday. This was a great relief as I was finding the residual inertia too heavy to shift and couldn't think how I was to keep the children happy for another week of holiday. Daisy and Alice had both had a glandular virus and had been in need of constant cuddles. Daisy had sensibly opted out for 24 hours after which she recovered but Alice remained tetchy, possibly also because she was finding Greg a bit overwhelming. I'd noticed this before during school holidays - the little ones need the peace and comfort of a one-to-one relationship for part of the day, which is interrupted when older children are on holiday from school. When it wasn't raining, we went for walks, usually very muddy ones and never more than a couple of miles. Alice could manage one but then had to be carried, Daisy managed the whole lot without complaint and with some semblance of enjoyment. She would get tired but saw the best way of relieving her fatigue as making a determined effort to get home. Greg would be deeply involved in fantasy games with every bush and tree, but once he'd given up, nothing would distract him so getting home was quite a slog.

I'd brought a bottle of Chris' homemade plum wine back with me from my earlier visit. It had sat in the larder unopened for a couple of months, unopened because of all the happy memories and associations it aroused. Even just seeing it reminded me of loving warmth, wholesome food and an ever-increasing lightness of the head and loosening of inhibition, completely incompatible with my existence with Zarek. Eventually I overcame my scruples and opened it and found that I only had to close my eyes while sitting at the table with the tele blaring and the children messing around with their food as usual, I was instantly transported for a few precious moments to the warmth and firelight in Chris' home. Dally a few seconds more and I'll swear I could feel his hands stealing gently over me, undoing buttons, hooks, zips, questing, caressing …….. miraculous wine …….. ambrosial …

38. Summer term

Once the children had gone back to school, loneliness and desperation really set in. Each day felt like a separate soggy balloon which I clambered into in the morning, floundered around for a bit, never quite able to get my footing, and then staggered out of at night. One day followed another but there was no connection between them, each day was an individual and isolated blob, no past, no future - just an existence. Which felt like a bloody waste of time.

 I was struggling with two sets of opposing feelings. One was connected to Zarek as a constant source of irritation, frustration and non-communication for which the only resolution was to leave him. The other set related to him as a sick person. He still looked ill, sallow, drawn, old. And glued firmly into my mind was the awfulness of taking the children away from him if he really was dying. We had no positive feelings for each other, but he loved the children, was consumed by it. OK so he used them as an extension for his inflated but shaky ego but that made them all the more important if it was to be extinguished for ever. What a dilemma.

It seemed to rain constantly, which made going out to collect envelopes distributed in aid of Samaritans, quite a chore, but at least it passed the time. Sometimes though, it was almost fun and even very touching. Old Mr. Barrett, the garage owner who lived up the road and must have been all of eighty, positively danced out of his door to give me his envelope and wish us well. But Eddie and Annie, who lived opposite on National Assistance and whose house reeked of poverty gave nothing, even though it would have done them good to sacrifice the price of a couple of Mars bars which they were forever buying from the newsagents next door. Another house seemed unoccupied until finally there was a querulous voice calling from the house's nether regions "I'm coming", accompanied by the creak of a walking frame. It took her hours poor old thing, but she had the envelope ready and was probably glad to have some human contact, even me, dressed up against the weather like an abominable snowman.

At this time, Greg and Daisy seemed to be finding each other particularly annoying. It usually started with Daisy goading him and ended when Greg lashed out in typical 'big' little boy fashion, a playful cuff which to her must have felt like a mighty clout, followed by much yelling and over-assertiveness from them both. At other times, Daisy was demure and helpful. Her latest game was 'Restaurants' when I was forever finding little tables beautifully laid, with old lace curtains for tablecloths and posies of flowers, cutlery, plates and the like while she stood in attendance with a towel over her arm, swathed in an over-long apron and clutching a pad for 'orders'. This may have had something to do with one of the effects of Zarek's treatment which was that he lost his sense of taste. It was a rare opportunity for humour - "I'm cooking this and this - which texture would you prefer ?" I'd ask him. He seemed worryingly tired and preoccupied but I didn't think he was helping himself too much. He'd go out to dig the garden in shorts and shirtsleeves when it was perishingly cold and the soil was like sticky toffee. He also attempted to repair the gatepost that I had knocked over six months earlier, but demonstrated few bricklaying skills. As a result it looked like the leaning tower of Pisa and as for pointing, he hadn't a clue. Anyway, it didn't matter too much as a week later, said gatepost developed CRACKS . This was not because of Zarek's faulty workmanship but because this time it was he who backed into it on account of it still being unfinished and too low to be visible when reversing !

This may sound odd but there was one unexpected and sort of positive consequence of Zarek's illness. It must be devastating when such a horrid thing hits a family which is well integrated and enjoying life together - a shattering contrast between a healthy life and a sick one. For us, with no family unity anyway, it didn't make that much difference in practical terms and if anything it was easier because Zarek had less energy to be nasty. It certainly didn't curtail any of our family activities because we had precious few. The only real issue was that I had to survive the prolongation of the divorce process, but it had little impact on our day to day existence.

In contrast to our under-stimulating routine, a trip to London on a gloriously sunshiny day, to see psychologist friend Terry, who I'd known since those long-distant Day Hospital days, was exhilarating. We sat by the river outside the Royal Festival Hall while Sunday London strolled, danced, sang, skateboarded around us. Terry had been having analysis for years which had helped him understand himself as well as preparing him for his own psychoanalytical career. He'd reassured me that my theory that Zarek's illness was a reaction to the situation wasn't barmy. Having known Zarek himself for many years, he knew him to be lacking in insight, his only outlet to our devastating situation being an extreme physical reaction ie cancer. He gave me an idea for further investigations and negotiations via our two solicitors. His suggestion was that it was time somebody, preferably Zarek's solicitor called his bluff and said "look mate, you don't stand a chance." Because what judge would be prepared to take the risk of handing three young children over to someone in the early stages of recovery from cancer ? Under these circumstances, Zarek might accept a legal separation with me having the children but staying in the area, until such time as he was deemed recovered ….. or succumbed. Terry felt it was about time somebody made it plain to Zarek that he was wasting everyone's time and money.

The next day it was back to the usual austerity regime and a letter from my father.

May 1983 Essex

Hullo dear Lizzie,

To turn for a moment to the less attractive side of life - we, too, find it difficult to understand the logic in Zarek's claim that 'there's all the more reason to go ahead with the custody contest' for the situation, to our way of thinking, hasn't really changed since you showed us the welfare officer's report and your affidavit (what we might call the 'pre-cancer' stage). If Zarek (as he apparently optimistically hopes) DOES recover from the throat cancer, we're back to the pre-cancer stage when the welfare officer stressed the fact that Zarek was not so young as he might be, and when we feel there would be no doubt at all that custody would come to you. And who's to say how full would be a full recovery ? I doubt whether a court would place much confidence in it when deciding custody. And if, after two, three months before Zarek submits his new affidavit (for we can't see him hurrying over it) it has to be admitted that he has NOT recovered, it becomes a simple and solid confirmation of the rightness of a decision to award you custody. So, in either event we seem to be back to the pre-cancer stage.

But what lies behind Zarek's claim that 'there's all the more reason to contest custody' does have one simple explanation exemplified by past attitude. He's determined to cause the maximum distress for, with common sense, he must know he stands little chance of securing custody. How else could he exercise an innate sadism arising from a sense of failure on the part of a psychiatrist to save his second marriage, and on being passed over on promotion stakes at the hospital, than to make his wife suffer.

He has been given good solid grounds for divorce, he instituted divorce and ostensibly wants it, but to dangle you on a string whilst having your services on the cheap and whilst enjoying the company of the children constitutes, in our opinion, just mental cruelty. So we wonder Liz, what does your barrister think of this ? Isn't she able to apply any 'push' to proceedings on the basis of mental cruelty and the wasting of the court's time, bearing in mind that the circumstances affecting custody will, as outlined above, not have changed in three months ?

A doleful letter, Liz - let's say how glad we were to learn that the lovely blue skating boots you bought for Daisy have brought some brightness into life, particularly because I suspect little Daisy must enjoy having her Mum with her when participating in an occupation which carries no competition from brother Greg ! You're right about the weather - the forecast this morning promised us something less chilly than of late, and it's surprising how much more inspiring a little sunshine is. It'll help Greg too, I guess, who will probably be back in good spirits by the time you receive this letter - Mother and I, and you too, of course, can be thankful that the recurrence of his asthma didn't happen while you were all staying here which could have given some credibility to Zarek's argument that our house was unhealthy !

I guess I'd better send this letter to Mrs. Jennifer. It's very good of her to act as a poste restante address, so do convey our gratitude to her for her help with this. I hope we're not being too much of a nuisance as presumably she has to 'phone you every time she receives one of our 'epistolary indulgences'!

So goodbye for now, me dear, and at the risk of being wearisome 'Nil illigitimus carborundum ……. !! … Dad.

If I was occupying one soggy balloon in Hampshire, there was another one flopping around in Suffolk with Chris struggling to find his way out of an emotional miasma which seemed likely to overwhelm him. He seemed to fall apart when he was alone and yet couldn't cope with close relationships. He saw himself as a catalyst, someone bringing about change whilst themselves remaining unchanged. This was perhaps the frustration. He set things off in all sorts of creative ways but was left with the same dissatisfied self at the end of it all. And yet all those people whose lives he had touched, me included, were so grateful for what he had done. Maybe this could be linked to his excessively high expectations of himself, never feeling that he had got anywhere, so never feeling that he had achieved anything or that his own life was any different as a result. But why should it be. He knew he was a good teacher, an inspired teacher amongst many who were bored with their daily slog. He knew that people loved and cared about him and that he was one of the world's special people. It seemed to me that there was no real reward for this, only the knowledge of it. And strong friendships, even relationships. Being at the super-cynical end of that particular spectrum, I couldn't personally believe in the possibility of achieving any ideals. I admired people who seemed to get there but the price to be paid was considerable, I thought. And it certainly didn't come easily to anyone. In this respect, we both seemed to be failures.

He struggled too with commitment and I wondered if it was because of not wanting to hurt, or presumably be hurt. I wondered who had let him down in the past, his Dad for dying when he was a baby, or his Mum for not being his Dad ? Going that far back made sense because subsequent relationships are all based on that early learning, whether it was coping with their presence or their absence. So it almost seemed too late to do anything about it, except understand why there was a basic lack of trust and hence insecurity.

Psycho-babble. We are all emotionally scarred in one way or another and have to learn to make the best of our battered selves.

There was evidence of this at a party I was invited to by some very old friends, Jeannie and Tom who were celebrating their fifteenth wedding anniversary. I'd been one of their bridesmaids and was Godmother to their first child. Looking round the room, I'd asked myself how many of the fifty or so people there, looking alert, happy, excited or plain bleary-eyed, were really satisfied with their lives but there was no knowing the answer. Several likely candidates for dissatisfaction certainly. One was Jeannie's plump younger sister, about thirty three and unmarried, who had made a sort of career out of a viral illness which had struck her down the previous year. She held forth at length about her condition but in fact looked healthier and more relaxed than I'd seen her for years. Then there was another rather grand double-barrelled lady (younger than me but with the behaviour and speech mannerisms of an elderly dowager) who made no secret of her tricky marriage. Similarly afflicted were Jazza and Bertie. Jazza was a part-time musician but in the real world as James, pursuing a career in stock-broking. His wife Bertie was French and quite chic but she prattled incessantly. As the evening wore on we heard details of the frightful underpants his mother was always sending him, his dreadful choice of clothes ("Just look at those awful shoes"), how he never brought her cups of

374

coffee in bed, only tea, how she couldn't stand him pouncing on her in the morning for a bit of ooh la la, on and on and on. At one point Jeannie had playfully said "Jazza, how have you stood her for all these years ?" and it was really difficult for him to answer.

The thing that I'd dreaded most of all at this party, was finding myself having to give explanations about my circumstances. This didn't happen which was a huge relief. Conversations weren't at such a personal level but even with people who knew each other, there was none of the endless chat about children, grandchildren, finding a gardener/cleaning lady, the benefits of solar panel installation, recipes from the latest celebrity cook etc. which was the flavour of social 'dos' in our small village.

Zarek had his final radio-therapy session in mid-May and had said he wanted to go away for a holiday. He continued to be very uncommunicative about his recovery. On good days, he seemed pretty normal but once I'd come home from the party, he retreated to bed and had drunk the whole of our weekend's supply of milk because of the 'heartburn', which he complained of. There was no knowing whether this was because of the treatment or the illness. He said the lump in his neck had gone but once or twice I caught him surreptitiously feeling around there and he was preoccupied and rather more absent-minded than usual. That Sunday, he stayed in bed, and feeling genuinely sorry for him, curled up there with his back to the world, I decided to take Alice who would otherwise have stayed at home with Zarek, along with Greg and Daisy to a children's service at the local church. The only concession made to any children present was to sing All Things Bright and Beautiful . Greg and Daisy behaved impeccably and were positively embarrassed at Alice's escalating kerfuffle level. She lasted half an hour which I didn't think was bad and we finally clomped out of the church just as they were praying for the sick and the souls of the dear departed.

Zarek wasn't the only one wanting a holiday. I was longing for another of my infrequent Chris visits, regardless of Zarek's health. If this seemed callous, by excluding me from the details of his illness and how he was feeling, I had little alternative. Even so, the fact that I was able to consider leaving this very sick man to care for three young children, even for a couple of days does seem pretty shocking. I found myself looking for reasons but it wasn't difficult to find them. Firstly, Zarek wanted me to go. He wanted me to be seen in the worst possible light to improve his chances in court, so what better demonstration of my fecklessness than this ? Another one, his denial of his illness because of how the prognosis could influence a court decision and the fact that we weren't communicating. Naively, I could have thought that he wasn't that sick so it was OK to go. Although I wasn't that naïve, I was certainly suffering desperately because of the prolongation of the situation, the recent awful turn of events and how I was being treated. I think two of these amounted to manipulation on his part, and the third, his illness, could in analytical terms be interpreted as him using everything, including his health and strength to fight me.

There were in addition, some mitigating facts as well as reasons. I had actually planned to depart after putting the children to bed on a Wednesday evening and return before lunchtime on the Friday after this. All three children were to be out during the day on the Thursday and I had arranged for a friend to give them tea that afternoon. This meant that their need for Zarek's care was minimised as much as I could possibly manage. Were these reasons good enough ? I really don't know. Our Australian friend James like my parents, seemed to feel that in the circumstances, Zarek's hope of keeping all three children was unlikely and that settling for just one, Greg, might give him more strength to fight his illness. Zarek was having none of this. His crazy determination to win all was what was keeping him going.

It was Chris who was keeping me going. His phone calls were like a life-belt, hurtling over the stormy sea and landing smack over my head and shoulders at the precise moment when I'd surfaced for the third and final time. I had worried that he would become too emotionally tied up with someone else to have anything left to share with me, but I needn't have done. It was Jodi who had pride of place in his heart, despite the passage of time. Or so I thought. It seemed the best place to keep such a treasure safe from the demands of the real world where all our relationships seemed to become distorted, scarred, uncomfortable. Even if she had to remain there for ever, at least she would remain inviolate, so long as he could bear the pain of such a burden. It had become a part of him, leaving him with no emotional resources left for further investment. That I could see. In effect he was emotionally bankrupt which in a way was fine for both of us at that point in time. I was confident that I was the best he could hope for because with the children, I knew I wasn't available for a living together sort of relationship. It seemed odd that I was stuck in a marriage that I couldn't get out of while he was stuck outside a relationship that he couldn't get into. His preoccupation with Jodi blocked his availability although he made no secret of quite a few women friends. He'd recently visited one called Julie who ran a craft shop in Aldeburgh and was selling his pots. She lived up a quaint unmade road, in a miniscule cottage which she had gutted, modernised, painted white throughout and filled with cow parsley, bluebells and sunshine in honour of his visit. Old-fashioned (he'd said she wore a long flannelette nightie) but pleasant and fun company was how he described her. Couldn't stop myself from wondering how *much* fun ....

39. Another visit

In Greek mythology, it was Sisyphus who spent all his time trying to push a heavy stone uphill which became everlastingly laborious because every time he was nearly there, it rolled back down again. That felt familiar. I was longing to get away but hadn't dared to share my plans with Zarek and it was driving me to drink. It started because quite often I didn't have lunch. By the time I'd collected a gaggle of little girls from school, ferried them home and got our meal organised, I felt distinctly frayed and my tummy needed some distraction. That was when the first glass of wine slipped down. Then there were a couple more with supper and hey ho, in no time at all half a bottle of the stuff had disappeared. The whisky night-cap which invariably accompanied my evening paper rendezvous with Chris didn't help. On one disastrous evening I'd made the mistake of starting with Pernod. Not a good idea. It lead to me practically throttling the cat, bawling the children out and then collapsing in a stupor until 8.30 when the phone rang and I suddenly realised that Daisy should have been in bed and Greg had got undressed but had settled down to watch the television. This led to a determined (but intermittent) effort to get on the wagon/take the pledge etc.

Finally, when I did ask Zarek about a visit to East Anglia, he said yes I could go, with barely a second thought, but even that worried me. He really wasn't too well, getting up later than usual and going to bed by 9.00 having spent much of the day in retreat. On the occasions when he did anything, it was usually a bit of gardening, and it looked as though he was dragging himself around but it was impossible to tell whether he was suffering physically or emotionally because we never talked.

I could see him secretly cherishing the children as they sat unconcernedly on his lap and could barely comprehend his particular hell. He had always felt himself to be absolutely omnipotent, utterly vital to their young lives. I could only guess that the worry of his uncertain future must have been driving him towards insanity. He saw himself as the children's total life support system, with my involvement as far as he was concerned as peripheral to what he considered to be their real needs. Of course I didn't share this view but I could understand his pain. I could feel the pressure of their demands increasing, as he withdrew, but there was still the feeling that he was acting as a censor on all my actions and decisions.

And I was worried that he really wasn't getting better - that this was going to be my last chance to escape albeit briefly for even a couple of days. I didn't know how long I could carry on without the reviving anticipation of time spent with Chris, the delight of being away and the poignant savour of all that we had shared. It kept me alive. I relived every time I pushed open his garden gate, ducked past giant fennel plants as I walked up the path, counted the cat pictures, cut from packets of Felix catfood that covered the front door and rang his lovely jangly bell, then entered …….. on this occasion he was playing some Andean pipe music and dancing around his sitting room waiting for me, in a bowler hat and the Bolivian poncho I'd given him for Christmas. Magic.

As usual, there wasn't enough time. There never was. Never enough time to develop and enjoy our sexual relationship instead of so urgently needing to relieve the immediate tensions and frustrations. Time to sleep and time to waken as we needed without thought of regular routines or external demands. So that I need not have thought that I shouldn't waken him with gentle caress or delicate exploration - or him me. I'd wanted to have freedom for both of us to escape all the emotional bogeys that bedevilled us so that our abandonment could have been total and without inhibition of any kind.

Zarek seemed much better when I returned so it appeared that the unpleasant side effects of his treatment were wearing off . He was soon back on fighting form again and his recent quiescence had clearly been as a consequence of his treatment rather than his illness. He continued with a programme of constant harrassment . "I told you last August that the easiest thing would be for you to go", he screeched at me and there were times when I wished I had. My one hope was that he wouldn't have to have the additional operation to remove lymph nodes so that everything could proceed but I doubted it. I had visions of hammering on some court house door and screaming in exasperation, "For God's sake won't somebody please divorce us" but then thought it might take so long that I'd be too senile to have the strength.

The summer holiday was looming on the horizon. With so many uncertainties, not least the date of the court case, it felt like a seven week yawning chasm. Whatever plans I might have wanted to make would have had to have been short term and inexpensive because of the possibility of unexpected cancellation. Also Zarek's power of veto which he'd exercised in the past, was intimidating and in any case my cash resources were limited. My first consideration was for the children and I felt it was mean of Zarek to in effect limit their opportunities. I could have taken them to Holland-on-Sea where my parents lived, which was at least a seaside resort but they had been there too often for it to feel like a 'proper' holiday. Even so, I had learnt from bitter experience that there was nothing more depressing than having no plans at all and living from day to day. Camping seemed like a possibility as my parents had all the equipment including quite a large frame tent, but the thought of coping with it all on my own was daunting. I hinted at this to Chris but he had his own plans. I knew of a caravan on a farm in south Wales which could be available at short notice so I clung to that as the most realistic possibility.

After my brief visit, Chris had written me a long letter :

May 1983 Suffolk

Hello, dear 'ol love. Glad you got back safely - thanks for phoning. Despite returning to Gloom City, it's always good to know your journey is over safely. I feel I neglect you so these days - I'm sorry I was in such a rush whilst you were here, but don't think for moment I didn't appreciate all you *did both <u>before</u> you came - that <u>superb</u> cake - and thanks for leaving it ! - <u>and</u> whilst you were here - that excellent supper, grass cutting - and the beautiful book you brought me. <u>And</u> all the shopping and phone calls - goodness, I <u>did</u> make use of you, didn't I. But maybe it helped <u>you</u> to feel useful and appreciated - and I <u>do</u> appreciate you, don't I ? - Hope I'll <u>never</u> take anything and more especially <u>anybody</u> for granted again. You are <u>so</u> willing and resourceful and capable and it's all <u>smothered</u> under layer upon layer of dead wood and debris from year after rotten year with Zarek.*

Never mind, gel - <u>I</u> know it's still there - you remember it too please. All just waiting to shoot up into new life again once the terror is over. And remember the <u>reality</u> is the tiny bit you are reminded of when you come up <u>here</u> not your horrid situation under that crazy man's pathetic thumb. It might not seem so now, but it can't last for much longer, one way or t'other.

Did I tell you I asked the P.E teacher at school if she'd like to come to the big thrash at the theatre tomorrow eve ? Left it with her to let me know - she didn't say anything but when I asked her again on Friday afternoon, beamed at me and said she'd <u>love</u> to, it sounded great fun. So I gave her my phone number - it was all so rushed at school, and said to buzz me and we'd fix arrangements up. So far no call. Now, do <u>I</u> call her ? After all these years of relationships with women, I <u>still</u> feel a reticence as if it was the first woman I'd ever met, to <u>drag</u> her to something - more to the point, <u>with</u> somebody she doesn't really want to go/be with. But she <u>did</u> seem enthusiastic - just being kind ? afraid to say no ?

Oh dear. It sends me <u>plummeting</u> right back to my failure to work things out with Jodi. If she hadn't got on so well back home, if she hadn't blossomed so, and seemingly found her academic/social/future feet, then I'd be kicking myself even harder in the head, than I have been for the past two years. But it had to be. Nevertheless I <u>do</u> realise it was the closest I'll ever come to <u>real</u> life with a partner - it <u>was</u> life together, with all our battles (mostly, virtually <u>all</u>, over the unreality/fantasy of another on/off relationship I was in when I met her. If only I'd met Jodi <u>first</u> ....).

If there's one thing that has corroded my vitals, it's the remorse I've felt, and go on and on feeling, at hurting someone who knocked herself out day in day out to demonstrate and prove her love for me and her worth <u>to</u> me. Her hurt must have been <u>fearful</u> - and all I could do was shrug it off at the time. I am a <u>fool</u>. I don't believe in myself as a worthy partner for anybody - I <u>have</u> to expurgate my remorse by exiling myself for good into the land of inner loneliness. Know it sounds <u>dreadfully</u> melodramatic - but as soon as I even begin to feel leanings towards anyone else I hear Jodi's footsteps chasing me down the lane, and her broken voice begging me to come back and talk - clogs going bonk, bonk, bonk in a hopeless effort to catch up. Putting the phone down on her, crying down in her cottage. Brushing away her hand as she asked, with such a loving smile, if she could hold mine as we walked down North Street - I didn't want people to feel we were that close. Making her <u>limp</u>, to catch me up in downtown icy Manhattan, blisters on her heels, irritable that we weren't on our sightseeing schedule. She doing her <u>utmost</u> to keep up with a bright smile. Making her cry in Princeton - I can't *even remember <u>why</u> now, save that the photo of her in the frame, small, cowed, blinking back tears, reminds me. And recalling all this makes me feel sexless, soulless, heartless, mindless - just the world's biggest fool. It's Jodi, <u>still</u>, I'm afraid Liz, that drives me to the blackest - no, not black - sad, grey, endless, perpetually erupting hopelessness.*

Sexual involvements are my biggest escape of all - a total involvement, for those few sacred moments, into the body and soul of a partner that obliterates completely all sadness and despair in a mutual ecstasy. And that's why I have to ensure that the other is completely involved in it too - she has to enjoy it as much as me, otherwise it's a futile exercise. We <u>both</u> have to leave this world for a moment. Does that explain it a little more positively ? I hope so.

It's been an excellent week teaching wise. No time to enlarge, save that the recent blackness has been dissolved, at least for a while, in the sweetness of young people and what we have achieved in the classroom. I'll phone XXX Chris.

Oh dear. What on earth was I doing with this man ? Our own relationship assumed the intimacy he desired but he was perfectly at ease talking of his curiosity about other women and then an escaped love that left him drained of that interest in others, which presumably included me. I simply didn't see it and felt myself to be somehow above tawdry daily passions. Couldn't see what he was telling me. What I saw was a hugely lovable man who was regularly questing for and achieving sexual adventures, which ultimately never satisfied his need for completeness. I wondered if he really knew what he was looking for. There had been any number of conquests with lovely women, who like me, had given him bucket loads of love and would have spent their lives continuing to do so, but every time, he scuttled away from real commitment. Making 'love' yes, but establishing a real relationship - that seemed to always elude him. But I just didn't see it. What was it about me which made me imagine that I could win his love when all others had failed ?

40. More letters

May 1983 Hampshire, again.

Hi Chris - a dear diary letter for you today but it occurred to me that you know so many details of my life, all the minutiae of my day to day living and breathing, that me in substance, is probably superfluous ………. maybe I'll send you a paper cut-out dolly with my complete wardrobe of clothes so that you can dress (or undress) me according to your whim, but do without the actual hassle of my presence altogether …..

<u>Saturday</u> - Rain, rain and yet more rain. And almost a relief to be able to rest and recover from my whirlwind trip to Sudbury. Children content to watch awful films on tele ! Missed you.

<u>Sunday</u>. No Sunday School so swimming instead in which Greg demonstrated his prowess at leaping off the diving board and actually coming to the surface. Daisy frolicked blissfully and looks a delight in her rose red swimming cozzie by Speedo. Long legs, knees which are just a fraction friendly and a smashing little bum. Alice is stockier in build but looks equally delightful in her diminutive pale blue gingham bikini bottom with its beaded tassels ! Zarek vile at lunchtime, upsetting everyone.

Afternoon - an unexpected trip out with heavily pregnant Katie and her two boys to their beach hut on Hayling Island -

even less like the seaside than Holland-on-Sea where my parents lived. We sat on deck chairs in the biting wind and cold, viewing a bank of pebbles - no sign of the sea as the hut is in a hollow. Dug in what sand there was with the children, mopped ice cream from their anoraks and pretended it was summer. Home to even more rain - missed you even more.

Monday. A Bank holiday family expedition. Whoopee. Went to Amberley Chalk Pits - an industrial museum where there are ancient engines, buses, road mending equipment, a forge where Alice thought the man was making 'snakes', a tanyard, a collection of wireless equipment, old cement and brick making works - and a pottery. You would have been horrified - the pots were less than mediocre and the potter himself had _mud_ up to his elbows and was wearing a filthy torn boiler suit. _So_ sloppy. The rest of the place was fun - a bit dusty and scruffy but seething with activity - rides for the children on anything that would move and lots of junky stuff to scramble over and enjoy. They loved it, especially some old water pumps where of course they all got soaked ! Zarek was stern, silent and aloof, taking endless cine films of nothing in particular. But thank God it was a diversion from my desperately unhappy state of mind. Am feeling so _dreadfully_ deprived of freedom and so frustrated. So _envious_ of your parties, holidays, plays - wondering all the time what you are doing, thinking, feeling - in the cellar, the garden, eating in the kitchen, in bed, lying in a field somewhere with eyes closed against the sun. Longing for that freedom.

_So_, yes, I missed you some more.

Tuesday. One of my regular attempts to translate feelings into _action_. Rang my solicitor, who reported that he's waiting for a date for my hearing. Two or three weeks from now he said. Probably be just as they slit Zarek's throat to get at his lymph nodes.

Afternoon. And a fun time at the local leisure centre where they are running Disco-roller skating sessions every day for the kids at half term. Dozens, hundreds of aspiring wheelie teeny boppers including Greg, Daisy and myself. Unbelievably loud music with everyone zooming round punctuated by games - a sort of tag where you sit down on the floor if you are caught, making the pursuit of the final few a _very_ hazardous affair for all, both sitters and skaters; then a great long conga with everyone snaking round the hall, then boy's speed skating followed by girl's speed skating. And for the first time, Greg really took off and _loved_ it. I watched him _tearing_ around on his skates with my heart in my mouth but he survived and was pouring with perspiration by the time he'd finished. He was thrilled to bits to be able to do it at long last which perhaps compensated a bit for the bashing, both emotional and physical he's had from Zarek over the last few days.

Honestly, his 'recovery' has made him _awful_. Nasty to Greg and me and constantly comparing Daisy unfavourably with Alice who seems to be the only one who can do anything right at the moment and even she isn't immune all the time.

I hear thunder, I hear thunder ….. only a distant rumble but let's hope it'll clear by tomorrow and give us another gloriously sunny day. At last it feels as though summer *might put in an appearance and it's such a relief when the children can play outside and enjoy the freedom they need. Whizzed into Chichester this morning to buy caps for Greg's gun (hundreds of them which are already nearly all used up) and a book I'd ordered for Daisy. Kept them both happy and didn't cost much. Super kids. They deserve better.*

Looking forward to your letter tomorrow - so until then, bye for now, Lonely Lizzie xx Can't resist sending you more hugs and kisses even though I suspect they're not good for you and merely add to your life's complications.

I am a worthy person. I really am. Good enough.

May 1983 Suffolk

By the embers - just in from theatre via coffee next door. Ha ! Well now ….. I thought she (Denise - called Dozey - I called her Dizzy all the time by mistake) was well on the way to 30. But no - 24, tho' she's done USA and Australia - friends with Tom and Watkin but intended as a sort of blind date for me. We all had supper in freezing garden and then to theatre party. Colossal crowds. Solid with people. Denise promptly met two ruggerbuggers she knew and spent whole evening talking animatedly to them. I butted in now and again and asked for a dance - then leapt off again to dance with all and sundry (new pumps, d'you see - magic !). I did enjoy it - at end, imagined Dozey Dizzy Denise would go off with her two blokes but no, she said she'd like coffee with us. I said (very kindly, not at all sarcastically) that she didn't have to be polite - it was quite OK , but she came. Afterwards drove her back to her car parked at the theatre and off she went.

And here I was, sitting by the fire when in came Tom and neighbour Brian from next door with three women. Awkward. I <u>really</u> didn't feel like a one night stand - Tom and Bridget (?) are in the room he rents upstairs, Bridget's sister is with Brian in my double room, and I put woman no. 3, Diana in back bedroom (all fresh and ready in <u>case</u> Denise had stayed !). And here I am in sleeping bag by fire - it's now 3.20 ! Feeling a bit of a party pooper - but I really <u>couldn't</u> have gone to bed with someone who'd just walked through the front door. Oh yes, just done a mountain of washing up. <u>What</u> a funny evening ! Very odd. Sort of heavy misfiring on all cylinders plus a gentle slap in the face.

<u>Lovely</u> fire going to waste - pity <u>you're</u> not here instead of all the strangers. Wonder if Tom will launder all the sheets for me ? So, I'll plug in Simon & Garfunkel and go to sleep with earphones on - thinking/dreaming of icy New York with Jodi and my life frittering away steadily. Night night, dear old friend. Thank you for all your loving kindness. Xxxxx Chris.

Later, or is it earlier, I'm not sure....

Wish we could read minds, Lizzie. There was something about Denise I found very attractive - spikey tomboy hair - such a flashing smile - she <u>looked</u> fun to be with ..... perhaps she's done a little research on <u>me</u> and discovered my age/background ? But it would be nice to make friends with somebody <u>new</u> ..... oh well, a nice thought ..... I really do forget I'm 48 and not thirty !

Take care dear Liz. Keep truckin' - so will I xxxChris xxx

Hm. 8.00 a.m Tuesday. Might have known Denise was not my type - she never drinks tea ! <u>Poor</u> old Chris ! Poor poor old lad ! - One little setback to his plans and he's drooping off in his mind to icy New York and snivelling into his hanky. Thank <u>GOD</u> (literally) for the coming of day-time and <u>REALITY</u> ! <u>And</u> the return of a sense of proportion and <u>HUMOUR</u> ! Liz it really was funny last night - talk about a French farce ! I'd just finished the first bit of this letter and was plugging in the headphones when down the stairs tripped Tom's bird Bridget to come over to me and sit beside the fire. I must say she was very pretty in a delicate rosebud/bone china kind of way. She sat down by the fire and asked where the other two were. Told her. "Oh" she said. "We must be off to Colchester" - 8 year old son and babysitter. Said it was the nicest house she'd ever been in and did I often have people dropping in like this ? Thank you, I said, then, yes. I said would she like to drop into <u>my</u> sleeping bag (ever a tryer, old Chris, despite his New York glooms). Said it wouldn't solve her problem. Too much of a gentleman to say it might solve <u>mine</u>. But sitting there all awry, wispy top and skirt - nice greens and purples and lots of tights showing - I mean, by then, with hoots and giggles and thumps coming from all over the house, I was <u>just</u> beginning to feel a bit left out, as was my member for Lower Crotchford. Up she went to Tom again to be swiftly followed by Brian coming <u>down</u> stairs - on his way home next door. I waited for a brick to come through the window from his wife Wendy. Just dozing off to Ommadawn when all three of the women appeared at my bedside - 6.00 a.m, off home to Colchester. "Thanks etc." - "Don't mention it - anytime at all etc. etc." "Bye." Dear oh <u>dear</u> !

And now it's tea and daylight - Tom staying in bed with the shock to his system - and your <u>delightful</u> letter. Should I reply with this ? Why not - we know each other too well <u>not</u> to and I <u>know</u> you'll enjoy a good laugh at the above ! Crazy. <u>What</u> a good yarn to add to my dinner party anecdotes.

But I <u>would</u> like to talk to you about Denise. Maybe these few lines will suffice to get it out of my system. How <u>wrong</u> I was about her - so off the mark. <u>Thought</u> my intuition was right - but what an odd mixture of sunny enthusiasm and careless indifference ?! It <u>seemed</u> a life and death conversation she was having with these two guys - <u>solid</u> for 2 hours ! And there I was beforehand, worrying that <u>she'd</u> feel left out!!

So it's off into the wet and gloom on the camping expedition with Charlie and Rosie. Nice. Am going to repack kit and put in a tracksuit, hot bottle, compass and emergency flares. Life's never dull Kiddo. Is it ? Have a hug, Liz baby. xox God Bless Cxxxx

June 1983 Hampshire

Oh crumbs. A jug-full, not a mug-full of coffee and a stab at a letter. Don't know if I can or should write - I'll just have to see what comes and then make up my mind about sending it. I hesitate to write because I'd much <u>much</u> rather talk to you about this sort of thing, but we seem to have drifted away from frank and free discussions when we're together or else there hasn't been time and we do communicate so openly in letters - or have done so. I feel I must say

393

something before you disappear entirely up the vortex of your frenetic activity.

Firstly - thank God you seem to be enjoying life again - or some of it ! Even if you do have to beat a hasty retreat to Simon & Garfunkel when the going gets tough. Six months ago you wouldn't even have gone to the theatre party and here you are, making the most, well, quite a lot of what sounds like a tricky situation without plummeting to the depths when it didn't work out as expected. Although maybe you did plummet a bit, maybe that's what you were really saying in your usual lighthearted way. But you emerged laughing, if a little wryly. It's a step in the right direction.

I wonder if it's occurred to you that although inevitably one makes initial assessments of people, potential partners, through their physical attractiveness - or lack of it, as one gets to know them even a little more, particularly if there is a difference in age, then the wisdom of experience does matter. So that although you are such a super person to be with, so charming and delightful company (that's not flattery - you know damn well) - you're just too mature in your outlook and attitudes to be really compatible with someone half your age. You're so good at being open, easy and seeing other people's point of view that perhaps you find this hard to believe but fifteen or twenty years must matter in ways more subtle than we realise. Maybe that's why Dozey Dizzy could be enthusiastic and indifferent all at the same time - she may not have had reason yet to even think about the effect her behaviour might have on someone else whereas the insights we have gained and regretted not having in the past, from all that has happened to us have an incredibly powerful effect on how we are with others. We'd like to think that we can slip into and out of relationships as we might have done years back but too much has happened in the meantime for it to be that easy. And I for one don't want it although I think it's maybe a bit different for women - for a start it's easier for an older man to attract a younger woman than the other way round. Dammit !

The next bit's the hard bit. Reading through your letter, you are so open and honest and light hearted about it all that I think how can I possibly mind. I know that our relationship, based as it is on such a long friendship and our more recent sexual loving, support, freedom to say exactly what we think and feel, is special and different and probably better than most of what we've experienced at the hands of others. But don't you think it would be odd, having said how much I care about you and how much I value what you've done for me, if it didn't hurt me just a little ? The stupid thing is that I know that I can't expect you to do otherwise and that it's me who's not facing up to the realities of the situation whilst you are being totally straight and honest. And not telling me wouldn't help because it would keep me that much further away from the reality. On the whole I'd rather know and try to understand and come to terms with it but it doesn't hurt just a little. It sears my soul.

I suspect you see, that we're both using familiar patterns and I'm wondering if there's any way we can help each other to take a look at them and consider alternatives - make use of the situation. Your honesty is totally disarming and makes me feel <u>guilty</u> about minding, but recently you've been <u>so</u> busy, it's helped to distract you from Jodi preoccupations but *has also created distance between us - distance which you needed, to escape from deeper commitment (to me) of which you are so fearful. (Not of course, that I'm the person to be committed to, as we both know - you still have the better grasp of reality. Or do you ?) My problem would appear to be the opposite. I'm honest too and haven't concealed my feelings from you but my tendency is to be over-committed to the extent that I rationalise things which deep down, I don't find acceptable - look what I managed for fifteen years with Zarek ! My sort of total loyalty is born of a desperate need to be accepted and I can't help relinquishing reason, when I find someone as worthwhile and valuable as you.*

The stupid thing is that for each of us to escape from these familiar patterns there is an opposite solution. I should do something I've never managed before and say OK, I need to save myself from further hurt and get out. Now. No anguished conversations, no more brief escapes, no thoughts of holidays, letters, a 'platonic' friendship. Ugh. Cut my losses and go. Despite the fact that my reserves after the last year are practically non-existent, that's how it would have to be. I suppose I should say "I quit" but that's happened to you so many times in the past, or you've set it up to happen, that I feel there ought to be something more constructive that I can do - something less hurtful to me and more helpful to you.

For you it would be the opposite. It would mean being prepared to admit to some sort of commitment, not to a fantasy future but to what you see as worthwhile in me in the here and now. What we share as being good and wholesome - and perhaps durable.

And yet I realise that all this is impossible for both of us so what do we do about it ? You keep on searching (regardless of age discrepancies)? Or hoping that Jodi will return ? Me keep on hoping ? And hurting ? And scribbling ?

I'm frightened at having written all this because I know you don't want the heavy stuff. And maybe that's why I'd hoped to escape for a quiet time with you to give it a chance to emerge without the constant pressure of the next thing to be done, people to be seen - or my having to rush back to horrid Hampshire.

And I guess I know what your reply will be. If you even feel like it. You sent me such a lovely warm, open, loving letter and this is what you get in reply. Poor recompense. And the odd thing is that whenever I have felt hurt or upset or in need of comfort, just at the right moment, as if by magic, that's what has come from you. Don't want to stop writing and give up what I have of you which I need and value so much. I suppose I've felt it for a while, the frenzy of activity which has helped to obscure the intensity of Jodi pain but has also made you less available to me. You register doubt yourself - "I do appreciate you, don't I ?" you ask, as though you're not quite sure whether, despite saying how much you appreciate me, I will really feel it. Because maybe you can't really feel it yourself ? Or it has no value for you. I almost feel as though I haven't existed. Feel maybe I've misled you and you've over-estimated my generosity in tolerating your obsession with Jodi, and the pursuit of possible future happinesses, without seeing what you have right here and now.

You see, despite the funniness of last Monday's situation, despite the wry humour with which you recount it, despite the fact that I know deep down that it hurt you and sent you scurrying for Simon & Garfunkel, I can't help feeling like an elderly dowager who's been relegated to the back seat of your charabanc while you sit in the front in your Biggles outfit with a fantasy blow-up dolly beside you, all cutie-pie lips, fluttering skirt/eyelashes and stocking top. You've made me incredibly comfortable in this back seat, all plumped up with cushions and kittens and chocolates and I know there are needs I can satisfy which Miss Cutie-Pie can't but nevertheless, there I am. Here I am.

I'm feeling - and I guess this is going to ring so many bells - in a horribly clanging, jangling sort of way - I'm feeling as though your regrets for what you haven't achieved in the past and your hopes for what you want to achieve in the future, are very much more important than what you have right now in the present, actually in your hand. The eternal search. You discovered what you had lost with Jodi and I'm not saying that the same situation prevails because I know it doesn't, but nevertheless, I'm feeling the same I guess, as she did, and Vanessa, and Annie. That in relation to your present, I don't sort of exist because you're so hung up on past sadnesses and future hopes. And the trouble is that there's gradually getting more of the past and less of the future - which is why something has got to happen to stop the rot. You'll go on doing it Chris - you can't help yourself.

Just realised.

I _know_ why I feel like a nobody in your present life - it's because I'm neither a 'romantic/tragic' figure from your past, nor a hope for your future. I'm just part of the hurly-burly of diversions with which you cram every available minute of the present to insulate you from both the other states. And it's meaningless to you, so therefore, so am I. One difference between me and the others is that, in spite of Zarek's attempt to crush me out of existence, because of my age/experience/_confidence_, you cannot threaten _my_ confidence in myself. I _do_ believe in who and what I am - hence my affirmation at the end of my last letter - I _am_ worthy. Which is why I don't want to quit. So there !

And don't you dare come bleating back about my three kids. _You_ have twenty-three, _fifty-three_ people at least with whom you share your life, to whom you make yourself limitlessly available - whom you enjoy beyond measure and who weary you ceaselessly with their endless demands - _just_ like children. So if anything, I feel that the balance is slightly in my favour !

OK so I can't do anything about my family - they need me. Well so does yours and it would be no more possible for you to wipe the slate clean and start all over again than it would be for me.

D'you know I think I might actually _send_ this letter ! My initial reaction to yours, after the amusement and awareness of your deep down hurt was of absolute emotional agony and desperation. _Not_ wanting to put pressure on you, not wanting to give up. It wasn't that you hurt me Chris. I felt demolished. At first I thought you had a better grasp of reality than me but now I'm not so sure - you've certainly less confidence. Poor old thing.

Do so want to talk to you - and make love too although maybe I've put you right off and other possibilities seem more attractive, less threatening. And I'm not sure that either of us is ready for the heavy stuff yet. So forgive me if I've hurt you or made you feel impatient or angry. You know I care too much to ever want to do that.

<u>Dear</u> Chris - <u>please</u> don't let's drift because of our neuroses. But let's try to use our combined <u>strengths</u> to help each other. Love Lizzie xxxx Wanting you without hassle and hang-up.

41. Painful progress

The good news at this stage was that Zarek's cancer had not spread. His treatment had been successful and there was no need for him to have lymph nodes removed. This meant that everything could proceed, as far as I was concerned, as quickly as possible. I hadn't realised how much his illness and enforced immobility had ground me down. I felt my dreams burgeoning again, like flowers warmed by spring sunshine. It was as though I had been in No Man's Land for weeks.

Good news was of course, tempered by bad and this came via my solicitor. Blackmail. Only if I relinquished the custody contest, would Zarek get off Pete's back and not inform his wife about his infidelity. Pitiful. Pathetic. Unbelievable. This appeared to be the opinion of both my solicitor and Zarek's, definitely not the reaction of a gentleman. Apparently he also thought I was lying about the duration of my sexual relationship with Chris and suspected my every move. One evening when I had popped out to see a friend whose husband was busy defending the Falklands, I found when I got home after less than an hour, that Zarek was also out. He arrived back shortly after me and immediately asked "How was Pete?" Told him to ring friend Katie who I had been with and left it at that but I did wonder if he'd been snooping round Pete and Stella's house to see if I was there. Barking up completely the wrong tree as I'd had nothing to do with Pete for over a year.

Managed to get a fiver out of Zarek for bottling some beer which he'd brewed at the Day Hospital for some party or other. Amazing what they did in the name of Occupational Therapy. It was a nightmare job. No clean bottles so I had to wash and sterilise them. Then had to collect Daisy from school and return for a hair-raising hour later in the afternoon with Alice, Daisy and her friend Victoria, to bottle and cork five gallons of the stuff. One bottle got smashed so there was sticky, beery swill and glass to clear up and then a rush to get home in time for Greg coming out of school. Worth a lot more than a fiver I'd say.

Chris accepted everything that I had said in my recent letters, which was a relief, but they unleashed a whole spate of negative desperation about himself and the world at large. It was the usual stuff about his need to escape from reality and commitment and responsibility, like Peter Pan not wanting to grow up, living on borrowed time, not having any real future, not using his considerable talents both practical and interpersonal, and so on. He described each new relationship as like darting out of a cave to test and check his power over women and to forget that this carried with it responsibility to use that power constructively. He felt his life, making pots and teaching to be futile. Yes, he earned money but to what end ? Having a good time ? Buying things ? Travelling ? He saw no point in any of it and although he felt he had been lucky enough to experience more joy, love and happiness than most people, the greater was his guilt at not spreading it around more. It was a very woeful response.

I'd heard it all before but never expressed with such vehemence and bitterness. I'd thought if he had misunderstood what I had to say, it might make him very angry and that would be that, misunderstanding and hostility making easy barriers behind which to retreat. But if I had been right and he'd understood what I was saying, then it would be forcing him to confront realities which were almost unbearable. His response haunted me, made me conscious of how unhappy I seemed to be making people. Zarek plainly hated me and would do so even more if I separated him from his children, and I felt as though any analysis of Chris' situation simply served to rub his nose in his own misery.

Zarek's health meanwhile was definitely improving. He was eating more normally, spending more time downstairs with 'the family' and being thoroughly obnoxious. To my surprise, I was genuinely pleased he was better. Alternatives would have been too awful, too complex to cope with. It was already bad enough. In the midst of all this drama, there were still things to laugh about, like the time when Alice and I came downstairs from tidying and bed-making to find water on the kitchen floor ..... and pondweed ...... and the cat, crouched furtively under the kitchen table and looking very guilty .... with something moving in her mouth. Could it be, no, surely not ? .... a GOLDFISH ? Flip flap went a little golden tail, crunch crunch gulp went Puss, and our Superfish was no more, gone to that greater fishtank in the skies/cat's stomach. Not completely gone however. For along came little Alice, bearing with the utmost delicacy, poor Superfish's only mortal remains. His head. I looked at that little fishy face, I who had decapitated and dismembered more fish than I could number, and felt that I had lost a friend. I'd dutifully tended the fish for eighteen months with little more than contempt and yet I felt I <u>knew</u> that fish. Ah me.

I wonder now why I'd waited to proceed with the divorce until Zarek's health had improved. If I'd been really intent on 'winning' mightn't it have been an idea to press on regardless in the hope that a very sick man would be seen as a risky custodial parent for three young children ? This didn't occur to me, nor was it suggested by anyone else. It was as though it was the 'decent' thing to do, to wait until both protagonists were squaring up on an even playing field. So it wasn't until Zarek was in better shape that my solicitor had finally received a copy of his affidavit . In addition to asking me for my comments, paragraph by paragraph, he had also suggested that I should make some kind of positive statement concerning my future plans with Chris as he might be called as a witness.

At this point I had challenged Chris to think very carefully about how much he wanted to be involved and I'd also reconsidered my decision to move to East Anglia, whether it was to associate with Chris or not. If I had decided to stay in Southsea, at least the children could have had educational continuity. Assuming that I would have to get a job there, the very last thing I wanted was to bump into Zarek or his reputation. The obvious difficulty was that the only place I was likely to find employment as an Occupational Therapist in mental health services, my only career option at that time, was in the hospital where he worked. The affidavit didn't completely demolish me but was extremely hurtful

and used up a fair bit of the self-confidence I'd been storing away for when the going got tough/tougher. Here it is:
ZAREK'S AFFIDAVIT

1. *I make this affidavit in support of my application for custody of the three children of the family - G.E.U, D.J.U, A.H.U.*
2. *At the present time the Respondent and I are still living in the same house and are both responsible for the upbringing of the children.*
3. *On the 18th August 1982, I issued a petition for divorce against the Respondent on the grounds of her adultery with two men (both named). She and they have admitted committing adultery and on the 16th. November 1982, I was granted a decree nisi on the grounds of the Respondent's adultery. The fact that the Respondent was committing adultery with two different men was a tremendous surprise and shock to me and I regard her behaviour as totally irresponsible.*
4. *The Respondent has not been a satisfactory mother. She swears in front of the children. They seem often to annoy her. She is bad-tempered and screams at them and on occasions has been physically violent with them. I remember on one occasion when her parents were having a meal with us, Greg was misbehaving in a minor way. I am usually in favour of ignoring minor transgressions by my children as I believe that to draw attention to them makes them worse, but she usually makes a fuss about them. On this particular occasion she caught hold of Greg's hand and pulled him violently off the chair and*

dragged him across the floor of the dining room. He was amazed and shocked and cried out "Mummy, what are you doing this to me for ?" When Alice, who was only two at the time, had thrown a piece of food from her plate, the Respondent spanked her causing the child great distress. The Respondent did it again when the child pulled a needle out of a piece of knitting. This sort of incident was repeated on many occasions. When the children were tiny, she used not to get up at night when they awoke and cried. Apart from the very early days when they were being breast-fed, I always got up to attend to the children at night and still do so as my wife habitually sleeps very deeply and does not hear the children crying in distress. I do not believe that the Respondent likes children or really wants the responsibility involved in bringing up children.

5. *From a bundle of correspondence in my possession and from various comments made by the Respondent, it is quite clear that she would wish to leave the matrimonial home and to go and either live with the first Co-Respondent in Suffolk or at least live near him there, taking the children with her. I would strongly object to this man having any part in the upbringing of my children. In the first place he lives in a small cottage which would be totally unsuitable for the children. Secondly, he is an impecunious potter who follows a Bohemian way of life. He has had, I understand, a number of relationships with women, all of which have broken down and I do not believe he has any wish to get involved in the long-term care of the children.*

6. *Throughout the lives of the children I have spent a good deal of time with them. As already mentioned, I used to get up to them when they were small and woke up in the night. All through the marriage, the Respondent seemed to be happy when she could get out of the matrimonial home. She developed musical interests which kept her often away, leaving the care of the children to me. She spent many weekends away from home, ostensibly visiting friends or her parents, but in fact, so I subsequently discovered, to stay with her lover. I welcomed every opportunity of being with my children whom I deeply love.*

7. *If the children were to stay with me they would have stability. My proposals are that they should continue to live with me in the house which has been their home all their lives. It is a four-bedroomed detached house with three reception rooms and a large garden. The children have their friends and animals around them and they all go to local fee-paying schools, where they are making excellent progress and enjoy school life including social activities and friendships that they have already established.*

8. *I state that I can provide the children with financial as well as emotional stability. I am a Consultant Psychiatrist earning approximately £20,000 per annum gross. My hours of work are flexible so that I could spend even more time with the children than heretofore. I have also ascertained that there is living across the road from me, a registered child-minder approved by the Local Authority. She would be able and indeed willing to look after the two*

eldest children after school and for periods during the holidays when I am at work. There is available at St. Mary's Hospital, a crèche for the children of hospital staff working within the Health District. The crèche is situated within a five minute walk of my place of employment, (you'd have to be fit !) St. James' Hospital, Portsmouth, which could take the youngest child, Alice. In fact Alice has been to the crèche for three days on a trial basis during the last half term ie 22 - 29 October. She was very happy there and did not want to leave. In fact the Respondent insisted that she should stay no longer. The crèche is open from 7.30 a.m to 6.00 p.m Monday to Friday, there are eight qualified staff, two trainees and two voluntary workers and they have a staff/child ratio of 1:1. I am also contemplating employing a full-time trained nanny and find from my enquiries that I could easily obtain one from one of the colleges. There is a room in the house available for a nanny. Finally, I have had offers of help to babysit from many of my friends in case of emergency. The children are in fact very independent. There would be no difficulty in taking them to school as there is a rota of parents.

9. There are a number of activities in which I would involve the children and in which the Respondent is not interested. For example, I would like the two eldest children to go to a local sailing school to learn to sail, to take them to judo lessons which the children enjoyed on one occasion, but this was actively discouraged by the Respondent. Although she pretends to be musical, she never tried to

encourage them to have music lessons with her, despite their active interest.

10. As a Consultant Psychiatrist, I feel that I understand better than the Respondent, the emotional needs of the children and I am confident that I can provide for them in a more satisfactory manner than can the Respondent. She is very immature and has her mind firmly fixed on her plans to go and live with the first Co-Respondent. From some of her remarks, it appeared to me clear that she wanted to have the children with her because it would provide her with enough maintenance not to have to work herself but to devote her time and energy to the first Co-Respondent who is himself impecunious.

11. I am prepared to devote all my time and energy, other than that which I have to devote to my professional life, to my children. The children are very well integrated in the local community. They have many friends, go to various parties and occasions and are very close to each other. I think it is essential that they should not be uprooted and most important that they should not be separated.

12. In all the circumstances I ask this Honourable Court to make an order granting me custody of the three children of the family.

For me, this affidavit was riddled with untruths, half-truths and misinterpretations, each of which I itemised in my response to my solicitor. It had me quivering with impotent rage, Chris too when I sent him a copy. At this time he was preoccupied by a production of A Midsummer Night's Dream in which he was playing one of the 'Rude

Mechanicals', but his reaction when he read it was quite something.

June 1983 Suffolk

D'you know Liz this makes me absolutely SICK, MURDEROUS, SO angry. This pompous B*****D !! P***K. W****R. Words fail me. How can he possibly think he can get away with it ?! I've SEEN your affidavit when you described all the things he has done to destroy your family life and any love that you might once have had for him, heard all about them from you over the recent years. How can he possibly think he will get away with it after you've spelt it all out in your own affidavit - the times he over-rode your decisions with the children, their food, their clothing, criticised your attempts to teach them how to behave, pushed you out of the way when you'd been to the GP to get help with Greg's chestiness, ignored your need for help when you had mumps and pneumonia, hit you - not just once but umpteen times, kicked you in the bum when you were pregnant with Daisy, moved out of your bedroom for eight weeks for God's sake when you'd thrown away a bit of toast !!!

Unfaithful ? My God I'm surprised you haven't killed him ! As for "understanding the children's needs" - he's clueless, couldn't understand the needs of a dead pig let alone three beautiful, intelligent, lively children and a beautiful, intelligent, lively, once loving and devoted wife. I KNOW you would give them your all and you've promised to do so. And as for us, we WOULDN'T get hitched because we know that neither of us wants it. Surely the Court will see that ?

How can he possibly think with his oh so important job that he can also care for three children, continue all of the lovely things you have done to try and make their childhood fun, happy and enjoyable ? It's outrageous. He DOESN'T STAND A CHANCE. Believe me. Cx

42. A date

The exchange of affidavits had at last triggered a date for our hearing which was to be on the 4th July. American Independence Day. Although it was a relief to know that this particular chapter was to come to an end, it also scared me silly. Scared me that the detached and not-bothering sort of attitude I'd lived with for so long, might have become the real me so that I was no longer capable of sustaining interest and involvement with my environment. Scared me that the children might be bringing too much of Zarek and his attitudes for me to be able to establish an independent way of life for all of us. Scared me that I wouldn't have the strength to reorganise things in the way I wanted for the children and that I'd go on muddling along and find that ultimately it hadn't been worth the long struggle. Scared me because of what I had to go through with the actual case, standing up in court while an unknown judge pawed over the wreckage of our marriage.

All of this left a sour taste in my mouth and a horribly wobbly and insecure feeling everywhere else but life had to go on. The next Saturday evening had been the village's annual Playschool Barbecue. It was always a very good 'do' and as Zarek was to be out elsewhere, I'd waited until Alice was asleep and had then taken Greg and Daisy. It was only a couple of hundred yards down the road after all and Alice never woke once she had dropped off.

It was a good do. Greg and Daisy were busy with their friends all evening so when it was time to go, it took me ages to find them. I had been helping to serve food most of the time and knew loads of people there but had this odd, sad feeling of regret and anxiety. Here I was with a crowd of people I knew, whose babies I had seen like mine, growing into children and with whom, although we hadn't that much in common, I'd shared a great deal over the years. Should I really be uprooting my children to start all over again in much less secure circumstances? Would it be worth it ? More guilt about deception. Maybe I really wasn't the person they thought they all knew. Wanted to escape and felt very low when I got home even though it had been a pleasant event.

Was busy getting Greg and Daisy into bed, very late for them and went into Daisy's room where Alice slept and found her bed empty. My heart stopped. Such a fright. Soon found her curled up and sound asleep in the big armchair in Zarek's room, tightly clutching his T-shirt. Couldn't imagine the horrors she had gone through when she had awakened and there was nobody there to answer her cries. More fearful guilt. Must never ever do that again. She seemed unperturbed in the morning and I didn't dare tell Zarek but I felt awful about it.

The next day, Zarek had been amazingly mellow, almost chatty at lunchtime, which made me feel fifty times worse about disliking him so much. He'd insisted on making some Polish potato noodles which none of the children liked so lunch was an absolute shambles and I wasn't sure what any

413

of them actually ate. It was like a running buffet with never more than two people seated at the table at the same time.

The afternoon was gloriously sunny which meant that the paddling pool came out, but oh, what a hassle. My lot and four 'friends' - swimming costumes, towels, wet children, cold children, running in and out, can we have a drink, yes, and ice cream, no, not 'til later. Greg keep the hosepipe down as I'm getting soaked, don't be rough in the paddling pool or you'll split it, let Alice have her bike, you're too heavy to go in that pram, Daisy stop hitting Esther with that cricket stump, wah wah wah from Alice, go home you lot, we're having tea and umpteen times - Greg, will you please stop yelling so much, the neighbours want their Sunday afternoon siesta. The noise level was unbelievable. Greg finally broke the handle of the very quaint little wooden pram my father had made for Daisy which made me feel both angry and sad. Didn't take it out on him but tried to get him to see why I minded. Poor kid.

And all the time, underneath, this growing fear and the most compelling need to escape and start again. But would it/could it be better ? I knew that my feelings of fear weren't going to go away. The case was seven weeks away, so compared with the forty it takes to grow a baby, it was just around the corner. Zarek at this time was back on fighting form and didn't miss an opportunity to belittle any effort on my part, so I didn't make much in order to diminish his chances. One of the basic tenets of his psychiatry was to give people responsibility for their own lives, even in small ways - things like not locking up all the scissors if they were potentially suicidal so that they had the chance (or choice) to rise to the occasion and behave responsibly, whatever that might mean to them. From my experience, the converse of this was also true. He'd wanted to talk about money but each of his proposals was depriving me of choice which made me feel very bolshie and mischievous. He proposed that he would do all the bulk shopping and I therefore wasn't to spend more than £10 at a time on purchases. (So perhaps £10 every day ?) Secondly, I was only to use the car for expeditions involving the children. (Perhaps I could 'hire' it from him for my own use ?) And thirdly, I wasn't to use the phone for my private conversations, only arrangements concerning the children. (Which gave me plenty of scope for chatting with friends.)

From whom, offers of help and support flooded in. Stella said she'd have the children at the time of the hearing, Mrs. Jennifer had said she'd come to court with me and sit around outside for whenever I needed her. Bronwen had said I could pop in for lunch as she lived just round the corner from the court and my parents also planned to come and stay at a hotel in Southsea while it was going on. I had started to get that tying up ends feeling, like when you have a baby or mend all your underwear before going on holiday. Wanted to get the house and garden sorted, altered a skirt that was too big, prepared everything, ready for The Next Stage. Whatever it might be.

Four book had appeared in Zarek's study which told me how he was preparing to fight the case. Firstly, there was The Feminine Mystique by Simone de Beauvoir which I'd read years ago but couldn't remember much about except that it had become a sort of feminist Bible. Then there was The

415

Myth of Motherhood and I can't remember that either. The third one was about the effects of divorce on children and finally there was a novel about a woman whose marriage was destroyed by a supposedly emancipated legal contract which was drawn up to establish that if the marriage broke down, she would only take exactly what she had put into it and not what the law said was hers by right. It looked as though Zarek saw himself as a champion for the cause of equal parental rights of fathers and was planning on taking on the whole of legal and social opinion in relation to mothers having custody of their children. It seemed a pity he hadn't shown more interest in the equal rights and responsibilities issue in our twelve year marriage so that we need never have got to the point of divorce. I'd wondered about suggesting to my counsel that she read the same books so that they could parry quote for quote.

The accruing stress and anxiety made me desperate for a brief respite. Chris' pressures were largely self-inflicted, optional and pleasurable - pottery production, lesson preparations at school and props for a Midsummer Night's Dream, easy-peasy, not like mine, so he was happy for me to pay a flying visit. Zarek didn't object either as he was delighted to have another opportunity to show what a competent father he was although when I was at home, he was quick to criticise my efforts whilst remaining splendidly aloof and detached from whatever was going on. It created a very oppressive atmosphere which evaporated, the minute he went out.

I managed to escape to Suffolk for a weekend and as well as seeing the final performance of the play, went to the

Summer Fayre at the school where Chris was teaching. The Fayre had a Second World War theme and It was odd seeing him wandering around in baggy old army shorts and tin hat, dispensing his subtle mixture of distanced familiarity with the kids. It gave me enormous pleasure to know what was going on under the tin hat, to know that I had the freedom to twine my bare legs in his, to feel his bare body against mine and to know that there was nothing that could impede the entry of him into me, despite our apparently decorous behaviour in such decorous surroundings. Very exciting.

That evening, in the play, Chris was his usual highly entertaining self, well suited to the part he played. He'd made himself a crude cardboard 'wall' with a very obvious crib of his lines, scrawled on the back and when he arrived in the auditorium for his entry he missed his footing and spewed peanuts all over the stage which the audience seemed to think was intentional. After the inevitable last night party, Chris said he'd had the same experience as me at the School Fayre, that 'secret places' knowledge hidden by clothes which generates a frisson of anticipatory sexual excitement, unknown to everybody around and even to the person who has generated it. Mmmmm.

At the play, Chris had obligingly got a seat for me , next to his friend Garry who I'd met on an earlier visit. Garry was one of those people who appeared to have an 'open' marriage. He and his wife had made no secret of their affairs tempered by their underlying devotion to each other. I suppose a long time ago, I might have succumbed to his man-looking-for-a-mistress line, but attractive though he was, he also appeared to be quite anxious and insecure, and troubled by his life. To me, Chris was in a different class, worth twenty, no, two hundred Garrys. One of the things that I had learnt about him through the months of our relationship was his absolute straightness, disarming honesty and trustworthiness. Because of this, I felt that I could never ever let him down.

43. Two worlds

As usual, once I'd returned home, it took time to discipline myself back into the daily domestic routine. The dreadful daily domestic routine. Once home, I guzzled peanut butter, cheese and chocolate as the usual final gesture of independence before settling into my more austere diet and routine. No more talking, laughing and loving time, except with the children. My final indulgence that evening was a letter to Chris and a generous slug of whisky. Just as well Zarek hadn't seemed to be marking the bottle as he was still paying for it whenever I replenished household supplies.

I'd been asked to do the church flowers the following week and had been looking forward to it until I realised that in mid-June, all the spring flowers had finished and later ones like roses weren't yet in bloom. I was reluctant to spend any of my miniscule income on buying flowers but with nothing much in the garden, there was no choice. I bought clusters of chrysanthemums, irritatingly unseasonal but pretty colours, palest pink, palest bronze and white, and found some nice leafery from our garden and mock orange blossom from Mrs. Jennifer's. My floral creation stood resplendent in the Sanctuary, a sort of organised chaos which looked alright to me but stuck out like a sore thumb, a tousled bed-warm head in relation to the three immaculate Constance Spry look-alikes situated elsewhere in the Church. Maybe I should have tried to compromise a bit, snip off the odd bird-shitty leaf or twig for the sake of the 'line' but I liked them to look as though they were still growing. As a compromise, I'd suggested to the lady who was responsible for the flowers that I wouldn't have minded in the least if she had hidden my effort behind a pillar but to be honest, I didn't think there was one big enough. In my mind, I was remembering twenty years ago, when Chris had sent me a rhododendron blossom from his mother's garden in a cardboard box, so carefully wrapped that when it arrived it looked as fresh as when he had picked it. The memory of my delight had remained with me throughout all the intervening years.

Daisy was curious to know what I'd been doing all morning in the Church, so I took her in later only to find a wedding in progress. Bride looked beautiful in decollete lace dripping off her shoulders, but I was reminded of Australian friend James who, when with Janet, his partner for ten years unwed, used to call out with great glee to emerging wedding couples, "You'll be sorry !" Actually, I suspect he was the one who was sorry as it was Janet who fled back to England after spending a decade with him in Australia.

That weekend, the weather was glorious. Zarek was on-call so out most of the time and Greg had his first experience of a Scout/Cub jamboree, which left me and the girls on our own to enjoy the sunshine in the garden. Knowing that no-one would come near enough to scrutinise me closely, I donned shorts and suntop which transformed any of my prominences, shoulders, collar bones, nose etc. from maggoty white to mottled pink. It was hard to understand why there was so little pigment in my skin when I had dark hair and brown eyes – no sign of a suntan.

Alice's birthday was the next day. I'd bought her a birthday card with a badge on it which I knew she'd like and a dear little doll's house. Zarek produced a diminutive Japanese violin which seemed a bit premature to me, it being her third birthday, but she liked it with little idea of what she should do with it. We had profiteroles, strawberry Pavlova and a clock birthday cake for tea having spent the morning at a local petshop where we had purchased a tortoise. We'd put it in the rabbit's pen with lots of shiny windmills and balloons so it looked very festive. As usual at a birthday tea party, Zarek was of us, but not with us, lurking with his cine camera and in the process being thoroughly disruptive. Alice too had excelled herself, first of all screaming blue murder because I didn't think it a very good idea for her to eat all of the clown candle which topped the profiterole pyramid. She seemed to prefer it to any of the other available food. Then she stood on her chair for a few moments, and concentrated hard before announcing, "Poo Mummy" by which time the telltale bulge had already appeared at the back of her pants, to the delight of the assembled company. This she managed to shed in a trail of little hard lumps like sheep droppings on her way to the loo.

All of this was soon overtaken by a phone call that I received from my solicitor the next day. Would I attend the Portsmouth court for a consultation with my Barrister. You bet I would.

She was a nice woman, around about forty, very easy to relate to, very matter of fact, and with no legal 'side' to her. I guessed she'd heard it all before. She had Zarek sussed and had an excellent grasp of the situation. I was advised that I had to have concrete arrangements for the children and our life elsewhere to present to the court, that I must decide on schools and arrange for the children to have places in them that September, that I should go ahead and arrange to start my job on the first of October and that I should have my tenancy of the hospital accommodation available to me, confirmed in writing. Bowled over. A lot of telephone calls. A lot of excitement mostly because I hadn't anticipated things moving so quickly nor suddenly becoming so real. Waiting for the house to be sold in order to have some money didn't come into it, she was telling me I should get started with my future with the children.

She also seemed to be more aware than I was of how oppressed I'd been by Zarek. So instead of allowing him to dictate the pace of events, I was to seize the initiative and start making things happen for myself. She thought it inadvisable to bring Chris into it as it might draw unnecessary attention to our relationship but she was very penetrating in the questions she asked, presumably wanting to make sure that I could withstand cross-questioning from 'the other side' because they would try challenging my assertion that Chris and I were not going to live together. I was told to emphasise that we had '.....a close and loving friendship but one within which we both needed space to operate independently.'

Feeling the future come alive, immediately sent all my doubts scurrying away so that I felt positive and confident about my plans. I started to see a future without having to constantly reconcile the differences between myself and Zarek. A mixture of sunshine and optimism filled my heart because I knew that I had something to build on. Zarek looked more and more like a loser and inevitably became more dictatorial as he saw the control of his family slipping out of his grasp.

The following weekend was my Sunday to play for Evensong and I'd been told there would be a baptism, two children from the same family, a baby and a toddler. This may not seem terribly relevant to my own story but it reminded me that our personal complications may be no worse than those experienced by others. Different, yes, but would I have wanted to exchange mine for those that I'm describing here ? No thank you.

When the family had noisily trooped into the Church, I was surprised to see that it was a former cleaning lady of mine, Norma and her postman partner. She'd already had two children by a previous relationship, one of whom was quite disturbed and attended a special school. Potts the Postie as he was known, had an unfortunate history as he'd been caught and prosecuted for knicker-picking from local clothes-lines which in our small village had caused quite a stir. About a week before Alice had been born, Norma stopped working for me on the pretext that her two children needed more attention. It wasn't wonderful timing from my point of view but I had a sneaking suspicion that she was a bit envious of my pregnancy and lo and behold, she produced her own baby ten months later. Then she had another one eighteen months after that and I can remember thinking 'blimey, but good luck to them. I hope they can manage.' The baptism went ahead, lots of relatives, doting Godparents, the older son behaving oddly, babies screaming, Norma grinning sheepishly, Potts the Postie looking detached and resigned as the whole business proceeded. I was glad to be playing for them and tried to do it as well as I could even though I knew that my efforts on the organ would be the last thing they were aware of. Afterwards I went to say hello to Norma (who looked so fat I wondered if she might be pregnant again) and admire the baby who had looked very sweet and animated as far as I could see from the mirror above the organ. I looked into her little face and had the saddest realisation - she was a Down's syndrome child. We had problems ? What would their life be like and what chance did those children have ? Norma's postie had been very reluctant to marry her but what did that matter ? As it was, he had looked utterly resigned, trapped.

Future becoming present

44. The real world

Suddenly, so much was happening I could barely cope. Up to this point it had been the inertia that had been getting me down but now that I had to establish a credible reality to demonstrate to the court that I meant business, it was the intense activity which nearly floored me. But I managed it. In the space of a couple of days, I'd visited Chris and gone to Bury St. Edmunds where I'd sorted out schools, my job and I had a hospital flat for me and the children to live in which was all included in another affidavit that my solicitor had compiled. Our future was definitely taking shape. However, there was something else that didn't only floor me, it literally swept the ground from under my feet.

I'd had an urgent phone call from my solicitor. Please would I go to his office as soon as possible. I arrived to see a great pile of photocopied letters on his desk. I saw my own writing, I saw Chris's. They were copies of many of the letters which had passed between us. These had been forwarded from Zarek's solicitor with the news that they were to be used by him in our court case. The shock of seeing them there, replete with purple passages, sexy drawings, loving and very personal descriptions of the passionate times we had shared together completely demolished me. I guessed that every time I'd been away, Zarek had turned the house upside down to find all my secret (ha !) hiding places. I took the letters home and tried to read them through but couldn't bear to. Worst of all was that I kept coming across odd sentences and phrases which taken out of context made me sound almost indifferent to having the children. What I had actually been doing, was to explore on paper, all aspects of my feelings in order to understand what I really wanted to happen but the bits Zarek planned to use had all been highlighted, and separated from their context, they completely misprepresented my true feelings.

My counsel had wanted a session with me to go through the letters. It could have been awful, cringe-making, but she was very sharp with a great sense of humour thank goodness. She said she'd roared out loud with laughter while reading them on the train and seemed to perceive all of us, Zarek, me, Chris, and the letters for what we were. She appreciated how they might be misinterpreted and what she'd have to do to get them properly understood. When I told her Zarek had been attempting to show them to his colleagues, in tones of utter incredulity, she had breathed "that's monstrous" and I felt she understood. I felt I could trust her although I suppose to her it was all in a day's work. It didn't occur to either of us at that time that the letters had in effect been 'stolen' and might therefore have been considered inadmissible evidence. Perhaps this was just as well. Our case felt complicated enough, without us embarking on a protracted journey across the legal minefield of intellectual property rights.

Living under the same roof as a man with whom this cat and mouse game was being played out was devastating. We barely spoke to each other but at the weekend, together we took the children to the beach. At least they enjoyed it, and the sea breezes were a wonderful antidote to the intense heat that would otherwise have kept us indoors all day. Feeling a bit stronger, that night I settled down and read the whole lot through. Every word. And honestly they didn't seem as bad as I'd thought and if anyone had taken the trouble to read everything, and providing they weren't too shocked by the explicit sexual content, then it was an accurate account of all that had happened. There was nothing I felt unable to defend nor anything that showed me up in a different light to how I'd been all along. But they were of course, my letters. Our letters.

Zarek must have been going through everything with a fine tooth comb to find bits to quote back in court. He'd found my reference to his blindness at not noticing all the letters flying backwards and forwards between me and Chris but he made no reference to all the worthwhile things I'd said or the sympathy I'd tried to show him, especially when he was ill, all the times I had tried to put ourselves in his shoes. Despite everything that I had written, it had always been tempered with sadness, sympathy for him and frustration that he couldn't unbend but that was never mentioned. He needed to show that I was a mean, uncaring bitch.

Because of his illness, he'd been at home for four months, at a time when we were least able to cope with each other. He was being absolutely vile, bossing, bullying, criticising, countermanding, taking over, denigrating, never missing an opportunity to put me down. Every contact gave rise to battles. One morning it was because Greg didn't have a clean shirt. Well he did but it simply needed ironing. To Zarek this was an obvious example of my inadequacy as a mother. Another time, Daisy had gone to play with Esther, a

429

rather clingy child from up the road and Zarek had said that Alice could go too. No sense of a six and eight year old playing together and needing minimal supervision whilst three year old Alice going along with them would need much closer attention and would therefore make demands on the other child's mother. No phone call with her to check that it was OK. There was also the occasion he'd called me a paranoid little schoolgirl who liked sleeping around and he was doing all this with a high sense of moral self-righteousness, the all-coping, all competent Father/Mother amalgam taking everything in its stride and knowing exactly how to handle everyone. Man handle. Ugh.

I knew that I had to get away from this man but felt so conscious of all that we lost by parting in this awful destructive way. The children might remember these apparently sunshiney days and wonder why their carefree existence with Mummy and Daddy together came to such an abrupt end. But it couldn't be otherwise. That was Zarek's game plan.

45. Delay

I might have known that something would happen to obstruct the whirlwind progress of the previous couple of weeks when so much had been settled and the future had started at last to feel real.

The first indication of a possible delay came from my solicitor who had said that the original judge who'd been scheduled to hear our case was no longer available. Instead, we had apparently been assigned a crusty and volatile old sod, much given to snapping pencils between his fingers at the least provocation. It appeared that he was impatience personified and would make up his mind in five minutes about the outcome to a case and then huff and puff if it took another day and a half to be completed. There was also a possibility that he might not hear the case at all because he'd recently refused to hear one about a pub where he'd once had a drink. And as predicted, he soon found an interest to declare which contaminated his impartiality. In his opinion, anyone who rejected the chance of sending their child to the school where Greg had been awarded a place where in fact Judge Crusty had once been a Governor, was clearly out of their mind, and so there was no way he could make an objective judgement in our case.

At this point I went numb. And stayed numb. No case. No nothing except more delay. More sitting it out in intolerable circumstances. Three problems. The first was the legal one about which I could do nothing. The second was that Greg was due to start his new school that September and with time passing, the possibility of him starting at one school because there had not been time to reach a decision and then having to be transferred to another if the court decided in my favour, became ever more real. This had always worried me above all else. The final problem was an emotional one, simply that I felt as though I had nothing left that would enable me to exist through another indefinite period. I'd scraped the barrel clean of all my coping resources.

There followed a series of quick fire telephone calls with my solicitor, who had been desperately attempting to find a space in different court schedules where our case might be heard. With courts depleted by summer holiday absences, even the High Court in London couldn't come up with an available date until mid-September. Then, miracle of miracles, an understanding Court Clerk in Winchester had grasped the urgency of our situation and produced two days, 30th. and 31st. August , when a court and judge were available. So be it. OK more waiting, but at least we had a definite end in sight, whatever the outcome. After so much uncertainty, I felt as though I'd waltz into the courtroom grinning broadly at the sheer relief of having got there.

Hold on a moment. The only person who apparently didn't know of this decision was Zarek, who just that day had arranged to take a week off, that particular week at the end of August, to take the children away on holiday. Obviously it was in his interest for Greg to start school in Portsmouth rather than anywhere else but his solicitor understood the need for him to be available especially as further procrastination on his part wouldn't look good. But yes, he was the only person to raise objection to this revised hearing date on account of the holiday he'd arranged and the disappointment the children would feel if they didn't go. Impossible to alter. Judge OK, Barrister OK, Solicitors OK, Defendant (me) OK, but not the bloody Petitioner. Fucking hell. What's more, I'd heard the swine desperately making last minute arrangements for a holiday cottage, over the phone when he MUST have known the date of the hearing.

Thank God, my solicitor had the presence of mind to arrange a special hearing before the Court Registrar to present my objections so that I had the satisfaction of hearing him say with incredulity "but you can't be meaning to take the children to Darlington, Darlington of all places for a holiday when a decision has to be made which will affect their whole lives ? The oldest child could end up starting in one new school and then have to be transferred to another. I have no patience with people who put holidays before such matters and I would suggest that the best way you can spend yours is in court causing the minimum inconvenience to your colleagues." So that was that. What's more, Zarek was ordered to pay the costs for that particular hearing.

August 1983 Hampshire

Very Dear Chris - poured myself a tumblerful of whisky an hour ago (in view of recent events it's surprising I didn't drink it straight from the bottle !) and was going to write to Hilda in Peru to tell her everything when I thought I'd just take a quick squizz at the letters again, THE letters. So read _all_ your letters and mine too. Numbness has overtaken me yet again since the hearing date has been moved forward. Now it's the thought of existing for another four weeks especially as it's the children's holiday and I've _got_ to make the effort to make things happen for their sakes. I'm _so_ glad you're trip to France has materialised so that you can get away from my nothingness which would just be boring and tedious for you. Another four weeks of Zarek poking into my letters, of keeping things going here - cutting the grass, cleaning the lavatories, endless tidying, hassles over meals. Day by day, day by miserable day, that's what it has to be. More weekends, more sinking feelings each evening as Zarek comes home. And the worry. Will it all happen in time to get the children off to school in Ipswich - endless unknowns, endless.

So. No point in dwelling on it.

Think the whisky is sitting in a puddle between my ears and it's Sunday School outing day tomorrow so maybe I'd better stagger to bed. Feel as though the real me has sort of evaporated somehow ….. love Lizziex

This almost feels like one of those "when you receive this I shall be already dead" type letters. Well, it's more than likely I shall be alive in the flesh even if the spirit feels as though it has reached an advanced stage of putrefaction. Hold your nose Chris. The smell is _dreadful_.

46. Apprehension

August 1983 South Wales (Written but not sent)

Dearest Chris - I'm sitting here with a pile of holiday postcards in front of me. Holiday postcards ? Yes, for here we are in a caravan in Wales, me and the children , eking out the time until the 30th August. CASE DAY. A friend happened to mention that her sister-in-law had this caravan to let on a farm so I'm here with the children until next Thursday when Zarek arrives and takes over for another week. Which all ties in wonderfully with your return from France since I shall just have got home and everyone else will still be in South Wales. So, two days peace for you and me before the storm breaks. I've letters to write, a good book and I can't do any of it because I've really buggered myself up inside. Thinking. That's the trouble with solitary holidays, isn't it - fortunately the children absorb most of my time but there's still enough left .....

Maybe this is the first or only letter you'll receive from me while I lie beside you in bed, wondering what is going to happen next. I can't send it to you now because you are in France and in any case, if I tried to say it, it would probably come out wrong. So, I write it because I have time and all my thoughts around me, and because I know I shall want to say something, to hear myself saying it, but may lack the courage to do so .....

You see it all started from my unanswered question when we were about to set off for the Midsummer Night's Dream. I'd asked why you had paired me up with Garry to see the play and you might have been about to say "No no, it wasn't the gentle brush-off, I simply wanted you to have pleasant company at the theatre." Nevertheless, I sat there in the theatre feeling strangely cold and quivering with anxiety for the whole of the first half, just wondering.

Wondering about things you've said recently like "but everyone thinks you're so attractive" and "you're young enough to start again."

Wondering if somehow when all my immediate troubles are over you'll want to evaporate out of my life so that I think I've imagined our involvement over the last eighteen months.

Wondering if I'll wake up in bed one morning and you'll say over tea and biscuits "oh by the way, I can't manage the play/film/concert next week because I'm getting married."

Wondering if , when you say (as after the Feydeau farce of that party a few weeks back) quite openly "but I didn't feel like a one-night stand," - if there have been other one-night stands or perhaps more importantly, if there are other relationships which might have seemed to pay off a higher dividend for your investment.

Wondering about all sorts of little things I've noticed or which you've been quite (fairly) open in telling me but which

I've been too polite (I suppose or maybe just dumb) to pursue.

Mrs. Jennifer said to me the other day "I really don't know how you've managed to survive through all this and I don't suppose you do either." And at the time I didn't, but since I've been thinking and started to feel the chill draught of insecurity, I realise that <u>you</u> have been the hearth at which I've warmed my emotions, my most constant and devoted friend always available to offer comfort and encouragement whenever my spirits were flagging. It's not that I've cherished secret hopes for the future, I don't think I have - at least I've tried to be as open and honest as I've always felt you to be with me and I can't imagine that anything would change this but now, alone with my thoughts, with the big ordeal so close and with you so far away, I'm obsessed with all sorts of fears which are probably meaningless but which I must exorcise somehow.

You see I feel this ever so slight distancing which I'd thought was due to a sort of mutual boredom with my seemingly endless situation. <u>I'm</u> bored with it too. Or maybe you've started to feel that when it's all over I shall put some sort of pressure on you - hadn't envisaged this - only that things wouldn't change, but perhaps you want them to. Or maybe it's because you've been too busy with school and seem to be really getting yourself together again. You don't seem to talk about you inside any more, letters have been less frequent and it's as though an indefinable personal component has slipped away from our communication. Mind you, with Zarek doing everything he can to intercept our letters, it would be hardly surprising if you were writing

437

fewer. To me though, the stage setting is still OK but I feel insecure - feel that it's something you don't want to share with me.

If this is so, and you know what it is, please tell me so that I can share in any plans or decisions that have to be made rather than washing around in this terrible sea of insecurity.

In a couple of weeks' time, I have to stand up in court and face the most hideous dissection of our intimacy, designed no doubt to make us both, and particularly me, appear as feckless and irresponsible as possible. Of course I'm at my most vulnerable now and if I'm chasing myself up a blind alley needlessly because of this intense worry, I'm sorry to drag you along with me. I know how in the past you've felt trapped by Vanessa and more particularly Jodi, coming at you with an acute attack of the 'heavies'. But you know I've never done this - it's just that I do like to be straight and know where I am with things. The biggest part of me inside is screaming no, no, not now, not with everything else falling about my ears and I can understand you, in your usual most considerate way, understanding this and wanting to protect me from it, but if it has to be now, well, it has to be. If you keep me going for my sake when you'd rather I were someone else, then it makes me feel such a fool somehow.

If I've got it wrong, then I'm sorry - sorry to have stirred things up when you have always shown me such love and consideration. It seems cruel to be untrusting but I'm about to enter the harshest fight for survival anyone could possibly face and which few people would have any comprehension of. I have to summon all my resources and I guess they aren't as tough as I'd once thought .....

August 1983 Hampshire

Lest the record be incomplete .....

Distraction. That's the name of the game now. Last few days. So it's distraction. And what more happy and delightful distraction could I have hoped for than your brief visit on your way home from your French holiday. One says thank you, hugs, kisses, waves, looks, but somehow writing has become closer to my feelings than almost anything else, except perhaps warm moist skin, and so I have to write it too. Not knowing what else I can say to demonstrate my utter gratefulness for that all too brief escape.

You see while I was plumbing the depths in South Wales, I wrote you this letter, which you will see sometime but not now, voicing anxieties and insecurities in relation to our situation - basically I suppose, my fears for a future which is so unknown. But I realise now that they hardly matter because in less than a week's time the whole scene will have changed so dramatically that <u>everything</u> will be different and it's going to take a long long time for me to be able to find my way around emotionally. Thank God you've got the sense to see this - I can barely comprehend how you've got yourself so knotted up in your life, your relationships, when you've handled me/us with such unfailing tact, consideration, generosity and compassion. I shall feel *gratitude for this for the rest of my life, whatever becomes of me. Or you. Or us.*

Stella's children were here all of today so I shared the French nougatine you brought back, between them - it was met with unanimous approval and thanks to my 'friend' for the treat ! Then I decided I'd had enough of toothache (I'm sure it's psychosomatic - whenever something stressful has been happening in my life it's associated with a trip to the dentist !) so telephoned the dentist who said he'd see me at 3.30. Off we went, me and six children for a couple of hours which were probably just as harrowing in their own right as anything I'm likely to experience in court. Dashed out during the interminable wait, for a supply of paper and crayons from the local art shop which was fortunately just round the corner. Alice was being utterly bloody-minded and eventually came and stood at my knees while the dentist performed. She sat down for a while and fell asleep but woke bellowing when she keeled over and bashed her head on his desk. Then had to chase round with all of them in the car to find a chemist still open to give me the antibiotic that had been prescribed. If it doesn't settle down after this, then it'll have to come out (the tooth) - I wonder how, on a bank holiday weekend with the case on Tuesday and Wednesday ? - String tied to a door-handle maybe ? Finally got home at sixish with all the children tired and hungry and me at the end of my tether. Zarek's attempt at helping was not "oh, what a lousy time you've had, what can I do to help ?" but "look how bloody-minded you are being, see how much better I can manage." Ugh.

All that's worth saying is thank you for being you and sharing so much of yourself with me. Thank you for French garlic and chocolate and sausage and cigarettes - lovely French Gauloises. And thank you for help with my bike - still firm and roadworthy, for puncture kit and pump. And thank you for driving and drinks and lots and lots of fun and laughter and bean shredding and chats and so much pleasuring with mind and bodies.

Thank you for scattering your gold dust so liberally in this part of the world and making yourself so available as friend and confidant and lover. Lover.

Hope that these last few days holiday here in Hampshire will have been every bit as enjoyable as the French cycling bit and that whatever the future brings for any of us will give the fulfilment that we are all searching for.

See you soon. Very much love, eternal respect, utter devotion, from Lizzie.

47. Panic

Dearest Hilda ,

I suppose it's crazy to start writing a letter at 1.15 a.m but I <u>have</u> to write. Get this.

Just supposing, after all that Zarek has done with <u>my</u> letters, I were to find one from another woman to <u>Chris</u> making it perfectly clear that he was sharing his favours. Wouldn't that be the wryest twist to the whole damn show ?

Well fucking sodding bloody hell, that's exactly what <u>has</u> happened. I'm still paralysed, choked with the pain of it and wondering what to do.

Chris had decided to go on a cycling holiday in Brittany. He came to cat-sit for a couple of days in Stella and Pete's house, just round the corner from us in the village, as we're not far from the ferry in Southampton and they were going to be away on holiday, so it suited everyone. Chris and I had a deliciously secret time together for a couple of days; after the children were in bed, and with Zarek at home, I'd escape for the evenings. Chris had left some gear behind at Stella's as he'd planned to do a bit of walking in Cornwall on his return and I'd said I'd wash some of it for him. He'd left in a frightful rush so I wasn't sure which bag the stuff would be in. I'd collected loads of rose petals to put in with his clothes once I'd washed them. The first bag I looked in had the clothes plus his address book and - a letter. What a punishment for my nosiness. It wasn't very intense but was obvious that they'd slept together. Recently. And who was it ? Julie from Leiston where "it's so relaxing and I can do nothing, absolutely nothing." Last time I went to his house there was a new picture on his bedroom wall, a stitched collage which he said she'd made. And I didn't enquire further out of politeness ..... nor was I brave enough to confront him with it when he returned from his French holiday, laden with presents for me and the children. My last letter to him promised my love and eternal devotion. To what, I'm wondering now ?

Funny thing is that I'd been wanting to talk about what he thought would become of us, wondering if he was hoping that once my troubles were over, he'd be able to evaporate out of my life, but now I simply dared not ask for fear it was true. Maybe he wanted me to find that letter to save him the bother of telling me or maybe it seemed not to matter to him. That's the most awful realisation. I've been feeling so insecure without knowing why (apart from the obvious) and when I was in Wales with the children, poured it all out on paper ..... but never sent it. How am I going to bear standing up in court, defending all that he has meant to me with the knowledge of what feels like a betrayal in my

heart ? I feel such a fool. An utter bloody idiot. Feel in a state of suspension and can't even free myself from the pain by crying. There's no-one I can tell either and by the time you receive this, it will all be over. I've felt so comfortable and secure with him but now, all that's gone and the real loss I'll feel when the divorce is through is not that of my husband, but of Chris.

Oh God Hilda, I really wish I was dead. Think about me. Love as ever, Lizzie.

So there I was, within days of having to stand up in court to fight for a future with my children, with the knowledge of Chris' duplicity staring me in the face. Stupidly I hadn't seen it coming so what hope could there possibly be for the outcome ?

48. Devastation

"So I am quite satisfied on detailed evidence that the Petitioner, Dr. Zarek Urbanczyk is not only capable of looking after the children but should continue to do so on the basis of care and control."

That's what he said, the judge, Mr. Justice Michael Roberts. A name I shall never forget. Nor shall I forget the date on which this pronouncement was made, 31st August 1983. Every year when it comes round, in spite of the many different, exciting, joyous paths that my life has taken since then, I recollect that quiver of utter desolation that enveloped me and the rage and indignation of feeling that I had been so misjudged. This is how it felt at the time:

I really feel ill. Very ill indeed. Not physically ill you understand. Not even ill with some kind of psychosomatic manifestation, a physical symptom of emotional turmoil. No, it is impossible to define this illness in terms of conventional symptomatology. There is pain certainly. But where is it ? Not in my head. Not in my body. But perhaps could it be in my heart ? Is it broken ? Is this what they mean by broken-hearted - a sort of total collapse of that part of oneself which is able to love and laugh and weep and mourn and show compassion, tolerance, understanding, concern for one's fellow sufferers ? Has that part of me gone ? Can it be mended ? My soul feels delirious, confused, fractured into a thousand splinters. What help is there in this strange world in which I feel I have no place ?

I am surrounded by loving 'nurses', my friends who tend my needs devotedly. But without a wish for recovery, there is no way in which I can reward them. I have no wish for recovery, no wish for reintegration into a world without my children.

I live in that courtroom a thousand times a day. Feeling again the judge's endlessly ponderous summary, knowing what he was to say at the end of it. Hearing over and over the words "and I have heard Dr. Urbanczyk say that he did not strike his wife and I believe him." So that I know that it has all been in vain, the barely endurable eighteen months, because as far as the court is concerned, I am the liar, fabricator of events, a worthless, feckless, irresponsible hussy. A bad influence on my children.

It really isn't true your Honour. You've got the wrong one. It's me telling the truth, not him. Look, it's in my diary, it's in the letters. <u>Please</u> read them again. <u>Really</u> read them and see if they show anything other than a decent, honest woman who's tried so hard to hang on to her integrity in spite of impossible odds. To hang on. To hang on ? Oh my God, can I .... ?

Just imagine …….

Consequences

49. Afterwards

"So I am quite satisfied on detailed evidence that the Petitioner, Dr. Zarek Urbanczyk is not only capable of looking after the children but should continue to do so on the basis of care and control."

These words had sealed my fate as a mother, and had relegated me to the ranks of an unusual and at that time, totally ignored minority of women, non-custodial mothers. Although a joint custody order was made, it was Zarek who was granted care and control whilst I got "very generous access indeed." This meant that the children would continue to live with him and that he would be responsible for their day-to-day well-being. To me, it felt like a face saving job to call it joint custody because my reality was that I had lost them. To the world at large, I felt like the ultimate failure, unable to sustain my marriage and unable to retain what should have been mine almost by definition, my role as a mother. Because of this, for several years my private life was a closed book to all but my immediate family and closest friends.

And so I followed through the plans that I had made, but alone. I hired a small removal van and drove it with such personal possessions and furniture that I could claim as mine from our family home across London to Suffolk and the flat which was to be my future address. I had a job to go to, yes, but no money and it was Chris who lent me the £500 that enabled me to purchase a serviceable car so that I could visit the children on a regular basis. Mobile phones didn't exist then, so I spent tearful hours in the dark and the rain that first month, outside a local phone box before my own phone was installed, longing for other people to finish their calls, hoping that the coins wouldn't get jammed or just tumble through, praying that I had enough change available. My flat on a housing estate, close to the hospital where I worked, was adequate but without money to purchase much in the way of carpets and furniture, the comforts were modest in comparison with the life-style I had been used to. My parents lent me money to help me get started and the first thing I bought, which was an emotional need rather than a practical one was a piano. This was a wonderful solace when the pain and loneliness of my situation overwhelmed me.

The children themselves seemed happy enough. At the time they were distressed and puzzled by what had happened, but they had had years of getting used to the ever-increasing distance between Zarek and myself so the fact of my actually moving out of the family home was possibly less shocking to them than it might have appeared. We established a regular routine of twice weekly phone calls, monthly visits when I went to see them and part of school holidays spent with me. I missed very much the intimacy of daily contact and learned not to read deep significances into what they told me about their home life because it was impossible for me to see the total picture. They were guarded about their feelings but desperately wanted to show me their happiest and most loving selves - possibly because their confidence in my love for them had been shaken by my absence and they were therefore trying to be as loveable as they could.

Without the children there were endless associations that brought pain. The run-up to Christmas was an agony of seeing the delight and eager anticipation on other children's faces and not of my own. On that first Christmas Eve, I can remember standing alone on the seashore near where my parents lived, playing with a flashing yo-yo that Chris had given me as a comfort present, but it did little to relieve the utter bleakness I was feeling.

Chris was helpful but clearly wanted to carry on with his life of multiple friendships and casual relationships of which I was but one. OK so this was what I had always maintained was what I wanted, but that was in anticipation of having the children with me. Without them, I had an unwanted freedom which was of little interest to him. Although we met regularly and spent enjoyable time together, within a year he had demonstrated that his romantic interests lay elsewhere.

At that time, of the three children, I missed my youngest daughter Alice the most. It's not that I loved her more than the others. Any parent will agree that their feelings for each child are different, not in quantity but just by nature of their different personalities and the response which one makes to them. The older two were achieving ever greater emotional independence while the little one and I still needed each other. Much later when she was in her early teens and there had been endless conflicts with her father, she climbed out of an upstairs window and took herself to

Social Services begging to be taken into care so that she could get away from him. Greg also needed to escape. He came to live with me and my second husband for his school sixth form years, a time that he describes as the happiest part of his schooldays.

Until then, non-custodial mothers had been an unresearched group. After all, we didn't matter to anybody, we were supposedly lying in the beds that we had made for ourselves. But what about the process of justice which brought us to this unthinkable situation. Was it really justice and for whom ? In my case I saw lies and distortions being accepted by a court of law as truth, and my ego took the harshest of body blows. I was not the person the judge chose to believe I was in order to make his decision, but there seemed nothing I could do to alter things. The day after the case had been heard, the hardest thing for me was when I saw my bicycle propped up against the garden wall with the child seat on the back which I would no longer need. And even now, the pain of this memory still lingers.

It is half a century since I fell in love with Zarek. Our children have children of their own whose lives bloom and blossom as ours begin to fade and die. At the time of the court case, I felt bitterly wronged and misjudged. I carried in my heart the knowledge that the decision was based on belief in his honesty, seasoned by his professional status, and as our tales contradicted each other in content, I was therefore judged to be the liar. Whilst reconciling myself to the awfulness of creating a different life, with my children no longer being the defining part of my existence, this hurt nearly as much as their absence. I subsequently heard from the wife of one of Zarek's colleagues that his solicitor had said I was "too honest" but this didn't help as I'd always assumed perhaps naively that honesty was an absolute concept - you either were or you weren't and if you swore an oath in court, then you were obliged to tell the truth. I am no longer sure of this. In present times, honesty could be called a social construct, something that is defined by what you can manage to get others to believe in.

In spite of all this, I eventually gained a PhD, and subsequently managed to carve out a rich and stimulating professional career including getting what I'd written into print. I embarked on new relationships and community involvements, maintained regular and committed contacts with my children and got on with living as best I could. My second husband made a generous contribution to this future, one which was greatly appreciated by my children, even though we eventually parted. We remain a close, loving and mutually supportive family and for this, I owe Greg, Daisy and Alice my undying gratitude. Theirs has not been an easy route into adulthood.

It was only after Zarek's funeral that I discovered what the children really thought about their father and what they would carry into the future in their memories. He had died a sad and sorry death although at 85, death is surely lurking somewhere nearby. Throughout his life he had retained his passion for playing his violin and always played in an amateur orchestra, wherever he was living. He had left the village where the children grew up and had bought a house next door to where Daisy lived with her husband and three children. Driving along a winding, wet lane prior to the final afternoon rehearsal for one of his regular concerts, he found himself behind a dawdling car. He was late and needed to get on. Ever an impatient driver, he took his chance, overtook the car in front but without realising that there was another one coming towards him. He clipped both the one he overtook and the one coming towards him but then lost control, ending up against a tree. Having broken his sternum, clavicle and nine ribs, which punctured his lungs, he was rushed to hospital where he lingered for two months, much of the time in Intensive Care, before expiring. During that sad and very demanding time, all three children did everything in their power to demonstrate their love for him, visiting as often as they could, given the constraints of distance, work commitments, new babies and demanding families. They willed him to go on living, knowing that long-term prospects were poor, but not wanting to lose him. And when he finally died, they all behaved with admirable dignity, respect and pride. An inquest later revealed that he had been quite a long way along the dementia path and shouldn't have been driving at all, so it was a mercy that nobody else suffered in this final accident.

Afterwards I asked each of them, about their memories of their childhood, especially after I had left the family home. Greg was reticent, saying that he was more concerned with the present and the future, than the past; but he did once say that without me, he felt his childhood had ended. Daisy was more forthright and in the process of negotiating a difficult divorce from the father of her three children said that she didn't want history to repeat itself, didn't want her children to go through what she had experienced as a child.

She said her father did his best but that it wasn't good enough. Alice produced detailed memories, the clothes I was wearing when I left, not having anyone to show her how to clean her teeth, saying "I want my Mummy" when I wasn't there. She summarised this by saying that what she missed most of all was the presence of what she called 'female energy' in her life.

So was the judge wrong to make what was for me, a truly terrible decision which it took me years to reconcile myself to ? Or did he with a wisdom that for many years I was blind to, create opportunities that I might never have otherwise enjoyed had I followed a more conventional maternal role ? I doubt though, if he was thinking about *my* future; his concern should definitely have been for the children. Should they have been deprived of a full-time mother, albeit a flawed one but left with an equally flawed father ? Was either of us any better than the other ? We each thought so but now I simply cannot tell and any parent would acknowledge the struggle we all have to make a good job of bringing up our children. We do our best. Ultimately it isn't a question of whether his choice was right or wrong, it felt to me as though it was made for the wrong reasons. Reasons based on lies cannot be good ones even when the circumstances appear to justify them.

So what of Chris, branded by the judge as a Duplicitous Bohemian ? Well, I guess I have to return to the huh of hindsight and acknowledge my own duplicity although unlike Chris, the person I most deceived was myself. If this is the case, then Chris and I were made for each other and as it happened, many years later, we fell in love afresh, but this time, we married.

(And did it last ? No, of course it didn't.)

25687866R00267

Printed in Great Britain
by Amazon